Praise for

AZING GRACE

"A com   werful portrait of the tragic harm so many c   urban America. As always, Jonathan Kozol's   elegiac, memorable and haunting."
—David   itzer Prize-winning author of *Bearing the Cross*

"Among   s of Jonathan Kozol's strong and often beautifu   cannot forget for even an instant that the poor   and live but a moment away. . . . There must be something special about Kozol—a warmth, a gentleness, a kind of mournful decency—that brings out the extraordinary in others. He knows how to ask questions, to listen patiently, and to treat the answers he gets with a respect that borders on courtliness. I have done enough interviewing myself to know that this is not so much a matter of art as it is a matter of person. Kozol is an important writer, but he is also an important presence. . . . There is no point in my trying to describe the portrait that Kozol draws of the children of Mott Haven, so I will content myself with recommending it for its calm power, its sensitivity and its almost painful clarity. As one of his young friends from the neighborhood might say, 'Thank you, Mr. Jonathan.' "   —Kai Erikson, *The Nation*

"*Amazing Grace* reads like an episodic novel, a pastiche of compelling characters, vivid scenes, and jarring observations. . . . A powerful and profoundly disturbing book that challenges all of us to take a hard look at the nation we are becoming."
                —William O'Brien, *Philadelphia Inquirer*

"It is powerful stuff: uplifting with its tales of those who survive amid the destruction, depressing because of the many lives that poverty kills, almost literally from the womb."
                —Lewis Beale, *New York Daily News*

"Surely deserving of a Pulitzer."   —*Philadelphia Daily News*

"In this stunningly simple and eloquent book, Jonathan Kozol continues to be our voice in the wilderness of America's childhood."   —Susan Campbell, *Hartford Courant*

"An often stirring and shocking . . . portrait of the dire poverty of these young inner-city lives. A labor of love by a deeply humane man."   —Lisa Shea, *Elle*

"At a time when Americans are struggling to see through the political, racial and economic walls that separate them, Jonathan Kozol comes along with a window. Like an Old Testament patriarch, he rages at what he calls the greed and 'theological evil' of our time."   —Anita Manning, *USA Today*

"A wrenching cri de coeur. . . . Kozol is a tireless witness to the travesty of childhood experienced by so many Americans."
                                                    —*Kirkus Reviews*

"Kozol wants you to step away from the comfortable. He wants you to see the children's magic and to be so shaken by their lives that you demand change. . . . A well-reported and crafted book that asks tough questions and hurts you to read."
                                        —June Arney, *Virginian-Pilot*

"The extraordinary thing about Mr. Kozol's writing is that God's presence in poor children comes through as light in the darkness. I believe *Amazing Grace* to be the finest book of its kind."   —Rt. Rev. Paul Moore, Episcopal Bishop of New York

"A superb book. I was alternately moved to tears and outrage."
                                            —Rabbi David Saperstein

"A profound book about New York, painting a portrait of where we really are in our municipal life and reminding all of us, but particularly those in government, of how much work we must do if we have any claim to having a moral center."
                            —Ruth Messinger, Manhattan Borough President

"I have just read *Amazing Grace*. I can hear these voices that are like flesh around the people I see every day. I can attest to their words. Jonathan writes like a transcendent Emerson without the privilege. He makes us believe in children again, and thus in ourselves."
                            —Luis Rodriguez, author of *Always Running*

Also by Jonathan Kozol

DEATH AT AN EARLY AGE

FREE SCHOOLS

THE NIGHT IS DARK AND I AM FAR FROM HOME

CHILDREN OF THE REVOLUTION

ON BEING A TEACHER

ILLITERATE AMERICA

RACHEL AND HER CHILDREN

SAVAGE INEQUALITIES

JONATHAN KOZOL

AMAZING GRACE

THE LIVES OF CHILDREN
AND THE CONSCIENCE OF A NATION

HarperPerennial

A Division of HarperCollins*Publishers*

First HarperPerennial edition published 1996.

Designed by Lauren Dong

Library of Congress Cataloging-in-Publication Data

Kozol, Jonathan.
    Amazing grace : the lives of children and the conscience of a nation / Jonathan Kozol.
      p. cm.
    Originally published: New York : Crown, c1995.
    Includes bibliographical references and index.
    ISBN 0-06-097697-7
    1. Poor children—New York (State)—New York. 2. Socially handicapped children—New York (State)—New York. 3. Children of minorities—New York (State)—New York. 4. Sick children—New York (State)—New York. 5. Inner cities—New York (State)—New York. 6. Mott Haven (New York, N.Y.)—Social conditions. I.Title.
HV885.N5K69   1996
362.7'09747'1—dc20   96-16817

98 99 RRD 20 19

This book is dedicated to the
children of Beekman Avenue and
St. Ann's Avenue in the South Bronx

and to Celeste, with every blessing

*And I saw a new heaven and new
earth, for the first heaven
and the first earth were passed
away. . . . And I heard a great voice
out of heaven saying, Behold . . . ,
I make all things new.*
                              —Revelation, 21

To The Reader

This is a slightly revised version of the hardcover printing of this book. Some of the revisions are updated
factual corrections. Others are minor changes in interpretation, prompted by some recent conversations with the
people I describe. A few are corrections that were made
for the initial printing but were not included as a consequence of problems in production. As in the hardcover
edition, the names of certain people have been changed
and certain identifying information is disguised. The precise locations of some conversations are disguised as well,
and some events and discussions of events have been rese-
quenced.

A brief word about the conversations of the children
in this narrative: Friends of mine who live or work in the
South Bronx and know some of the children I've
described share my sense of admiration for the clarity
and honesty with which so many of them speak.
But readers may well wonder if these youngsters are not
ever simply vague, or boring, or repetitive, or just plain in-
coherent.

The answer, as most of their teachers will attest, is that
they are sometimes every bit as boring as some grown-ups
are, and often hopelessly repetitive and, in the case of at

least one child I particularly like, almost inventively and maddeningly obscure. They also get distracted or get interrupted and forget what they were saying and take quite a few long detours sometimes before they return to what they had begun to say.

In these cases I have chosen to excise and bypass a good deal of talk that seems to be of little interest even to the person who is speaking. Robert Coles, a thoughtful writer and physician whose extensive interviews with children have enlightened, challenged, and inspired me for nearly 30 years, has spoken of the selectivity that is inevitably present in the process of assembling and reproducing many lengthy conversations, particularly those of children, in a form concise enough to fit within the confines of a book. It is a reminder worth repeating here, though it is also true that certain children quoted in this book are so direct, and so clear-headed, and so pleasantly determined to pursue a theme or an idea to its conclusion, that virtually the only interruptions in a conversation are my questions.

In the months since publication I have made approximately 50 visits back to the South Bronx, riding the same subway train, visiting the same streets and same neighborhoods, knocking on the same doors, sometimes early in the evening, and then sitting up until the early hours of the morning in the homes of people who became my friends while I was working on this book. During these visits I have seen some changes in Mott Haven. The homicide rate is down and crack cocaine use seems to have declined, though heroin use is on the rise. There have been some school improvement programs and a number of new medical initiatives, and there are more promises that housing reconstruction, which has been proceeding at a good pace in some other sections of the Bronx, may soon be introduced into these neighborhoods as well.

Still, when I look for hope these days, I tend to look less often to external signs of progress such as housing reconstruction—which can be too rapidly arrested and reversed by shifts in public policy—than to the words and prayers of children and the spiritual resilience of so many of their mothers and grandmothers. It is, above all, the very young whose luminous capacity for tenderness and love and a transcendent sense of faith in human decency give me reason for hope.

Readers who would like to know of certain advocacy groups, religious groups, and other organizations that are working to advance the interests of some of the children in this book, and of low-income children elsewhere in the nation, may write to me in care of my publisher. Documentation for matters of public record, and for sources I've relied upon, is in the notes beginning on page 257.

Chapter One

The Number 6 train from Manhattan to the South Bronx makes nine stops in the 18-minute ride between East 59th Street and Brook Avenue. When you enter the train, you are in the seventh richest congressional district in the nation. When you leave, you are in the poorest.

The 600,000 people who live here and the 450,000 people who live in Washington Heights and Harlem, which are separated from the South Bronx by a narrow river, make up one of the largest racially segregated concentrations of poor people in our nation.

Brook Avenue, which is the tenth stop on the local, lies in the center of Mott Haven, whose 48,000 people are the poorest in the South Bronx. Two thirds are Hispanic, one third black. Thirty-five percent are children. In 1991, the median household income of the area, according to the *New York Times,* was $7,600.

St. Ann's Church, on St. Ann's Avenue, is three blocks from the subway station. The children who come to this small Episcopal church for food and comfort and to play, and the mothers and fathers who come here for prayer, are said to be the poorest people in New York. "More than 95 percent are poor," the pastor says—"the poorest of the poor, poor by any standard I can think of."

At the elementary school that serves the neighborhood across the avenue, only seven of 800 children do not qualify for free school lunches. "Five of those seven," says the principal, "get reduced-price lunches, because they are classified as only 'poor,' not 'destitute.'"

In some cities, the public reputation of a ghetto neighborhood bears little connection to the world that you

3

discover when you walk the streets with children and listen to their words. In Mott Haven, this is not the case. By and large, the words of the children in the streets and schools and houses that surround St. Ann's more than justify the grimness in the words of journalists who have described the area.

Crack-cocaine addiction and the intravenous use of heroin, which children I have met here call "the needle drug," are woven into the texture of existence in Mott Haven. Nearly 4,000 heroin injectors, many of whom are HIV-infected, live here. Virtually every child at St. Ann's knows someone, a relative or neighbor, who has died of AIDS, and most children here know many others who are dying now of the disease. One quarter of the women of Mott Haven who are tested in obstetric wards are positive for HIV. Rates of pediatric AIDS, therefore, are high.

Depression is common among children in Mott Haven. Many cry a great deal but cannot explain exactly why.

Fear and anxiety are common. Many cannot sleep.

Asthma is the most common illness among children here. Many have to struggle to take in a good deep breath. Some mothers keep oxygen tanks, which children describe as "breathing machines," next to their children's beds.

The houses in which these children live, two thirds of which are owned by the City of New York, are often as squalid as the houses of the poorest children I have visited in rural Mississippi, but there is none of the greenness and the healing sweetness of the Mississippi countryside outside their windows, which are often barred and bolted as protection against thieves.

Some of these houses are freezing in the winter. In dangerously cold weather, the city sometimes distributes electric blankets and space heaters to its tenants. In emergency conditions, if space heaters can't be used, because substandard wiring is overloaded, the city's practice, according to *Newsday,* is to pass out sleeping bags.

"You just cover up . . . and hope you wake up the next morning," says a father of four children, one of them an infant one month old, as they prepare to climb into their sleeping bags in hats and coats on a December night.

In humid summer weather, roaches crawl on virtually every surface of the houses in which many of the children live. Rats emerge from holes in bedroom walls, terrorizing infants in their cribs. In the streets outside, the restlessness and anger that are present in all seasons frequently intensify under the stress of heat.

In speaking of rates of homicide in New York City neighborhoods, the *Times* refers to the streets around St. Ann's as "the deadliest blocks" in "the deadliest precinct" of the city. If there is a deadlier place in the United States, I don't know where it is.

In 1991, 84 people, more than half of whom were 21 or younger, were murdered in the precinct. A year later, ten people were shot dead on a street called Beekman Avenue, where many of the children I have come to know reside. On Valentine's Day of 1993, three more children and three adults were shot dead on the living room floor of an apartment six blocks from the run-down park that serves the area.

In early July of 1993, shortly before the first time that I visited the neighborhood, three more people were shot in 30 minutes in three unrelated murders in the South Bronx, one of them only a block from St. Ann's Avenue. A week later, a mother was murdered and her baby wounded by a bullet in the stomach while they were standing on a South Bronx corner. Three weeks after that, a minister and elderly parishioner were shot outside the front door of their church, while another South Bronx resident was discovered in his bathtub with his head cut off. In subsequent days, a man was shot in both his eyes and a ten-year-old was critically wounded in the brain.

What is it like for children to grow up here? What do they think the world has done to them? Do they believe that they are being shunned or hidden by society? If so, do they think that they deserve this? What is it that enables some of them to pray? When they pray, what do they say to God?

* * *

Walking into St. Ann's Church on a hot summer afternoon, one is immediately in the presence of small children. They seem to be everywhere: in the garden, in the hallways, in the kitchen, in the chapel, on the stairs. The first time I see the pastor, Martha Overall, she is carrying a newborn baby in her arms and is surrounded by three lively and excited little girls. In one of the most diseased and dangerous communities in any city of the Western world, the beautiful old stone church on St. Ann's Avenue is a gentle sanctuary from the terrors of the streets outside.

A seven-year-old boy named Cliffie, whose mother has come to the church to talk with Reverend Overall, agrees to take me for a walk around the neighborhood. His mother cautions me, "He does tell fibs," then gives him a hug and tells him, "Be as interesting as you always are."

There are children in the poorest, most abandoned places who, despite the miseries and poisons that the world has pumped into their lives, seem, when you first meet them, to be cheerful anyway. Cliffie, as we set out onto St. Ann's Avenue, seems about as buoyant, and as lively, and as charmingly mysterious, as seven-year-olds anywhere. He also seems to feel no shyness and no hesitation about filling the role of guide that he has been assigned.

Reaching up to take my hand the moment that we leave the church, he starts a running commentary almost instantly, interrupting now and then to say hello to men and women on the street, dozens of whom are standing just outside the gateway to St. Ann's, waiting for a food pantry to open.

At a tiny park in a vacant lot less than a block away, he points to a number of stuffed animals that are attached to the branches of a tree.

"Bears," he says.

"Why are there bears in the tree?" I ask.

He doesn't answer me but smiles at the bears affectionately. "I saw a boy shot in the head right over there," he says a moment later, in a voice that does not sound particularly sad, then looks up at me and asks politely, "Would you like a chocolate chip cookie?"

"No, thank you," I say.

6

He has a package of cookies and removes one. He breaks it in half, returns half to the package, and munches on the other half as we are walking.

Leading me across the avenue, he hesitates in front of a bodega, looks in both directions up and down the street, then seems to come to a conclusion.

"Okay. I think we need to go up here."

We head north for a block or two, then turn right and walk a long block to a rutted street called Cypress Avenue. After crossing Cypress, he hesitates again.

"Do you want to go down there?" he asks.

I say, "Okay," not knowing what he means.

"They're burning bodies there," he says.

"What kind of bodies?"

"The bodies of people!" he says in a spooky voice, as if he enjoys the opportunity to terrify a grown-up.

"Is that the truth?"

He acts as if he doesn't hear my question and begins to hum.

The place that Cliffie is referring to turns out to be a waste incinerator that was put in operation recently over the objections of the parents in the neighborhood. The incinerator, I am later reassured by Reverend Overall, does not burn entire "bodies." What it burns are so-called "red-bag products," such as amputated limbs and fetal tissue, bedding, bandages, and syringes that are transported here from 14 New York City hospitals. The waste products of some of these hospitals, she says, were initially going to be burned at an incinerator scheduled to be built along the East Side of Manhattan, but the siting of a burner there had been successfully resisted by the parents of the area because of fear of cancer risks to children.

Munching another cookie as we walk, Cliffie asks me, "Do you want to go on Jackson Avenue?"

Although I don't know one street from another, I agree.

"Come on," he says. "I'll take you there. We have to go around this block."

He pauses then, however—"wait a minute"—and he pulls an asthma inhaler from his pocket, holds it to his mouth, presses it twice, and then puts it away.

Silent for a while as we walk to Jackson Avenue, he stops when he sees a dog he knows. "That's Princess," he explains. To the dog, he says, "Hi, Princess!" Then, to me: "You see? We're almost there."

He stops again to ask if he can hold my tape recorder. When I hand it to him, he studies the red light to be sure that it is working and then whispers, "We are going to have a conversation."

As confident and grown-up as he sounds, he has the round face of a baby and is scarcely more than three and a half feet tall. When he has bad dreams, he tells me, "I go in my mommy's bed and crawl under the covers." At other times, when he's upset, he says, "I sleep with a picture of my mother and I dream of her."

Unlike many children I have met in recent years, he has an absolutely literal religious faith. When I ask him how he pictures God, he says, "He has long hair and He can walk on the deep water." To make sure I understand that this is an unusual ability, he adds, "Nobody else can."

He seems to take the lessons of religion literally also. Speaking of a time his mother sent him to the store "to get a pizza"—"three slices, one for my mom, one for my dad, and one for me"—he says he saw a homeless man who told him he was hungry. "But he was too cold to move his mouth! He couldn't talk!"

"How did you know that he was hungry if he couldn't talk?"

"He pointed to my pizza."

"What did you do?"

"I gave him some!"

"Were your parents mad at you?"

He looks surprised by this. "Why would they be mad?" he asks. "God told us, 'Share!'"

When I ask him who his heroes are, he first says "Michael Jackson" and then "Oprah!"—like that, with an exclamation on the word. I try to get him to speak about "important" persons as the schools tend to define them. "Have you read about George Washington?"

"I don't even know the man," he says.

We follow Jackson Avenue past several boarded buildings and a "flat fix" shop, stop briefly in front of a fenced-in lot where the police of New York City bring impounded cars, and then turn left in the direction of a highway with an elevated road above it, where a sign says "Bruckner Boulevard." Crossing beneath the elevated road, we soon arrive at Locust Avenue.

The medical waste incinerator, a new-looking building, is gunmetal blue on top and cinder block below. From one of its metal sliding-doors, which is half-open, a sourly unpleasant odor drifts into the street. Standing in front of the building, Cliffie grumbles slightly but does not seem terribly concerned. "You sure that you don't want a cookie?"

Again, I say, "No, thank you."

"I think I'll have another one," he says and takes another for himself.

After we cross Bruckner Boulevard again, he stops to consider the direction we should go. "You want to go the hard way or the easy way back to the church?"

"Let's go the easy way," I say.

"Well, actually, they're both the same," he says. "But, if we go up this way, I can show you where my store is."

When we get to the grocery that he calls his store, he walks right in and says hello to the man behind the counter, who is friendly to him, then walks out again and sees a young man standing in a doorway who, he tells me, is his cousin, then another man who is, he says, "my other cousin," and to whom he says, "Hi, Woody!" He holds up the tape recorder, which he is still carrying, and asks his cousin, "How old are you?"

The man replies, "I'm 32."

"Okay," says Cliffie, fiddling with the tape recorder. "I think we can give this thing a rest." He turns it off and hands it back to me.

Next to another vacant lot, where someone has dumped a heap of auto tires and some rusted auto parts, he points to a hypodermic needle in the tangled grass and to the bright-colored caps of crack containers, then, for no reason that I can discern, starts puffing up his cheeks and blowing out the air.

"The day is coming when the world will be destroyed," he finally announces. "Everyone is going to be burned to crispy cookies."

A car stops at that moment so that we can cross a busy street. "See that?" he says. "They let us cross." As we cross, he waves at the driver, who doesn't seem to know him but waves anyway. After we cross, he asks me, "Can I have the tape recorder back?" I hear him whispering into the microphone, "We're out of cookies. I ate a whole bag of cookies. They're all gone."

Back again on St. Ann's Avenue, he sees a man he knows close to the church and says hello to him. The man nods. "How you doin', little man?"

He holds up the tape recorder to the man. "Say how old you are."

The man says, "Sixty-five."

"Okay," says Cliffie. "That's enough. So long!"

Inside the church, his mother looks at me with some amusement on her face. "Did this child wear you out?"

"No," I say. "I enjoyed the walk." I mention, however, that he took me to the waste incinerator and repeat his comment about "burning bodies," to which she responds by giving him a half-sarcastic look, hesitating, and then saying, "Hey! You never know! Maybe this child knows something we haven't heard!"

After giving him another pleasantly suspicious look, she leans back in a chair and folds her arms like someone who is getting ready to say something she has planned to tell me all along. "The point is that they put a *lot* of things into our neighborhood that no one wants," she says. "The waste incinerator is just one more lovely way of showing their affection."

I ask, "Does it insult you?"

"It used to," she replies. "The truth is, you get used to the offense. There's trashy things all over. There's a garbage dump three blocks away. Then there's all the trucks that come through stinking up the air, heading for the

10

Hunts Point Market. Drivers get their drugs there and their prostitutes.

"Did he take you down to Jackson Avenue?"

When I say he did, she says, "You see a lot of prostitutes down there as well. Further down. By the expressway.... Then we get illegal dumpers. People who don't live here come and dump things they don't want: broken televisions, boxes of bottles, old refrigerators, beat-up cars, old pieces of metal, other lovely things. They do it in the wee hours of the morning.

"Actually," she says upon reflection, "I've got quite a few nice things that way. Not long ago, somebody dumped a pile of chairs and tables in the street. Brand-new. I was offended but I was also blessed. I took two chairs."

A small and wiry woman wearing blue jeans and a baseball cap, a former cocaine addict who now helps addicted women and their children, she tells me that more than 3,000 homeless families have been relocated by the city in this neighborhood during the past few years, and she asks a question I will hear from many other people here during the months ahead. "Why do you want to put so many people with small children in a place with so much sickness? This is the last place in New York that they should put poor children. Clumping so many people, all with the same symptoms and same problems, in one crowded place with nothin' they can grow on? Our children start to mourn themselves before their time."

Cliffie, who is listening to this while leaning on his elbow like a pensive grown-up, offers his tentative approval to his mother's words. "Yes," he says, "I think that's probably true."

He says it with so much thought, and grown-up reservation, that his mother can't help smiling, even though it's not a funny statement. She looks at him hard, grabs him suddenly around the neck, and kisses him.

In the evening, I go back to look more closely at the corner lot that I had passed with Cliffie, where he pointed out the stuffed bears in the branches of a tree. In the semidarkness, I can make out several figures, some of them standing, some squatting on their knees, then many more, perhaps two dozen people, some of whom are talking to each other, some apparently transacting business, others who are sleeping. It is, I later learn, one of many drug parks in the South Bronx that police sometimes try to shut down but, for the most part, leave in peace for those who have no other place to shoot their drugs or drink their wine. The stuffed animals are tied by strings to the branches of the tree, a curious sight, which I later share with a woman cleaning up the kitchen in the basement of the church, who simply nods at this and says, "They're children's bears," but does not attempt a further explanation.

The pastor tells me that the place is known as "Children's Park." Volunteers arrive here twice a week to give out condoms and clean needles to addicted men and women, some of whom bring their children with them. The children play near the bears or on a jungle gym while their mothers wait for needles.

At nine P.M., Reverend Overall offers to drive me downtown to Manhattan. Three hungry-looking dogs run past us when she pushes back the gates to the garden of the church to get her car. The dogs disappear into a section of the churchyard where, she says, one of our nation's Founding Fathers, Gouverneur Morris, who wrote the preamble to the U.S. Constitution, has his resting place. His wife, Anne Morris, is buried here beside him.

Alice Washington lives on a street called Boston Road, close to East Tremont Avenue, about two miles to the north of St. Ann's Church. Visibly fragile as a consequence of having AIDS and highly susceptible to chest infections, she lives with her son, who is a high school senior, in a first-floor apartment with three steel locks on the door. A nurse comes once a month to take her temperature and check her heart and her blood pressure.

The nurse, says Mrs. Washington one evening when we're sitting in her kitchen, has another 16 patients in the building. "Some are children born with AIDS. Some are older people. One is a child 12 years old shot in a crossfire at the bus stop on the corner. The bullet ricocheted and got her in the back. She's lost her hair. Can't go to school. She's paralyzed. I see her mother all the time. They wheel her outside in the summer.

"This happened last year, on the Fourth of July. Summer had just begun. I feel so sorry for that child."

I ask how many people in the building now have AIDS.

"In this building? Including the children, maybe 27 people. That's just in this section. In the other building over there, there's maybe 20 more. Then there's lots of other people have it but don't know, afraid to know, and don't want to be tested. We're livin' in a bad time. What else can I say?

"The girl across the hall, she died last week. An overdose of drugs. Fifteen years old. Her uncle came around and knocked at all the doors for contributions so that he could bury her. I saw them bringin' the body out on the meat wagon. You know, the coroner. This was a pretty young lady. Freckles and red hair. She's Puerto Rican but looked like an Irish girl. And now she's died."

She speaks of a generous woman who was kind to her some years ago when she was homeless, living in Manhattan's Martinique Hotel, a notorious shelter where she spent nearly four years and which has since been closed. "I got a beautiful letter from her and I put it on my bedroom wall," she says. "Beautiful handwriting. . . .

"During that time, I was trained as an AIDS worker. Social worker asked me did I want to get into this program. I said yes. I told him I'd do anything to get out of my room. So I went through the training and got certified to work with people who have AIDS. Those were the days when everyone was scared. No one knew exactly what it was and no one wanted to find out if they had been infected. I didn't know then I was sick myself."

Speaking of another child in the building, a nine-year-old who died of AIDS two months before, she says, "This little girl was also Puerto Rican. Name was Sylvia, but people called her Angel. Her mother died six months before. An intravenous user. The mother's boyfriend was 42 years old and he had AIDS as well. He raped the little girl right in her bed. The grandmother of this child is a woman that

13

I know. She said, 'They got my daughter. Now they got my baby.'

"This woman, the grandmother, is an interesting person. Strong as a rock. She knew that the police would not arrest the man. She told me, 'I ain't waitin' for the law.' In less than 48 hours he was dead. The body was found in front of a nightclub with a bullet in his head. I hate to say it but he got what he deserved.

"The grandmother's gone. Moved back to Puerto Rico. She lost her daughter and granddaughter. She had no one else. Why would she want to stay here in New York?"

She mentions another friend of hers, whose son was a high school senior and had won a college scholarship. "Cops show up one day, bang at her door. She asks them, 'Why you bangin' like that on my door?' Cop says, 'Open up the door.' She opens the door. Cop comes in. 'Do you have a son?' 'Why you botherin' with my son?' she says. Cop says, 'Wait a minute. Come outside.' They go outside. Her son is sitting out in front buck-naked. She says to the cop, 'What did he do?' Cop says, 'I'm sorry to tell you this. Your son is a drug addict.' He'd sold every stitch of his clothes, even his underwear. A few months later, he was dead. . . .

"His mother worked at Chemical Bank. Now she's walkin' door to door, tryin' to save other mothers' kids. What can I say?"

A person who works in a real job at a place like Chemical Bank, she tells me, is a rare exception in the neighborhood. "Almost no one here has jobs like that. Some are too sick. They live on SSI"—a federal program for sick and disabled people. Maybe five or six in 25, she says, have some legitimate employment. "Another five or ten are selling drugs or doing prostitution. The ones that are infected—some of them don't think twice about infecting someone else. Almost too scared to think of it at all."

The hospital to which she goes for care is called Bronx-Lebanon.

"Every time my doctor says I have to go back to the hospital, I cry," she says. "He called me last time after I had had some tests and said he wanted me admitted. I told him I didn't want to go. He said, 'Mrs. Washington, you've *got* to go.' He said a bed had been arranged. They told him they would have it ready in two hours. I went to the hospital and, when I get there, it's six hours before they can put me in a bed. Then, when I go upstairs, the room is not prepared. The bed is covered with blood and bandages from someone else. Flowers are scattered on the floor. Toilet's stopped with toilet paper. Bed hasn't been made. I'd been through this once before. Either you wait for hours until someone cleans the room or else you clean the room yourself.

"David [her son] went out in the corridor and found some linen for the bed. First, he had to wash it down. I don't blame my doctor. He cannot control what happens if he isn't there. Nurses are overworked. My nurse had 22 patients and was working two shifts end-to-end.

"Once you're in bed, if you call the nurse, you wait for half an hour. 'You know, Mrs. Washington, you've been here before,' they say. 'You know that we are understaffed.' How do they know, when someone calls, that you're not dying?

"I know most of the nurses. Some are like old friends to me by now. But, still, why should a patient have to make her bed and wash her room?"

The privately run hospital, which I have since visited, is an uninviting place, but she assures me that it's better than the other major hospital that serves the area, a city-run institution known as Lincoln Hospital, which has been denied accreditation more than once over the years because of the failure of the staff to monitor patients after surgery and to enter critical data in their records. At least 12 people, including two infants, says the *Times*, have died because of staff mistakes at Lincoln, which is the hospital relied upon by families in the St. Ann's neighborhood.

Mrs. Washington tells me, nonetheless, that both Lincoln and Bronx-Lebanon are generally considered better than another nearby public institution, Harlem Hospital, which the minister of Harlem's leading church refers to as "a cesspool" and which has also lost accreditation several times. "They keep running out of penicillin there," she says.

15

A nurse who works there, according to one press account, carries a card in her wallet with the message: "Do Not Take Me to Harlem Hospital in an Emergency."

The relative merits of Bronx-Lebanon, however, do not offer Mrs. Washington much solace. "It's the difference between terrible and worse than terrible," she says. "The time before, when I had a fever, my doctor said I had pneumonia. I waited in the emergency room two days to be admitted."

I ask, "Where were you waiting?"

"Waiting in the waiting room with everybody else," she says. "Right there, in chairs, with all the other people who were waiting. Sick children vomiting up their food. Men with gunshot wounds. People with AIDS. Old people coughing up their blood. On the third day I gave up and went back home. My doctor said I was right to leave because it isn't safe for me to be there with so many other people with infections."

Although there are flashes of impatience and sarcasm as she speaks, her comments on these matters, for the most part, are subdued, not openly indignant, and there is a quietness about her words as if she is already looking back upon her life and on New York itself from a considerable distance.

Only once in the course of a long evening does she voice something like open anger, and this comes up not in reference to the hospital but in speaking of the New York City press. Seeing a copy of the *Daily News* on one of the kitchen chairs, I ask her if it covers stories in this neighborhood. "It does," she says. "Sometimes David goes and gets me *Newsday* too." She adds, "We do not buy the *New York Post*."

"Why not?" I ask.

"It's prejudiced," she answers.

I ask if she ever reads the *Times,* which is the paper that I read to keep in touch with news in New York City.

"It's the best paper that we got," she says, "but I can't get it at my store."

Surprised by this, I ask her if she knows some reason why.

"I don't know why. A lot of people ask for it. Maybe they figure people in our situation couldn't buy the things they advertise so they wouldn't see us as good customers."

"Do you believe that?"

"I don't know. Maybe I don't. But it makes sense. Why else? I know that they don't think that we're so stupid we can't read it. If they can get it all the way to where you live in Massachusetts, why can't they get it to the Bronx?

"Sometimes," she says, "David goes and gets it for me at another store on Sunday. They sell it in a couple of places but they run out fast."

I ask her why she goes to so much trouble to obtain it.

"I like to look at the ads and read the social pages," she replies. "It gives you a feeling that you know what's going on."

These are almost the only things she says that have an edge of indignation; even here, it is more sadness than real indignation. She seems resigned to things the way they are. "That's how it is. What can I say?" she often asks.

On a steamy afternoon in late July, I return to New York City. In the early evening, in front of my hotel, I try in vain to find a taxi-driver who will take me to East Tremont, so I end up going there by train.

When I enter the train, which isn't crowded at this hour, the passengers are people of all races. By 86th Street, most of the white passengers are gone. At 96th Street, all of the other white people leave the car I'm in, but several black and Hispanic women, two of whom are in maids' uniforms, come in and sit together on a seat beside me.

Mrs. Washington's son is waiting for me at East Tremont. He tells me she's been cut from welfare since I saw them last. It's a complicated story, but it seems that her food stamps and her welfare payment had been stolen from her in the street some months before. When she began the process of replacing them, there was a computer error that removed her from the rolls entirely. He also mentions that she needs to go into the hospital again and speaks of "a spinal tap" but isn't clear about the details.

As we head up the street, black and Hispanic kids eye me uneasily. Signs advertising beepers are displayed on walls or in the windows of the stores on almost every block. Aimless men in sullen groups are gathered on the corners. We pass a burnt-out building with a makeshift altar and a crucifix and many little jars of flowers on the sidewalk by a blackened door—an illegal nightclub, he explains, where more than 80 people died when fire broke out on the second floor. As we stand there, a police car pulls up with its siren screaming. An officer gets out and walks up to a group of men in front of an abandoned house. A sign nearby announces in Spanish, "Christ Is Coming."

A block away, we pass a Mister Softee truck and, on the opposite corner, a *coquito* stand, where children can buy coconut ices—"in a cup," David explains. Nearing his apartment house, we pass an elderly woman pushing a grocery cart, a small dog walking as quickly as he can beside her. She smiles at us as she passes. "People call her 'the lady with the Bible,' " David says. "You usually see her with a Bible in her hand. She goes out with her dog collecting cans."

When we get to his building, he unlocks the door to his apartment (three locks, three separate keys) while three men standing nearby in the corridor watch us closely. I feel a long way from Manhattan.

Mrs. Washington is in bed when I arrive. Her bedroom is darkened, but she isn't sleeping and she soon gets up, puts on a robe, and comes out to the kitchen. The heat in the kitchen, unrelieved by a fan or breeze, because the windows in the room are closed, is oppressive and my shirt sticks to my skin.

"The heat drains everyone of energy," she says. "Every little gesture that you make becomes so hard."

She speaks of a woman who lives upstairs, a friend of hers, who has a number of young children. "She loses all her strength to keep them clean. The place is roach-infested. The roaches crawl on the table and she doesn't have the energy to brush them off. The faucet drips in the sink. She lets it drip. She's diabetic and she has no strength. When I'm feeling well enough, I go up there to help her."

Wiping a cloth across her throat, she says, "It was

93 degrees today. The air was so sticky you could hardly breathe. Hotter inside—but I'm afraid to open up the windows."

On all sides of the building in which she and David live are blocks and blocks of other buildings like this holding infants miserable from rash and soiled frequently from diarrhea, elderly people trying hard to breathe, younger people who, if they dare to do so, lean from their windows hoping to detect a breeze and fanning themselves sometimes with a folded magazine.

"It's so humid in July," she says. "People lie on their beds but cannot sleep."

Her daughter, she tells me, lives on 141st Street in Mott Haven, very close to St. Ann's Church. "On a hot night like tonight, everyone there is outside on the stoop because nobody has a fan. You know it's dangerous to do it but you got to go outside. You either go outside and take your chance or else you roast inside the house."

The temperature tonight, according to the paper, is going to go down into the 70s; but if it has started to go down, the difference can't be felt here in her kitchen. She gets out a pitcher of ice water and pours me a drink and then sits down.

"This is what happened with the welfare. . . ." She then relates a story that, with minor alterations, I've heard many times from people who have lost their welfare payments in New York. "To get an emergency replacement for my check," she says, "I needed to bring three letters to the welfare office—one from my doctor, one from the hospital, one from my social worker.

"I got the doctor's letter and the social worker's letter but the hospital's letter didn't come. So I went back and forth from welfare to the hospital—it took a week and finally I got the letter. I brought in all the letters and I waited for another week and then I went to the computer. I put my card in but it didn't work. Sometimes that happens, so you put it in the next computer. I tried all five. It didn't work. Then the man there said, 'Your card is dead. You've been cut off.' "

In order to get reinstated in the system, she explains,

"you have to go to 16th Street and get a new ID. Your relatives are not allowed to do it for you. You always know that when you do it, there will be some other problems and you'll have to go again and file some other papers. So you go to 16th Street, an hour's ride, and get the new ID, and then to 34th Street to the food stamp center. . . ."

At first it isn't clear to me why she would need a letter from her doctor to get reinstated in the welfare system. When I ask about this, it becomes apparent that she has condensed two pieces of the story.

"My doctor said that I should be on SSI. He said, if I have to start all over, that's the program that I should apply for. I told him I applied for it before, when I had cancer, but they said I wasn't sick enough. He said I needed to go and try again.

"I don't know how sick you have to be to qualify for SSI. My girlfriend died from AIDS in March. She never did get SSI. After she died, the checks began to come. Now they keep on coming. Her boyfriend cashes them each month. She's dead! They *have* to know she died. They paid to bury her. They had to see the death certificate.

"My doctor says, when it comes to the poor, they can't get nothin' right. Anyway, they got me runnin' uptown, downtown, to the hospital, to 34th Street, to the welfare, with the streets so hot and everyone at welfare so impatient. I've got no choice but I don't think I can go through it anymore. I feel like somebody beat me up."

We talk for several hours. Because it is quiet outside on the street, David opens the kitchen window to let in a little air. As the room cools off and she seems more composed, he asks his mother if she'd like something to eat. She looks toward the refrigerator for a moment, then says no. "I don't think I can hold it down."

Before I leave, she mentions the 15-year-old girl who lived across the hall, whose uncle had been trying to raise money for her burial. "The girl who died, the city had to bury her. Her uncle couldn't raise the money for a funeral. That means that she don't get no stone over her grave."

"What do they put on it?" I ask.

"They say she gets a number," she replies. "City don't

have the money for the living. I guess they think: Why waste it on the dead?"

Sometimes, she tells me, people in her building borrow burial money from a man across the street who sells cocaine. "A woman I know borrowed $500 from him. Before she was done, she'd paid him back $1,000. He used to wait for her at the check-cashing first of every month. If you're a woman, he has ways to make sure that you pay.

"Check-cashing places also handle Western Union. Send a Western Union to somebody and you pay them $25 for $100. It's a different world from where you live. What can I say?"

"If poor people behaved rationally," says Lawrence Mead, a professor of political science at New York University, "they would seldom be poor for long in the first place." Many social scientists today appear to hold this point of view and argue that the largest portion of the suffering poor people undergo has to be blamed upon their own "behaviors," a word they tend to pluralize.

Alice Washington was born in 1944 in New York City. She grew up in Harlem and the Bronx and went to segregated public schools, not something of her choosing, nor that of her mother and her father. She finished high school, studied bookkeeping at a secretarial college, and went to work, beginning at 19. When she married, at the age of 25, she had to choose her husband from that segregated "marriage pool," to which our social scientists sometimes quite icily refer, of frequently unemployable black men, some of whom have been involved in drugs or spent some time in prison. From her husband, after many years of what she thought to be monogamous matrimony, she contracted the AIDS virus.

She left her husband after he began to beat her. Cancer of her fallopian tubes was detected at this time, then cancer of her uterus. She had three operations. Too frail to keep on with the second of two jobs that she had held, in all, for nearly 20 years, she was forced to turn for mercy to the City of New York.

In 1983, at the age of 39, she landed with her children in a homeless shelter two blocks from Times Square, an old hotel in which the plumbing did not work and from which she and David and his sister had to carry buckets to a bar across the street in order to get water. After spending close to four years in three shelters in Manhattan, she was moved by the city to the neighborhood where she now lives in the South Bronx. It was at this time that she learned she carried the AIDS virus. Since the time that I met Mrs. Washington, I have spent hundreds of hours talking with her in her kitchen. I have yet to figure out what she has done that was irrational.

On an evening in August, when I'm home in Massachusetts, David calls me around midnight after his mother's gone to bed and asks if we can talk.

I ask him how she's feeling and he says, "I can't get her to eat. She's vomiting and coughing. She keeps waking up at night and going to the bathroom, usually at two or three. Her doctor wants her in the hospital but she's afraid to go. She says it's so upsetting when she goes there that she comes back feeling worse.

"I keep waking up myself. Even if my mother isn't up, I wake up anyway. I go in her room to see if she's asleep. If she's sleeping I just sit there by her bed." When she's feeling very sick, he says, he stays in her room and sleeps at the bottom of the bed.

"Sometimes in the afternoon, when I come in, I find her crying. I try to get her to talk to me but she won't talk. I know that she doesn't want to make me sad, but when she won't say anything, her being silent makes me sad. She thinks that she's protecting me but she cannot protect me.

"Once she said, 'I don't think I'm going to be here very long.' That was the only time she ever talked to me like that. . . .

"Last night I couldn't sleep, so I sat up for a long time. I got the thought that maybe she's not eating so that she'll be sick enough for SSI. I wondered if she's starving herself so that she'll qualify, so that they'll say, 'This woman's sick enough. She qualifies.'" He doesn't cry but sounds as if he's struggling to control his voice.

"I don't think my mother's asking for something she does not deserve. She worked hard all her life. She's a very honest person. She's kind to other people. She's a nicer person than a lot of the rich people that I notice on TV. She gives more of herself to other people. My mother means a great deal to me. I don't know what I'll do after she's gone.

"Sometimes I wish I could turn back the calendar to 1980. I have a lot of thoughts like that at night. I wonder how powerful God is. He must be wise and powerful to make the animals and trees and give man organs and a brain to build complex machineries, but He is not powerful enough to stop the evil on the earth, to change the hearts of people."

I ask what he means by "the evil on the earth."

"Evil exists," he says, not flinching at the word. "I believe that what the rich have done to the poor people in this city is something that a preacher could call evil. Somebody has power. Pretending that they don't so they don't need to use it to help people—that is my idea of evil.

"I went to the clinic last week with my mother. Out in front there was a table set up on the street. On the table there were paper bags with condoms and clean needles. I saw the prostitutes lined up waiting for the condoms. I saw drug users lined up waiting for the needles. It was like seeing a line of ghosts. It looked like all the people there were dying.

"Most of the addicts and prostitutes are black. Some are Hispanic. But they're all people of color. It made me feel frightened for my race. The men are killing themselves with needles and the women are laying their bodies down with anyone they meet, not knowing who they are. Some are only 15 but look 25. Then you have the older women, 35 or 40, and they look so sick you wonder how someone would want to sleep with them.

"Quite a few times, when I have had to go to St. Ann's Avenue, the dealers open their hands when I go by. They say, 'What do you want?' I walk right by. You try not to look at them but you can feel the hatred in their eyes as you go by."

I ask him what it is he thinks they hate in him.

"I think they hate you because you are not in their condition. 'I am in hell and you are not and so I hate you and I have to try to bring you down to where I am.' I feel pity for them, and fear, because they're lost.

"My teacher says, 'We came here in chains and now we buy our own chains and we put them on ourselves.' Every little store sells chains. They even have them at check-cashing. . . .

"Some of the prostitutes are very bold. They come right up to you. Not the younger ones. The younger ones don't bother me. The older women do. I think to myself, 'This woman is the same age as my mother.'

"I believe that we were put here for a purpose, but these people in the streets can't *see* a purpose. There's a whole world out there if you know it's there, if you can see it. But they're in a cage. They cannot see."

The newspapers, he notes, keep saying that tuberculosis has come back to the South Bronx. "That's one reason why my mother's scared to go back to the hospital. As soon as they know that someone has TB they're supposed to isolate him in a room, but sometimes it's a day or two before they get to him. So he could be sitting there right now and it could be tomorrow night before they know he has TB. Meanwhile, you might be sitting next to him all of that time. You try to keep off at a distance in the waiting room, but sometimes you can't.

"Heroin's making a comeback in our neighborhood. There's something different in it from before, so it's stronger and, I guess, more lethal." He tells me one of the street names for the drug is "DOA"—dead on arrival. "If you walk on St. Ann's Avenue at night, you hear the dealers call it out. It's like they're saying, 'Come on over here. I'll show you how to end your life.' The dealers are sometimes jittery. They look at you with this strange smile. It's not just hatred. It's as if they're laughing at their lives—and yours."

Chapter Two

According to a textbook for children published in 1987 by the Bronx County Historical Society, virtually all of what is now described as the South Bronx was purchased between 1670 and 1692 by a man named Richard Morris with profits made from sugar production on a slave plantation owned by his family in Barbados. Slaves, imported to New York to till his lands, also built the manor house in which the children and grandchildren of the family lived.

Gouverneur Morris, the great-grandson of Richard, was born in 1752 near what is now the corner of East 132nd Street and Cypress Avenue. At 25, he was one of the youngest delegates to the Continental Congress. In 1787, "by himself," according to the text, "he wrote the preamble to the U.S. Constitution" and, because he had a graceful style, was given "a major hand" in writing other portions of that document as well. His half-brother, Lewis, we are told, was one of the signers of the Declaration of Independence.

The textbook, written primarily for the use of teachers in the schools of the South Bronx, attempts to reconcile a sense of reverence for one of the Founding Fathers with an honest recognition of the contradictions in his life and background. While noting, for example, that his family did not merely use slaves on their lands but also traded slaves and used their labor as the workforce in an iron foundry that they operated in New Jersey, the author tries to place these enterprises in a mitigating context. "There is reason to believe," she writes, that the slaves owned by the Morris family "were treated more humanely than slaves elsewhere."

Gouverneur Morris himself, according to the text,

grew up to be a critic of slave-holding, which he termed "the curse of Heaven in the states where it prevails," yet retained some of the slaves he had inherited to tend his manor house and raise his son.

An apparently complicated man, enlightened in some ways although not in others, he "distrusted the 'masses,' " did not believe that "poor people should vote," and tried "to shape the Constitution so that it protected the rights of property owners at all costs," yet he was willing, in principle at least, to infringe the rights of people who owned slaves and later helped to found a charitable society intended to make slavery less onerous and to encourage the manumission of a slave upon the age of 25.

"Ironically," however, the writer says, "the last slave in the State of New York" was living—unemancipated—on the Morris lands in 1827, more than ten years after his master's death.

Morris did not marry until the age of 57. When he died at the age of 64, he left one survivor, Gouverneur Morris II, who later erected the church on St. Ann's Avenue in honor of his mother. The two vaults in which the Founding Father and his family rest, the textbook says, are to be seen today on the grounds of the church—where, in fact, at the time when I first visited, the burial site overlooked a trash-deposit just behind the area where drug needles were exchanged in Children's Park.

In a lesson plan included in the text, children are urged to imagine what it would be like to be "a ten-year-old slave boy" in the manor house while Gouverneur was growing up. "You hear young Gouverneur speaking French," which he has studied at the private school that he attends, in which he also studies Latin grammar, English composition, and arithmetic. He also "studies French with his tutor, who is preparing him for college," and will later enter "the school . . . now called Columbia University," where "he will have the best education" possible.

"You wish," says the text, "that you could have such an education. . . . You hope that things will change someday."

Students are encouraged to visit various South Bronx sites named for the Founding Father's family—among them, Morris High School, "oldest high school in the Bronx," and the Port Morris Industrial Park, where "thriving factories . . . are now located" near the place on the East River where the ships transporting slaves and sugar once were moored. A site called Gouverneur Morris Square is briskly mentioned too.

There is a noticeable awkwardness and tension in some of the passages that recommend "field trips and walking tours" to these historic sites. Morris High School is, after all, one of the most beleaguered, segregated, and decrepit secondary schools in the United States. The Port Morris Industrial Park is flourishing to a degree, but any jobs there that may go to South Bronx residents tend to be in menial labor at the lowest scales of pay. Gouverneur Morris Square, which the writer candidly describes as "an all-but-forgotten tribute to the penman of the Constitution," is a bleak, abandoned spot close to a stretch of Bruckner Boulevard that has become a thriving stroll for youthful prostitutes.

Still, the writer tries to give the South Bronx children reasons to identify with the historical traditions of the neighborhood. As a boy, she tells us, for example, Gouverneur Morris took delight in writing "verses and poetry," which, she emphasizes, were "popular in his time the way rap songs are today." She also mentions that Brook Avenue, which lies today at the heart of the narcotics trade, is named after a mill brook where the Morris children "used to play and take long walks" in fields and woods where bears and foxes once roamed free. "Notice how Mill Brook Apartments"—a reference to a dangerous public housing complex in Mott Haven—"corresponds to the area where the Mill Brook formerly flowed. . . ."

In one of the many interesting details that the Bronx County Historical Society provides for use of teachers in the classrooms of the area, it is noted that the original name of the Bronx River was a Native American word that means "the place of peace."

*   *   *

Back in New York City in late August, I find a taxi-driver at the airport who agrees to take me directly to the Bronx. Like many taxi-drivers in New York, he has a foreign accent. When I ask him where he's from, he says, "From Russia." He seems good-natured and slides open a small panel in the bulletproof partition at his back so we can chat. But when we come off the bridge into the Bronx, he opens his window, spits in the street, then rolls the window shut and locks his door. "All this is scum here. No one works. Look at this."

I ask him where he lives.

"I live in Queens, in a nice section."

The children I'm going to meet are members of a group that has been organized by workers at a storefront program close to Shakespeare Avenue on Featherbed Lane, run by Covenant House, an independent Catholic organization based in midtown on the West Side of Manhattan. The program's director, Gizelle Luke, is a young black woman who has lived in Europe for some years but came back to work here in the Bronx about eight months ago.

Before the children have assembled, she takes me a couple of blocks from Shakespeare Avenue to an overpass that crosses an expressway, which, she says, leads to the suburbs and the interstate, I-95. Standing on the overpass, she gestures back toward Featherbed Lane and at a housing complex on a hill that rises just behind it. There are, she says, few economic possibilities for people who reside here. "There aren't many branches of the major banks. The 'banks' are loan sharks—or check-cashing places. If you want to open a small business, there's no banker that you've come to know that you can talk with to obtain a loan. No libraries open in the evening. Few recreational opportunities for children. Many abandoned houses and abandoned people and abandoned cars. But I want you to see something interesting."

Turning to the highway, where the cars are speeding by beneath us, she points in the direction of some buildings just beyond the road.

At first I can't tell what she's pointing at. Then I notice

30

the pictures of flowers, window shades and curtains and interiors of pretty-looking rooms, that have been painted on these buildings on the sides that face the highway. It's a very strange sight, and the pictures have been done so well that when you look the first time, you imagine that you're seeing into people's homes—pleasant-looking homes, in fact, that have a distinctly middle-class appearance. I ask her if people who live here did these pictures.

"Nobody lives here," she replies. "Those buildings are all empty."

The city had these murals painted on the walls, she says, not for the people in the neighborhood—because they're facing the wrong way—but for tourists and commuters. "The idea is that they mustn't be upset by knowing too much about the population here. It isn't enough that these people are sequestered. It's also important that their presence be disguised or 'sweetened.' The city did not repair the buildings so that kids who live around here could, in fact, *have* pretty rooms like those. Instead, they *painted* pretty rooms on the facades. It's an illusion."

I ask if the people around here have made comments of this sort.

"I don't know what they say," she says. "I haven't asked. To me, it's just outrageous. The first time I saw it, I thought, 'Oh, Lord! Well, what a dirty thing to do!' Really, it is far beyond racism. It's just—'In your face! Take that!' We don't clean up your neighborhood, don't fix your buildings, fix your schools, or give you decent hospitals or banks. Instead, we paint the back sides of the buildings so that people driving to the suburbs will have something nice to look at."

Most people, she adds, soon realize that the pictures are just that—mere paintings—so they can't accomplish their objective. "Maybe it works for tourists who are here for the first time." The city, she says, denies unkind intentions and insists it's simply decoration. "Decoration for whom? It makes me angry. Look at my hand. I'm trembling."

The children I meet a few minutes later in her office range in age from seven to 12 years old. The conversation, which is desultory and a bit forced at the start, becomes more animated when I ask about the public schools that they attend, one of which is housed in a former synagogue built in 1897. Another school, to which some of the kids commute, was ranked "dead last" in reading scores of all the elementary schools in New York City two years earlier. Both schools, according to one of the children, an 11-year-old named Kimberly, have mostly Hispanic and black children—"not many white students," she says.

"How many white students—Anglo whites—do you have in your class?" I ask.

"In my class?" she answers. "There is none."

The other children answer, "None," except for one girl who says, "One."

"I used to have a white boy in my class," says Robert, nine years old. "He was Irish."

"Did you like him?"

"He was my best friend."

"Since 1960," says a 12-year-old named Jeremiah, "white people started moving away from black and Spanish people in New York."

The specificity of the date intrigues me. "Where do you think white people went?" I ask.

"I think—to the country," says another boy.

"It isn't where people live. It's *how* they live," says Jeremiah.

"Say that again," I ask.

"It's *how* they live," he says again. "There are different economies in different places."

When I ask him to explain this, he refers to Riverdale, a mostly white and middle-class community in the northwest section of the Bronx. "Life in Riverdale is opened up," he says. "Where we live, it's locked down."

"In what way?" I ask.

"We can't go out and play."

"Why not?"

"You go in the park to play," he answers sharply. "You'll see why."

Gizelle Luke, who is standing behind him, looks at me and lifts her eyebrows when he says this.

I try to draw in the other children by asking them to tell me someone they admire. Several children answer, "Marcus Garvey," who is hardly mentioned in most textbooks nowadays. Others speak of Malcolm X. No one, however, mentions Martin Luther King, even though the major street within the neighborhood is named for him. When I comment on this, some of the children groan.

"He's mentioned too much," says Jeremiah.

" 'Name a hero of black people,' " says Chevonne, a nine-year-old, mimicking a teacher. " 'Dr. Martin Luther King. . . . I have a dream. . . .' "

I ask her why she doesn't like to hear of it.

"One," she says, "because you hear it too much. Two, because it isn't true."

"If everyone looks up to him," says Jeremiah, "you have to try to find somebody of your own."

"Who do *you* look up to?"

"I look up to God," he says, "my mother, and myself."

A number of sirens from police cars in the street interrupt the conversation for a moment. When the sirens subside and the police cars have moved on, I ask the children if they think of the police as people they can trust.

"I don't," says Kimberly.

Virtually all the children answer, "No."

"You have nothing good to say about the people who protect you?"

In one voice, they answer, "No."

Kimberly describes a night, a couple weeks before, when she and her brothers thought their house was being robbed. "It was late and we were looking at TV. We called the cops. They never came. We called my grandmother. My grandmother came. The police never came. They didn't come."

Feelings of distrust for the police are not unusual among young people nowadays, not only in the cities; but the unanimity in the distrust these children voice is somewhat startling.

I ask them, "Is this a good country?"

"No," says Chevonne.

"Somewhere," says Kimberly.

"Where?" I ask.

"Maybe in Connecticut," she says.

"Why Connecticut?"

"It's quiet there," she says. "They have green places."

"At school, do you sing 'America the Beautiful'?"

"We don't sing that anymore," says Kimberly.

"In some schools they do," says Robert.

"Do you think America is beautiful?"

"It was beautiful when they wrote that song," says Jeremiah.

Kimberly and Robert speak of killings that have taken place within the neighborhood, and Jeremiah speaks about "the little altars in the streets" that people make by setting candles in a circle on the sidewalk where someone has been shot down. "You hear shooting in the night," he says. "Next day, you see a lot of little cardboard boxes, each one with a candle—sometimes flowers, and you see a picture of the person who was killed.

"Sometimes," he says, "they tie a flower to a tree and sometimes they paint the person's name against the wall and put one candle underneath."

I ask him, "Can you sleep after you hear about these things?"

"I pray that someone in my family will not die."

Like many children I have come to know in the South Bronx, Jeremiah and his friends do not speak during our meeting in the jargon that some middle-class Americans identify with inner-city kids. There's no obscenity in their speech, nor are there any of those flip code-phrases that are almost always placed within the mouths of poor black children in the movies—a style of speech, I sometimes think, that may be exaggerated by the media to lend a heightened sense of "differentness" to children in the ghetto. Children, however, are good at psyching out a stranger; it may be that these children would speak somewhat differently to someone they know better.

As the meeting breaks up, the youngest child in the group, who sat at my side but did not say a word for the entire hour, whispers to me that she did not like what the other children said about not trusting the police. I ask her why. She says, "My father's a policeman."

The child, who tells me her name is Monique, seems to have been saving up this one idea to share with me in private. "I trust my daddy," she says, "but I don't know my daddy." Whispering still, she says, "I never saw him but I know that he's in the police."

I ask Monique if she lives with her mother.

"I never saw my mother either," she replies.

She's a tiny child with two pigtails and a pair of bright-red sneakers. On the front of her jersey are these words: "The Power of Little People."

I ask how old she is.

"I'm seven," she replies.

Standing outside on the sidewalk after the children have gone home, Gizelle comments on one of the sharp-edged statements Jeremiah made. "When you asked him about the reason that he feels 'locked down,' his answer to you was rather curt. There was an abruptness and impatience in his tone. I think it's because he didn't want to make it easy for you. He wanted to leave it for *you* to speak about racism. He didn't want to hand it to you on a platter. It's part of his maturity and dignity, I think. But you can sense the edginess in that: forcing a white person maybe to go further than you wanted, to make you name reality, not letting himself be used by you as a convenient voice. A lot of black people feel like that. They want America to name its crime and not keep squirming to avoid the risky words." She adds, "I found his description of 'the little altars in the streets' particularly moving."

Since that time, I have become more aware of just how many of those little altars there are on the sidewalks all over the South Bronx. People in the neighborhoods water the flowers sometimes and replace the candles. Even when the flowers are dry, the altars often remain in place for months, sometimes for years.

*   *   *

The following day, I spend some hours in the neighborhood where Jeremiah lives. Walking in Featherbed Lane, past Shakespeare Avenue, to a broad commercial boulevard named for Martin Luther King, I stop in front of a local branch of the New York Public Library, which is in a narrow building that was formerly a Chinese restaurant. I knock at the heavily barred door, but no one answers; and when I try the door, I find it's locked, although it's only two P.M. Outside the barricaded library, I watch an emaciated woman weaving her way to a public phone, to which she then clings, holding the receiver in her hand, but not depositing a coin, and seeming to be frozen in some terrifying indecision. A half-hour later, when I return to the same spot, she is still there.

Avenues named for Dr. King transect a number of the most unhappy inner-city neighborhoods in the United States; some of the most drug-infested buildings in New York and other cities bear his name or names of other notable black figures. One particularly dangerous housing project in New York is named for Langston Hughes, another for James Weldon Johnson.

Many words one sees and hears within these neighborhoods convey this unintended sense of mockery. Sometimes, however, the mockery is obviously intentional. One of the gang names found in several cities I have visited is "Niggers For Life." One of the popular brand names for the heroin sold this year in the South Bronx is "Jungle Fever." Other names for heroin in widespread use in New York City are "Black Sabbath" and "True Power" and "Black Death."

The romanticized self-mockery in names like these brings to my mind the anguish of a young black woman who grew up in one of New York City's ghetto neighborhoods but goes to college in the Berkshires. In a story she wrote about her younger brother, whose given name is Malcolm X, she says that he dropped out of high school and now wanders through the city with a beeper and a friend whose nickname, she reports, is Tragedy.

"My brother's head is so close-shaven," she says, "it's almost bald." Her brother tells her, "This is how everyone is cutting their hair. . . ." The name of the hairstyle, he explains, is "25 Years to Life."

She asks him, "Like in prison . . . ? This is how you want to wear your hair?"

"You don't have to be in jail to be in prison," he replies.

Her portrait of her brother Malcolm walking the streets with Tragedy in shaven heads summons up one of those journeys poets wrote about during the Middle Ages. The pilgrimages of that era, however, usually had clear-cut destinations. There is no destination for the pilgrimage that Malcolm X and the young man called Tragedy have chosen, any more than for the men with beepers here along King Boulevard.

A man on a corner that I pass, just off King Boulevard, keeps saying a word that sounds like "works." After repeating it several times, he pauses, then says it again. It has a bored and humdrum sound. "They're selling hypodermic needles," Mrs. Washington later explains to me when I ask her what this means.

On a hill beside King Boulevard, a number of women are seated on chairs outside the door of an apartment building, playing cards while keeping their eyes on children and grandchildren. A strangely austere old man with long gray hair sits on a milk crate by the curb, one of his arms draped over a crutch, a hot and tired look within his eyes. Nearby, enough small kids to make up the full enrollment of a good-size summer camp are filling the sidewalks with their shouts and cries. The temperature today is 96 degrees. The children are doing what they can to have some fun, but there is little sense of freedom in their play.

A few months earlier, some children in the neighborhood had opened a hydrant to create a kind of river in the street, then mobbed and attacked a number of firefighters who were sent to shut the hydrant off because of the danger to the neighborhood in lowered water pressure in the case of fire. Nobody on King Boulevard, today at least, has opened any hydrants, even though the day is humid and uncomfortable.

A ten-year-old standing near a sno-cone cart strikes up

a chat with me, perhaps with the goal of getting me to buy a sno-cone for him and a friend of his, which I do. In the course of talking with him, I inquire if his family has air-conditioning in their apartment.

"Our family doesn't have time or money to bother with air-conditioning," he says. "We open the windows and we don't have any problems." His body looks hot; he's drenched in sweat and he has a somewhat awkward expression when he says this, but he displays no sense of feeling pitiable or wanting any pity.

I ask him if he had a chance to go away during the summer.

"No, I couldn't go," he says.

"Have you ever been away to camp?"

"No," he answers.

"Are there places here where you can play?"

"Not really," he replies, his eyes fixed on the ground.

At six P.M., in Featherbed Lane, there is the busy hum of voices and a slightly fevered sense of expectation in the air as milling groups of adolescents take the place of younger children, mothers, and grandmothers who were on the sidewalks and the front steps of the buildings earlier. In a deep gutter, one small child, wearing only underpants, lies on his stomach in a pool of dirty water about six inches deep, splashing joyfully, pretending he can swim.

On another afternoon a few days later, I talk with a group of adolescents who have gathered in another storefront office that is being used as a youth center, this one not in the South Bronx but in a Harlem neighborhood about a dozen blocks west of St. Ann's. When I share with them the statement Jeremiah made about the feeling that he is "locked down," a 15-year-old student, Isabel, jumps right in and says, "I think that that's too strong. I would put it differently."

I ask, "How would you put it?"

"It's not like being in a jail," she says. "It's more like being 'hidden.' It's as if you have been put in a garage where, if they don't have room for something but aren't sure if they should throw it out, they put it there where they don't need to think of it again."

I ask if she believes Americans do not "have room" for her or people like her.

"Think of it this way," says a 16-year-old named Maria, who is Isabel's half-sister. "If people in New York woke up one day and learned that we were gone, that we had simply died or left for somewhere else, how would they feel?"

"How do you think they'd feel?" I ask.

"I think they'd be relieved. I think it would lift a burden from their minds. I think the owners of the downtown stores would be ecstatic. They'd know they'd never need to see us coming in their doors, and taxi-drivers would be happy because they would never need to come here anymore. People in Manhattan could go on and lead their lives and not feel worried about being robbed and not feel guilty and not need to pay for welfare babies."

"Do you think that's how they really look at people in this neighborhood?"

"I think they look at us as obstacles to moving forward," she replies.

The students go out of their way to make it clear that they do not subscribe to rhetoric about "conspiracies" or "genocide," perhaps because I'm white, perhaps because they know that rhetoric like that is frequently discredited, perhaps because they truly don't believe it.

"It's not like, 'Well, these babies just aren't dying fast enough,'" Maria says. "'Let's figure out a way to kill some more.' It's not like that at all. It's like—I don't know how to say this. . . ." She holds a Styrofoam cup in her hands and turns it slowly for a moment. "If you weave enough bad things into the fibers of a person's life—sickness and filth, old mattresses and other junk thrown in the streets and other ugly ruined things, and ruined people, a prison here, sewage there, drug dealers here, the homeless people over there, then give us the very worst schools anyone could think of, hospitals that keep you waiting for ten hours, police that don't show up when someone's dying, take the train that's underneath the street in the good neighborhoods and put it up above where it shuts out the sun, you can guess that life will not be very nice and children will not have much sense of being glad of who they are. Sometimes it feels like we've been buried six feet under their perceptions. This is what I feel they have accomplished."

"Put them over there in a big housing project," says a boy named Benjamin. "Pack them tight. Don't think about them. Keep your hands clean. Maybe they'll kill each other off."

"I have a few statements to make about that," Isabel says. "When we talk about the people who are making these decisions, we keep saying 'they' and most of the time we think of 'they' as being white. We don't even know who 'they' might really be, yet we keep saying 'they.' This is because we know we have no power to decide these things. Something's always happening where the last and final vote was not the one we made. So we say 'they did this' and 'they' seems extremely powerful, but we do not know who 'they' are.

"Sometimes it seems that 'they' are the welfare workers or the supervisors, who can be very rude to people, or maybe the nurses at the hospitals, or the doctors, or police, but most of these people do not have much power. So you always want to know who does have power and you ask this question but you can't find out. You see destruction around you but you do not know who the destroyer is."

"Some people," I point out, "would say that the 'destroyers' are the people right here in this neighborhood." I run through a list of some of the people who are likely to be named most frequently—drug dealers, or the kids whose parents do not give them proper supervision, or teenagers who cause havoc in the housing projects, absent fathers, women who refuse some kinds of jobs that they may find demeaning. . . .

"The drug dealers don't have any power over the economy," Maria says. "They don't control the hospitals. They don't run the schools and they don't run New York."

"Okay, I have a few points to make," says an extremely shy and dark-skinned girl who tells me she is from Honduras.

She speaks softly at first; the others turn to her, and

even a group of somewhat restless boys who have been whispering to one another quiet down and pay attention.

"My mother can't speak English, so I go with her to welfare. I always feel like crying when I see the way she's treated. 'Fill this application! Hurry up! Sit down! It's not your turn!' This is not the way that people should be treated. It's not even the way you talk to dogs because you wouldn't bark at dogs. I hear this lady say to another lady, to a social worker, or a supervisor, 'Why are they here if they don't speak the language? Why don't they go back to where they're from?'

"But it isn't only language, because no one talks that way to a rich lady who does not speak English. Go downtown. You'll see what I mean. Sometimes these women come from Italy or Argentina or from Spain. They go in the stores in their beautiful clothes. They're treated like celebrities. It isn't the language. It's skin color and it's being poor. This is something more than disrespect. It's as if they wish that you did not *exist* so they would not have to be bothered."

"If you go downtown to a nice store," says Maria, "they look at you sometimes as if your body is disgusting. You can be dressed in your best dress but you feel you are not welcome. They follow you sometimes but they do not want to touch you. You pay for something—she pulls back her hand—like that! as if my hand is dirty."

White people who feel saddened by Maria's words may nonetheless tend to discount the accuracy of her perceptions and may even hear in them a hint of paranoia. Yet countless statements in the press would certainly reinforce her paranoia, if that's really what it is. Images of moral dirtiness and overflowing worthlessness, identified with poor black and Hispanic women and their children, fill the pages of our daily papers; and even young people who don't read the papers are exposed to the same images in conversations heard all day and night in New York City on the mainstream radio stations.

"They are not like you, and they are not like me," says a popular talk-show host who broadcasts in late evening hours on New York's top-rated A.M. station. "They are

41

something apart. They are distinct." He wonders if there's "a factory" where they " 'drop' those kids . . . what? ten a minute?" At first, it seems he's speaking only of black teens who have committed serious crimes. But his language has a sweep that seems to go beyond the law-and-order issue. "No amount of food stamps . . . no amount of punishment," he says, will help the situation. "There is nothing to do but segregate yourself from them." They are "a different species. . . ."

Black and Hispanic adolescents speak a lot of being disrespected—"dissed"—by other kids in their communities. But the sense of disrespect these youngsters hear over the radio and see sometimes in some of the tabloid papers is in a different league entirely from the sort of thing they may experience from their own peers. The statements of Maria and her sister, one after another, leave no doubt that they have understood the message being given to them by a large and, it appears, expanding sector of American society. They also strike me as so very, very different from the abstract, cautious commentaries about "racial sensitivities" and "racial tensions" made at times by the more serious newspapers in their editorials about these matters. A sense of justified and prophetic rage is usually absent from these commentaries, but the students here in Harlem voice it freely.

"Do you ever hear of cities that existed long ago and are extinct today?" asks Isabel. "I believe that this will happen here. Everyone will get so sick of life in Harlem and the South Bronx that we'll just give up and move to somewhere else. But it will be the same thing there again until the new place is so sad and ugly it's destroyed and then we'll move again to somewhere else, and somewhere else, until the whole world is destroyed and there is nothing to look back on but the ashes."

Startled by her words, I ask her, as I find I will be asking many times throughout this year of visits to New York, "Do you honestly believe that?"

"Yes. I do," she says. "I believe that to a full extent."

*   *   *

Cooler weather finally arrives. I lose touch with Mrs. Washington and David for a time. On a weekend in October when I'm in New York to talk with teachers, I stop by to visit them one night a little before dark.

Mrs. Washington does not get out of bed when I come in. She seems much weaker than she was during July. When I ask how she feels, she answers, "Better . . . worse. . . . It comes and goes," then shows me a notice she has just received from the company that manages her building. "It's a dispossess. Eviction order." She takes it back and puts it by her lamp. "My rent is paid directly by the city. I don't see the money. When the city's computers make an error, I get one of these. In '92 I got one and it said I had to be 'recertified.' I went to welfare and I told them that I was already certified, so they said, 'Okay. You're fine!' Two months later, I got the dispossess.

"The problem is they have no continuity. Every other month, it seems, the welfare staff gets fired and my social worker disappears."

When I ask the name of her social worker, she says, "I don't have one. I had one but her husband died and she went back to Puerto Rico. She came by and told me that she wasn't breaking down her caseload since there wasn't anyone to take her place. I still don't have a new case worker." Picking up the dispossess again, she says, "It says I owe $6,000. I got three of these last week. They push them underneath the door. I have to try to get a lawyer."

She asks me what I'm doing in New York and I describe the teachers' conference I'm attending. I also tell her of the children I've been meeting and relate my conversation with Maria and her sister and their friends.

"How they doin'?" she asks, as if she knew them.

I repeat what Maria said—that if "we . . . died or left for somewhere else," the people in the city would be glad.

"How old is this girl?"

I say 16.

"I feel the same and I'm three times her age."

"Do you think these feelings go that far?" I ask. "Wishing poor people literally would *die?*"

"Not all of them feel like that, I guess. Maybe the majority. Maybe not. I bet close to half. Most of them probably don't think of it at all. . . ."

She thinks it over and then qualifies her words. "Maybe once a year they do. Some of them have parties around Christmas to raise something for the poor. If we wasn't poor, maybe they'd have no reason to have parties."

"You don't see kindness in these acts?"

"I wish I could. But if they want to help the poor, they don't need to have a party first. They could skip the party and just send the money up to feed the children who are hungry." After a moment, with more energy, she adds, "Come on, Jonathan! They do this once a year. What's goin' to happen on December 26? Who is this charity for? In a way, it's for themselves so they won't feel ashamed goin' to church to pray on Christmas Eve. Maybe they think this way they won't end up in hell."

I ask if she believes in heaven and hell.

"We have our hell right here on earth. They'll get theirs after their last breath."

A Bible that was on the kitchen table in July is open on her quilt. I ask what part she reads.

"New Testament mostly is the one I read. Sometimes I read Ecclesiastes. If you want to know what's happening these days, it's all right there.

"Truth is, I don't know it like his grandma did." She nods in the direction of the kitchen, where her son is sitting. "She knew the Bible from first word to last. My father had his Bible by his bed on the night table. At meals he used to read to us from the Old Testament. I don't dwell so much on the denominations. . . ."

Somewhat lethargically now, as if she may be just a bit sedated, she says, "All of us in my family had their Bibles. I have another little one I carry in my bag. To tell the truth, right now it don't give me much strength."

"Are you eating anything?" I ask.

"I got a chicken in the freezer," she replies. "David cooks broccoli for me. Last night he made me chicken and a baked potato. When I can't eat, he puts some vegetables and fruit into the blender. You can't believe how nasty it tastes but he insists I eat it."

I ask her about the woman I saw the last time I was here, who goes out with her dog collecting cans—"the lady with the Bible," David called her.

"This lady," she says, "is just a very friendly person. She'll stop and say, 'Have a nice day.' You can tell she's lonely. She's not young. Could be 75 years old, or 80. Lives by herself. The Puerto Ricans call her 'Mama.' There's a lot of people like her in the neighborhood.

"This woman's dog is always dirty-looking, but she loves him. Always hurryin' after her on little feet. Everyone around here knows the dog, though no one knows his name. Store-owners put out food for him. He drinks his water from a fountain near the zoo, same place homeless people do. I guess he leads a good life for a dog.

"Sometimes if I don't see her for a while, I start to worry. During the winter you don't see her much. I guess she stays inside. You feel concerned. . . . There's something about this lady that's mysterious. She knows all the verses of the Bible. It makes everybody happy when they see her."

"I didn't know there were homeless people at the zoo," I say.

"There's homeless people everywhere," she says. "Newspapers say Manhattan is the part of New York City that has all the homeless. That's not true. It's just because they see them there, in Central Park and other places like Penn Station. They don't know how many men are living up here by the zoo.

"Women too. . . . They're chased out of the subway, chased out of Central Park. They make their little huts down by the river and the city burns them down. Some of them spend the whole night on the ferry that goes out to Staten Island. They go back and forth all night because, if they get off, they'll be arrested.

"Up here, no one bothers them. They're not harassed."

Although I've been to the zoo with children on a number of occasions, coming up here on the train and walking through the neighborhood leave me disoriented. I ask her, "Which direction is the zoo from here?"

Gesturing north, she says, "Right over there. That's

where they stay. They go in there and hide, right by the zoo. I guess that they feel safe in there, close to the animals. They know that no one will arrest them. I don't know. I guess it's better than walkin' in the streets and bein' driven about from place to place.

"One night last December close to Christmas, it was down to ten or 12 degrees. Wind was strong. You heard it beatin' on the windows all night long like somebody was bangin' on the panes. I said to David, 'They're goin' to freeze out there tonight.'

"All night long I heard the wind. I looked out the window and I couldn't get no sleep. I didn't even see no stray dogs out there in the street. I kept thinkin' of the time when we had no place of our own."

Listening to her voice, which now does have an obviously sedated sound, I soon forget to take notes and almost forget that I am here in search of information. I find myself searching for something other than information but can't tell myself exactly what it is. There will be other evenings like this in the year ahead. Often during times like these I have to fight off the feeling that I am about to cry. I do fight it off because I do not want to be embarrassed. Outside the apartment, when I leave, I sometimes give in to these feelings, which I never can explain because they do not seem connected to the things we talk about. It's something cumulative that just builds up during a quiet time.

She doesn't say much about her problems with the welfare system during this conversation; nor does she speak about the hospital, except to mention that the elevators in the clinic building are not working—"so I got to walk up four floors if I want to see my doctor. People who are too sick to walk—somebody comes down, a nurse or social worker, whoever is available, usually a man—comes down to carry them upstairs. . . .

"Hospital's started a soup kitchen. People line up early in the street, just like they do to get free flour. Flour comes in five-pound bags," she adds with little energy.

Her weakness is so pronounced, her body so much thinner than before, I wonder if she'll be in the hospital again the next time I am here. Her son stays in the kitchen while I'm with her, leaning on the table with his hands pressed to his eyes.

At midnight on November 1, a 150-year-old church two blocks from Mrs. Washington's apartment is consumed by fire. Flames, according to the *Times,* destroy the church's 100-year-old organ and its stained-glass windows and the records of the births and deaths of all who prayed here for six generations.

Arson is suspected; and although there is no evidence to prove this, many people, including David, take it as a logical assumption. His frustration with some of the men in the community is reawakened by the fire.

"Some of these men," he tells me on the phone one night a few days after this event, "would burn their own house with their mother in it if they didn't like something she said."

"But why—a church?" I ask.

"I don't know why," he says, "but that's the way it is. I feel afraid of my own people, my own race, black people, students my own age. You step on someone's foot or look at somebody the wrong way—if he doesn't like your attitude, he might pull out a gun and kill you."

"What does that mean—'he doesn't like your attitude'?"

"It means he doesn't like the way you look at him. He wants to change it for you, take you down a little. That's what some people call 'an attitude adjustment.'

"The trouble is, they don't just take you down. They take you *out.* These are young kids, 12 or 14 sometimes, but they look much older.

"A time might come when we will have to treat these children who kill people like adults—keep them in prison for much longer periods of years. Right now, they're in and out too fast. My mother says New York is the only place where you can kill someone and still be home for dinner.

"A couple of months ago," he says, "this girl was raped

and burned and murdered under the expressway—
Bruckner Boulevard. It's a kind of overpass. Under the
overpass there's this dead-end area. That's where they
found her body. It was in a Pampers box that somebody
had soaked in gasoline. The medical examiner said he
thinks she was 11 but he can't be sure. I wanted to ask
someone, 'What's happening to my race? Why do we murder our own people?' "

The child of whom he speaks turns out to have been
13, but very small. Her family, according to one press account, had been transferred by the city from a homeless
shelter in Manhattan to a "bleak apartment" with "no table,
no dresser, not a single piece of living room furniture."
Soon after that, she began to run away from home and
travel on the subway late at night. After her death, she was
remembered by the teachers at her school as "an ugly duck-
ling" who smelled so bad that other kids would not sit next
to her. Her teachers said she was aware of why she was
avoided by her classmates. When children said to her, "You
smell," she would reply, "I know."

When I ask David how his mother's feeling, he says
that her appetite is better. "I cooked beef stew last night. I
put in a can of kernel corn and some green vegetables,
some green peas and fresh string beans, which I know she
likes. We had Italian bread. They bake it every day here.
The grocery store is overpriced but everything they sell is
good and fresh. My mother's doctor says I've got to keep
her eating.

"She had some ice cream for dessert," he adds.

He mentions, too, that he has applied to John Jay College, which is part of City University, for admission to a
program that trains prison officers. "I'm pretty sure I'm
going to get in but I don't know if I'll receive financial aid.
They say that they're not giving out as much now as they
used to."

The details of what he cooks to spark his mother's appetite—the "kernel corn" and the "green vegetables"—
seem so important to him. He still sounds very young at
times. When he speaks of his mother, he sometimes calls
her "Mommy," then corrects himself and says, "My

mother." At other times, he sounds more grown-up than most adults that I know.

"I have a friend," he says one night in mid-November when he phones again a little before midnight. "His cousin was in the hospital with AIDS. I went to visit him last month and I got scared. I knew him before. He was an athlete and he used to work out on machines. I didn't recognize him in the hospital—he looked so thin. He couldn't eat or drink. They had him on an IV tube.

"I'd never seen an AIDS case so advanced. It frightened me to see him. I thought, 'Is this what's going to happen to my mother?'

"He died this week. He passed away on Thursday. I didn't expect that it would come so soon. He was only 29.

"They had a service for him at a funeral home today. His mother and brothers and sisters and grandmother were there, and his great-grandmother. I think he was going to be cremated, being that they didn't have much money. People who'd been close to him stood up and spoke. Everyone said something they remembered.

"His mother is a poor lady. Something about her clothing told me she is poor. She said that she had fought with him to keep him alive in the last days, but she could not.

"His sister is religious. She said when she went to see him Wednesday, on the day before he died, his eyes were closed and he was very still. She thought he was sleeping. She was talking to her friend, who went with her, sitting in the room next to his bed. She said she told her friend he was a good man who did not do harm to anyone. He woke up then and held out his hand to meet her friend and said that he was glad to meet her. His sister told him, 'God is with you.' When she said those words, she said she saw a light in his eyes she'd never seen before. He squeezed her hand and said, 'I love you,' and she said she knew then that he'd be all right—he looked at peace. That was the last time that she saw him living. He died the next morning.

"People ask why God is taking the good people. But his mother said she has accepted it because he's in a better place. I still don't see the fairness, but it's not for me to judge.

"This family came here from Puerto Rico. There were little children at the ceremony, nieces and nephews of Willie—that's his name, the man who died. They ran around and played because they didn't understand why we were there."

"Do you know," I ask, "how Willie got infected?"

"His cousin says he'd met a girl and dated her awhile. Then the relationship broke off. A couple years later he found out he was sick. His cousin says he had no other girlfriend in those years, but I don't know if that is true.

"I didn't say anything at the ceremony because I didn't know him well and didn't know what I should say. My mother says when you're 90 years old and see your children and your grandchildren grown up, then you expect to die. But when someone is 29 years old, it's harder to accept. Children know they have to bury their parents, but for parents to bury their children shouldn't happen."

I ask if he believes in God.

"I have to. He's the one who makes it possible for me to have my mother with me still. I hope He lets her die without the pain that Willie just went through."

"Another boy got killed in front of the building next door," Mrs. Washington remarks when I return to visit a few days before Thanksgiving. "A Puerto Rican kid, 16 years old. His parents are quiet people.

"See? It's just that quick. Their son is gone. Eleven P.M. Boston Road. It just takes a second. Now his mother and father have to bury him.

"He shouldn't have been outside there at that hour in the first place. He could have been a dealer. Or he might have been a lookout. He might have been killed for something he was doin'. Or it might be he was doin' nothin'. Whatever he was doing or wasn't doing, now he's dead. The funeral's tomorrow.

"It wasn't in the paper. I looked in *Newsday* and the *Daily News*. Maybe it will be in the Bronx paper. I'm going to find a nice card for his mother and father."

She speaks with terror of the apartment building in Mott Haven where her daughter, Charlayne, lives with her two children. "The building's full of dealers, just like ours, but in much worse condition. There's a hole in the ceiling of the bathroom. You can't take a shower. You look up and you can see right in the next apartment. When people above her use their shower, water pours down on your head. Electric sockets get all wet. The plaster's crumbling. . . .

"Drug dealers down there are so brazen that they ripped the metal front right off the mailbox. They used to just break off the locks. Then the tenants put a steel grate over the whole row of boxes. The dealers got enraged at this and ripped the grate off too.

"I'm petrified of going there to see her. Costs six dollars for a cab if you can find one. Six dollars is a lot of money for me but, if they're in danger, I don't have no choice.

"As soon as you get out of the cab, it doesn't matter who you are, the dealers run right up to you and ask you what you want and tell you what they have. You go inside, you see somebody shooting drugs right in the hallway.

"I had the children with me for a weekend. When I bring them back on Sunday night, we see this woman with her needle shooting up on the front stairs. She has the needle in her arm. I'm trying to get the children past her, so I ask her, 'Could you do that somewhere else?' She tells me, 'I'm sorry. I don't mean to disrespect you, but I can't get up.' "

"Little children shouldn't have to see that," says her son, who's standing in the doorway of the kitchen, "but they see it all the time. Last time I was there, I saw two women in the hallway. One of them had the belt around her arm, the needle in her other hand. The other one's eyes were droopy, as if she was nodding off."

"Nobody's s'posed to live like this in the United States," his mother says. "Did you ever read about this in the books you used in school? I never heard about this in no textbook."

I tell her that her daughter's apartment building

sounds a little like the Martinique, the homeless shelter where she used to live, which Mario Cuomo, who was governor at the time, described as "a scene out of Dickens."

"Trust me. The Martinique was like the Hilton in comparison to this. At least they had guards in the lobby." She says that nearly a dozen families who were in the Martinique when she was there now live on Charlayne's block. "Like I say, the city moved whole floors of people wholesale from the shelters into certain blocks. . . .

"Sometimes I think that we were better off when we were in the shelters in Manhattan. At least we were close to better hospitals and we were in the middle of an area of normal life, normal activity, and you could walk along Fifth Avenue and take your kids to Central Park. You could see nice stores and walk by restaurants and theaters and nice buildings, even if you couldn't go inside.

"When I got out of the Martinique, I was hoping, 'Maybe this time we will get a chance to lead our lives like normal people in real neighborhoods.' Now I see that I was wrong. Instead of putting two of us here, two of us there, two others over there, they kept us all together and they put us all in places where the drugs were bad already. So you took a place of death and added more death, and more danger, and this was intentional and it was spiteful and it was a conscious plan.

"Every time I go to Charlayne's neighborhood, I see someone that I remember from the Martinique. We look at each other and we think, 'Well, there we are! Oh boy!'

"Nobody thought that they was goin' to put us into fancy neighborhoods on the East Side. You're not goin' to put poor people into neighborhoods like that. But no one believed that they would concentrate us in the places that were most diseased because this would amount to a death sentence. Put a lot of families in a place like Charlayne's building and you can begin to write obituaries."

"Why do you think they did this?"

"They put us all together in one place, I guess, so that we couldn't do no harm to no one else. They don't want no one poor and nothin' ugly in the places where they live. Some time ago, I don't remember when, they took a smelly sewage plant and stuck it down in Harlem. This ain't new. This is an old story in New York. . . .

"We was sittin' the other day in Charlayne's kitchen and I'm lookin' out the window and I see these boys outside there on her fire escape with hoods over their heads and baggin' dope and puttin' bullets in their guns. I'm just sittin', lookin' at them.

"So I go to the window and I say, 'Could you please do your business somewhere else?' This dealer in his damn hood asks me, 'Lady, what's your problem?' I said, 'This is my daughter's fire escape. Please do what you have to do upstairs so your own mother has to watch you.' "

Her daughter's apartment, she mentions, had been robbed a month before. "We was at the store. When we came back, her lock was broken and her TV and her radio were gone. We called the 911 number and we gave them the address and then we waited for three hours. Finally two policemen came, two little cops. They looked afraid, like little boys. When they came in, I asked them why it took so long. One of them told me, 'Mrs. Washington, the truth is, when your call came in three hours ago, a number of us heard it but we all knew the address and no one wanted to respond because nobody wants to come here to this building. Everyone is scared.'

"I said to him, 'I don't blame someone for bein' scared. But if you're scared of comin' here when somebody is robbed, then you are in the wrong profession.'

"The cop was being honest and polite. Like I said, he looked like a young boy. 'Ma'am,' he said, 'I'm 24 years old. I got a new baby that was just born and I got a wife and I don't want to die.' I understand it, but my daughter and her children have to live there.

" 'We was passin' the buck the last three hours,' says the cop. I can't blame him. Cops think of the building like a death camp. But if the police are scared to come there, why does the city put small children in the building?

"People," she adds, "don't like you calling this a death camp. I know why. I understand. But I don't know what else to call it. There might be some other word that you should use. . . .

"When I'm mad I think, 'How can you blame this on white people? This is poor folks doin' these things to themselves.' Then, when I'm calm, I think, 'Why did they put so many of these hopeless people in this place to start with?' I go back and forth on this. You don't know who to blame."

A copy of *Newsday* is on the sofa in the living room. "We've been gettin' it for free," she says. "Somebody steals it from the trucks. They sell it for a dime or something on the street. Then, when they get tired of sellin' it, they stand there and they give you a free copy.

"The doughnut man—he's a Puerto Rican man—he gives you a copy sometimes with your doughnut and your coffee. I think he gets it from the ones who steal it.

"My mother used to read the *Journal-American* and the *New York Times*. This was maybe 40 years ago. Once a week she got the *Amsterdam News*. It comes out on Thursdays. I get it on Friday."

Her health, she says, has been better. "I'm eatin' again. Ate a pint of ice cream last night after dinner. Häagen-Dazs—I love it. We get it at a store down by the train."

This familiar detail ("Häagen-Dazs"), something that belongs to the everyday world, something I buy at my store too, seems reassuring, safe, and normal. It shuts out the sense of peril for a while.

"The weather was beautiful this afternoon. Crowds of people were outside. I went out for a while and took a walk."

As I'm putting on my coat, she pulls a frame down from a bookcase and holds it beneath a lamp. In the frame is a color photo of two women. One is a pretty and youthful version of herself. The other is a light-skinned woman with thick glasses. "That's my mother," she tells me, brushing the surface of the frame with the soft sleeve of her wool sweater. "This one's me when I was 22." Her eyes fill up with tears. "I miss my mother."

Chapter Three

Christmas at last in New York City, but there is no snow. Riding the train on December 21, I find it hard to understand the muffled voice of the conductor who announces stations. I ask a woman seated beside me with a bag from Bloomingdale's if this is the right train for Brook Avenue.

"Where is that?" she asks.

"It's in the Bronx," I say, "near St. Ann's Avenue."

"I don't know what happens after 96th," she says.

A woman sitting across from me says I'm on the wrong train. "This is the express. Get off at 125th Street. Take the local, Number 6."

On the local there are many heavily dressed men and several women with babies, but few with shopping bags and none with those bright-colored Christmas bags from Bloomingdale's or Macy's. The women look weary. Some of the men sleep in their seats, swaying slightly with the rhythm of the train. Some of those who are awake have stoic looks, neither particularly unhappy nor contented. A startlingly beautiful olive-skinned Hispanic girl, maybe 16 or 17 years old, sits directly opposite me in black shoes, black pants, black pea jacket buttoned to the throat, and black beret, her hands folded and her eyes closed.

At twelve-fifteen on St. Ann's Avenue, three people from the needle exchange are setting up boxes on three tables underneath a sheltered area at Children's Park. The box on one table contains condoms. On the second table are written materials in English and Spanish. On the third table are two kinds of needles. The needles wrapped in blue are longer and stronger and can be dismantled. These, according to a former user who tells me she became an addict at 15 but has been clean for nine months and now works for the exchange, are for cocaine injectors and for others who "inject deep in their bodies." The needles wrapped in orange, which are shorter and are known as "diabetic needles," are the needles of choice for the skin-poppers. On the same table as the needles are a box of "cookers" (bottle caps) and bleach kits wrapped in plastic.

The space occupied by the park is about the size of a single building lot. From St. Ann's Avenue to the apartment building in the back, the distance may be 50 yards. The width of the lot is less than 15 yards. The shelter where the tables are set up, an open-sided structure with a tin and wooden roof, is roughly halfway back. Behind the shelter, in a field of weeds and trash, there is a rusted jungle gym. Between the shelter and the street, the ground is paved with bricks. Four thin trees, from one of which the various stuffed animals are hanging, stand beside two wooden benches in the section of the lot that borders St. Ann's Avenue. On the wall of the building to the right side of the lot, there is a sign in faded paint.

THIS PARK WAS BUILT FOR AND BY

THE PEOPLE SO THAT CHILDREN

WOULD BE TREATED WITH RESPECT

At one P.M., addicts begin to line up at the table with the needles. Some are elderly men in tattered clothes with ravaged faces and intense eyes. Others are young black and Hispanic women who are neatly dressed, composed and patient. Of about 1,000 addicts who are registered with the exchange, according to Joyce Rivera-Beckman, a political scientist who began the program in August 1990 when it was still prohibited by law, between 150 and 200 show up on an average afternoon.

Each addict provides a registration number and is questioned about frequency of use, then counts out the dirty needles he or she has brought to the exchange, deposits them in a plastic waste-container, and receives an equal number of clean needles. One young black woman says she uses six needles a day, counts out 60 needles, and is given 60 clean ones for ten days. Those who have never been here before and have no registration number are asked to bare their legs or arms or throat to show fresh tracks.

"A good vein for injecting is one that feels like a small rubber tube under a sheet," says one of the pamphlets on the second table, which also explains in pictures and words how to know if you hit an artery ("when you pull back, the blood is frothy"), how to rotate injection sites, and what to do in case of overdose. Although this material seems frightening to me, the atmosphere among the addicts and Rivera-Beckman's staff is friendly and relaxed, and the whole thing seems almost as normal as a visit to a doctor or a dentist with the one important difference that the staff here is much nicer and the waiting time much shorter than in many medical clinics I have visited.

The needle exchange is over at three. A quiet period follows in the park, because no dealing takes place at the times when kids are coming home from school. A little after four o'clock, I go to get a cup of coffee at a nearby store and then return to Children's Park in time to see a woman in a purple sweater standing where the needles were distributed and, in a slightly brusque voice, calling, "Next!" to men and women who appear from all directions to buy heroin.

Two blocks away, in Rivera-Beckman's office, she describes what she calls a "protocol" or "etiquette" by which the various sections of the park have been apportioned to diverse groups that make use of it. "Mothers come with children to sit under the stuffed animals. Homeless people who get meals next door at a soup kitchen come and sit there too. The drug dealers use the section in the back. In good weather, an evangelist sometimes comes to preach and while he's preaching the drug dealers stop dealing.

"I asked a dealer once why he would let the preacher preach. I can't remember his exact words, but he had a clear sense of 'entitlement' or 'right' for various people to use the park for different purposes, but only in particular areas. In other words, there are understood domains, none of it ever formally agreed to but evolving somehow by a mutual acceptance.

"I don't want to romanticize the situation, but we do see something here that's curiously functional, highly structured on a microscale, as in a plaza in a Mexican or Puerto Rican town. Life in their cramped apartments is compressed, so this little park becomes a natural extension. No matter what the destructive forces on all sides, this life force does break out and organize itself, and it *is* organized. The timing of drug dealing is precise: nine to three, and four to ten on weekdays, nine A.M. to midnight on the weekends. The dealers, moreover, get job benefits. They're paid well and are given breaks to shoot their drugs if they are users too."

Until the previous year, she says, the heroin trade in the neighborhood was dominated by a druglord named George Calderon. "He'd been a heroin user himself since he was ten years old. By 1986 or '87, he was renting certain corners to the lower-level dealers for $200,000 yearly." The druglord, she says, was believed to be the leading private employer in the neighborhood, providing more than 250 jobs "for women and men both—he was an 'equal opportunity' employer."

On holidays, like dictators in some foreign countries in past decades, he would throw out thousands of dollars in the streets, she says, to be scooped up by children and teenagers. When, in May of 1992, he was shot dead at the age of 35, hundreds of his former customers and neighbors filed past his coffin at the altar of St. Ann's. He was, according to press accounts, buried in his white suit and gold chains.

"Calderon," says Rivera-Beckman, "was an outgoing man, gregarious, and something of a showman. The guy who ran things for him in the park was less outgoing; he was quiet, reticent, polite. He asked me questions about HIV infection. I gave him information. He seemed grateful, maybe guilty. It may be that he felt it gave him status to be seen conversing with me."

At six P.M., a light rain falls on Children's Park. The woman in the purple sweater who sells heroin is gone. The place is temporarily abandoned. It doesn't look much like a Mexican plaza. It looks more like the stage set for a play by Beckett or Kurt Weill. I walk into the trash-strewn lot behind the park. On the wall of the building in the back is a memorial in ornate graffiti:

CALDERON SUGAR

REST IN PEACE

The script of the druglord's name is blue. A heart is drawn in red. "Sugar," I am later told, refers not to Calderon but to his younger sister, who took over the drug operation on his death when she was 27 but was murdered two months later. The dates of their births and deaths are given also.

Mrs. Washington's daughter lives with her children three blocks from the park in one of the 1,273 apartments of the 38 buildings of the privately owned but publicly subsidized Diego-Beekman Houses, a complex of some of the most physically repellent and profoundly dangerous buildings in America, which are owned by a company called Continental Wingate, based in Boston.

"Only 12 percent of the people who live in these buildings have real jobs," the security director of the complex tells me when I meet him in his office on December 22. "The rest receive Aid to Families with Dependent Children or some other form of welfare. A two-bedroom apartment is rented for $800 to $900." Families on welfare pay about one third of their public assistance allocation, generally between $200 and $250; the rest is paid with federal funds. "Between 30 and 40 percent of tenants have no telephones," he says.

"The biggest problems, healthwise, are respiratory. Some is TB. But asthma is the greatest. Guys who work for me carry breathing pumps." The total population of the complex is, he says, between 4,000 and 5,000 people.

"Here's the reality: a mother, a baby or two babies,

maybe one older child, maybe two, and a grandmother. Most of the grandmothers are in their middle to late thirties. Great-grandmothers could be 55.

"The greatest need in the neighborhood," he says, "is real employment. Some of the men come in here and they want a job so bad. You see it in their eyes. They ask. They question me continually. I have to tell them honestly that there is nothing there."

A feeling of discouragement, he believes, has deepened in the past few years. "I don't see as many Christmas lights as I saw even a year ago. Three years ago, in one of those high-rise buildings further down on St. Ann's Avenue, you'd see every window lighted up. Everyone had something little to be happy for. Last night, in a 20-story building, there might have been seven windows that had lights."

Hunger, he says, remains a constant problem. "I give out food every two months. I get it from a warehouse out in Brooklyn. About 10,000 pounds. Cornmeal. Canned pork. Flour, rice, and butter. It's donated by the government.

"I get enough to feed 500 people. I need enough to feed 1,000. Whatever I get, I could use twice as much. The line goes out the door and down two blocks. If I say it starts at noon, they're lining up by nine.

"Drug dealers sometimes make donations. When we have a party on the block, they do give money. One time— it was during a block party—one of the dealers went up on the roof and, I don't know how much it was, he threw down fives and tens and singles in the street."

Putting on his coat, he asks if I would like to see some of the neighborhood. As we walk, he points to trash-deposits in the streets, says hello to children that he knows, and nods politely to their mothers. A tall black man, he seems to have protective feelings toward the tenants, which may war somewhat against his necessary loyalty to his employers.

Halfway down on Beekman Avenue, we turn into a narrow street that dead-ends at a ledge from which a granite stairway leads down to another street below. The metal railings of the stairway have been ripped out of their sockets. Slabs of stone have fallen from the steeply graded stairs.

Whole sections of the stairs are missing. One step is balanced like a seesaw and tilts when I walk on it. "When it freezes," says the security director, "this right here is murder. An elderly person who tried to use these stairs would be in danger."

"Can't the local politicians deal with this?" I ask.

He looks at me and shrugs. "This is the South Bronx."

When the security director had agreed to talk with me, I had told him that I needed to get answers to specific questions about demographics, rent, and income in the neighborhood; but some of the things he's said encourage me to share with him a different kind of question. "When people in these buildings talk to you about the problems that they face," I ask, "do you get the feeling that they have much satisfaction in their lives? Do you think they ever stop and reckon up their sense of happiness?"

He stares down at the heap of granite slabs. "If you ask some tenants, 'Is your life worth living?'" he says after standing like that for a while, "some of them, I think, might not know how to answer. Some, too, walk right through the gloom without it touching them. Others won't let you get inside of them to know. The depression is always there, though, as an undercurrent, and sometimes it's not just an undercurrent. Sometimes it's so thick it feels like you could cut it with a knife.

"I was down at Rockefeller Center yesterday. Seeing the lights and the excitement, I was thinking to myself, 'There seems like so much happiness down here. If you could just bag it up and sprinkle some up there. . . .'"

The principal of P.S. 65, the public school two blocks away, a gracious man named Manuel Rodriguez whom I meet by simply walking into the open school around midday and going to his office, speaks candidly of the depression that he sees in many children. "In the past two weeks I've had three children speak of suicide. I mean, they 'indicate' suicide. These are not just casual remarks.

"I have one child in the sixth grade who is so depressed he stays up until four A.M. He takes a shoe and hammers at roaches all night long. He's not destructive, just so terribly unhappy.

"Sometimes, though, the ones who *ought* to be depressed don't seem upset at all. We lose a lot of parents to AIDS. Mothers come in and tell us they are dying. One little boy whose mother died over the weekend came in on Monday as if nothing much had happened. I would have expected to see some emotion. Nothing. He was flat, as if it was an ordinary day and nothing special had occurred."

When I mention what Cliffie's mother said about the prostitutes who congregate near the expressway, he replies, "Yes, they're there. Sometimes at seven in the morning when I come to school. Very young. Everybody knows."

He also speaks of many children in the school who have been scarred by household fires. "Some of our children have been horribly disfigured in these fires. I notice, though, that the other children treat them kindly and do not make fun of them. There is a protective feeling that can be extraordinarily moving. There is nothing predatory in these children. They know that the world does not much like them and they try hard to be good to one another.

"No matter how disfigured they may be," he adds, "I find these children beautiful."

Mrs. Washington makes arrangements with me on the phone to meet at her daughter's house for dinner. She urges me, however, not to try to talk with anyone I meet while I am walking there and not to take notes on the street. I mention that I was on the street this morning with the security director, but she doesn't sound impressed. "The security director has a gun. You don't. Besides, it will be dark by then and nobody there knows you.

"This street is not like mine," she says. "I told you that. People get shot around there every day. Two months ago, a boy was shot in Charlayne's building, on the first floor. Nine years old. It was a mistake. He was watching television with his brothers and his sisters. The bullet came right through the door. Now he's in a wheelchair. Charlayne says that you can see the bullet holes."

Two men, she adds, were critically wounded just outside the door in the same shooting.

She repeats her warning about being circumspect. "Don't take out your pad of paper when you go there. Don't take out your camera. Just go to the second floor: 2B. There isn't any bell. She'll watch for you."

Walking from St. Ann's Avenue to get to the apartment around six P.M., I hear the voice of a woman crying, *"Venga! Venga! Venga!"* Turning east on 141st Street, I pass a man who says in a half-whisper, "Check it out," but turns away as I go by. A woman on the corner of Beekman Avenue addresses me as "Papa."

At Charlayne's apartment house, I make my way through a group of six or seven men on the front steps, two in the small lobby, and two on the landing of the stairwell halfway to the second floor. Charlayne is waiting for me and opens the door before I knock.

Mrs. Washington arrives five minutes later. She comes in crying because the cab-driver got lost and she ran out of money so she got out of the cab and walked the last 12 blocks and, she says, "got scared." The children, who have been to Rockefeller Center with a group of kids from St. Ann's Church to see the Christmas tree, arrive soon after.

Charlayne's younger child, a boy, is five years old. The older child, Sara, who is six and is adopted, is the daughter of a crack-addicted woman who was once a friend of Charlayne.

"The doctor," Mrs. Washington tells me while the children are in their bedroom playing with a toy computer, "said that Sara had so much cocaine in her when she was born it could have killed an elephant. They gave her phenobarbital and whatever else you give a baby who is born addicted. She only weighed three pounds. Her eyes were heavy-lidded.

"The doctor says these things will be with her all of her life. Even now sometimes she seems to go into herself. You say, 'What's wrong?' She answers, 'Nothin'.' But you feel something is wrong."

"I was tryin' to get her a psychiatrist," says Charlayne. "I put her name down, but her teacher said they couldn't see her for a long time because there are many children like her in the school."

"When she learned Charlayne was not her mommy," Mrs. Washington goes on, "she asked me, 'Nanny, you are not my grandma?' I said to her, 'Sweetie, who does your clothes and cooks your food?' She said, 'Mommy.' I said, 'That's your mother.' And I told her, 'You are my grand-daughter. Period.' She calls me 'Nanny.' Sometimes, when she's feeling scared, she puts her hand on mine. The other night around nine-thirty, my telephone rang and when I picked it up, it was just silence. I said, 'Hello.' She didn't speak. I said, 'Hello' again. Then she says, 'Nanny, I love you. Will you come and visit?' "

"When there are gunshots," Charlayne says, "they fall to their knées and crawl over there into the hallway where there are no windows. I taught them to do it like the men do in the army, crawling on their stomachs."

Some of the men who hang out on the stairs, she says, treat her politely; others do not. "This particular night I had to go out to the store at nine o'clock. There was two guys standing out here on the stairs. One had a sawed-off shotgun. This dealer knows that I don't like him. He followed me down the stairs and down the street right to the store and followed me into the store. He had the shotgun with him. He said something to me but I didn't answer. So I bought what I had to buy and came back home."

No one in the building tries to cover up the sale of drugs, she says. "In the summer, there's one family brings a bunch of lounge chairs outside with their children and they have a barbecue and sell cocaine all day from maybe nine A.M. to twelve or one at night. Music playin'. Puerto Rican music and rap music. Hundreds of people comin' by. The guys with their fat ropes and Gucci links. This goes on every weekend in hot weather.

"Right here in this block it's crack cocaine. Down there at the park it's heroin. If it's cars, it's people from New Jersey or upstate.

"Oh yeah! You see people noddin' in the streets. Yeah! It's open. Everyone sees." Some of the bodegas, little Puerto Rican stores, sell drugs as well as food, she adds. "You'll see dealers in there, prostitutes with children, buyin' Pampers, buyin' what they need. . . ."

"Do the children know that they are prostitutes?"

"My children do."

"Does it upset them?"

"I don't know. It upsets *me*. I feel sorry for them, some-times. Other times I don't. Sara's mother—every day she's doin' it, doin' what she has to do, right out there in the street.

"The places where you see them most are underneath the Bruckner and the Major Deegan. It's dark under the Major Deegan, but you see them, seven, eight, or nine of them on this side, seven, eight, or nine of them on that side."

"Some of these women are buck-naked," Mrs. Washington reports.

I find this impossible to believe, but Charlayne says, "It's true. They're naked. They have nothin' on."

I ask her, *"Literally nothing?"*

"Nothin'!"

Seeing the look on my face, she says, "Some of them wear G-strings or a pair of tiny shorts."

"Is this only in the summer?"

"Even in October, in November."

Many of the customers for the prostitutes, she says, are truckers. "But you also see some men in cars—men of all races, every kind. The woman climbs right in, does what she has to do, then goes and gets a hit, then back out on the street to find another one. Sometimes they make him buy the drugs first. Then they do it."

"How much do they make?"

"Three dollars . . . or five dollars. . . ."

"How many are addicted?"

"All of them are. You wouldn't do that for three dollars otherwise."

"I saw a woman on the train not long ago," says Mrs. Washington. "A young-looking woman. Wasn't clean. She had a giant block of surplus cheese: a ten-pound box. A man said to her, 'Sister, you got you a big block of cheese.' She told him, 'You can have it for three dollars.' He hurried up and gave her the three dollars. As soon as he paid her, she got off the train. Like I say, you can't save the whole world. . . .

"They don't give out the cheese no more. Now they give canned ham, some kind of combination. Not the kind you buy in stores. You see the signs, 'Surplus Food' on such or such a day, and 'Bring a Bag.' I don't do it because I don't need it and somebody else might need it and I don't want someone else's children goin' hungry. I know what it's like."

She mentions a woman who comes in the evening once a week to a corner close to Lincoln Hospital and gives away free food out of her station wagon. "She was there a week ago, giving out hot stew. It was maybe five o'clock. The afternoon dealers were goin' in, the evenin' dealers comin' out. A lot of people lookin' sad and scared. I don't know who she is. Her car is burgundy. She wears a long white gown. It looks like a choir robe and she has beads that look like rosary beads around her neck. She brings a little girl with her who gives out ballpoint pens and miniature Bibles."

The children come into the living room for supper. They bring the toy computer with them and sit down with Mrs. Washington to show her a number game they have been playing. They are well behaved and both politely say "excuse me" if they want to ask a question. Sara seems perfectly normal and shows no apparent signs of damage from cocaine addiction, but in this easygoing setting there is no real way to know if anything is wrong.

Charlayne is in her last year at a two-year college and is holding down a part-time office job at the same time. Over a spaghetti dinner, which the children struggle to scoop up with forks and fingers, she tells me that they go to after-school at St. Ann's Church, where they receive an early meal. She picks them up there at six-thirty when she's done with work.

After chatting with us for a while after dinner, the children go back to their bedroom, where, because it is Christmas vacation, they are permitted to stay up and watch a movie on TV. Once the children are out of hearing, Charlayne tells me that her son "cries all night long" when there is shooting. "Sometimes I'm cryin' too, because I'm scared to get too near the door."

"Do all the dealers out there carry guns?" I ask.

"Every dealer on this block is strapped," she says. "Some of the girls are too."

I ask if any of the older women carry guns for their protection.

"I can't say for right here in this neighborhood," her mother says, "but I can tell you I'd feel safer if I had one." She mentions a fast-food restaurant on Boston Road, not far from where she lives, a place that sells fried chicken, where police not long ago broke in and found a large supply of guns. "It turned out the man was selling them. They say he sold more than 2,000 in a year. Sawed-off shotguns for $25, 38-caliber pistols like the ones policemen have for $50. All you needed to do was order chicken and your gun was the side order. Whatever you bought, he gave you a free box of ammunition. He told the police, 'What's the point of havin' a gun if you don't have no bullets?'

"To tell the truth, I wish I'd known about it before this person got arrested. I would have went and got one for myself."

"I can't imagine you with a gun," I say.

Before she can reply, however, Sara comes into the room again to ask a question about something she is watching on TV. Charlayne gets up and goes into the kitchen to stuff paper towels underneath the sink where the hot-water pipe is spraying scalding water on the floor.

At ten P.M., before the children go to sleep, I stand in the doorway of their bedroom as they kneel beside their beds and clasp their hands and close their eyes.

God bless Mommy. God bless Nanny.
God, don't punish me because I'm black.

"Do they say the same prayer every night?" I ask their mother after she has tucked them in and closed their door.

"Every night," she answers.

"I wish that I could help them to get out of here," says Mrs. Washington.

The following day, I visit a soup kitchen where more than 200 people, about two thirds of whom are children, come to eat four times a week. The mothers of the children seem competitive, and almost frantic, to make sure their children get their share. A child I meet, a five-year-old boy named Emmanuel, tells me he's "in kiddie garden." His mother says he hasn't started yet. "He starts next year."

"You have to remember," says one of the priests with whom I share my thoughts about these meetings, "that for this little boy whom you have met, his life is just as important, to him, as your life is to you. No matter how insufficient or how shabby it may seem to some, it is the only one he has"—an obvious statement that upsets me deeply nonetheless.

"Many of these children," says the priest, "get literally nothing in the way of 'extras.' There are many children here who don't get birthday presents, who never had a gift at Christmastime and never even had a Christmas tree, which would not be included in the welfare budget. It's particularly hard here in December when so much of life in New York City has to do with buying gifts and giving gifts, when everything—the music, decorations, fragrances, the giant ribbons wrapped around some of the stores—makes Christmas inescapable. You wish that you could wrap one of those ribbons around certain of the children. I mean, some of them have *nothing*. Their bedrooms are empty. They don't hang up stockings. If they have food for Christmas, they are fortunate. It is a bare existence.

"Sometimes, in front of a wonderful place like FAO Schwarz, you wonder if poor kids like these have fantasies of breaking in and stealing toys or games, electric trains—whatever children play with nowadays. If they ever did it, if they just went in one night and cleaned the whole place out, you have to ask if they could ever steal back half as much as has been stolen from them."

During these days I walk for hours in the neighborhood, starting at Willis Avenue, crossing Brook, and then St. Ann's, going as far as Locust Avenue to look at the medical waste incinerator one more time, then back to Beekman Avenue. In cold of winter, as in summer's heat, a feeling of asphyxia seems to contain the neighborhood. The faces of some of the relatively young women with advanced cases of AIDS, their eyes so hollow, their jawbones so protruding, look like the faces of women in the House of the Dying run by the nuns within the poorest slum of Port-au-Prince. It's something that you don't forget. Seeing these women in the street, you feel almost ashamed of your good health and worry that, no matter how you speak of them, it may sound patronizing. "The rich," said St. Vincent de Paul, "should beg the poor to forgive us for the bread we bring them." Healthy people sometimes feel they need to beg forgiveness too, although there is no reason why. Maybe we simply ask forgiveness for not being born where these poor women have been born, knowing that if we had lived here too, our fate might well have been the same.

On a gray afternoon at Children's Park, I stand for a long time looking at the Calderon memorial behind the little hut where needles are exchanged. Nearby, scattered in the weeds and trash, are several rusted 55-gallon barrels bearing "Toxic Contents" warnings. The barrels are empty. Whatever residual poison they contained has long since seeped into the soil. The cumulative ugliness of things contains its own toxicity, however. It's hard to think that any city that has love for children would allow them to grow up in such a place.

Eight blocks north of St. Ann's Church, on St. Ann's Avenue, a community organizer named Lee Stuart, who has worked in the South Bronx for eight years and now directs a church-supported branch of the Industrial Areas Foundation, points to a construction site on which the city is about to build a new reform school—"a real fort," she says, "right opposite a junior high." Twelve blocks farther to the north, and slightly to the west, she points to the future site of a court complex, a $460 million monolith that will cover three square blocks, casting its shadow on three

71

public schools. She also shows me the prospective site of a new police academy, which, she says, "may or may not be built right now," depending on the outcome of a political dispute. The Bronx House of Detention, she says, is nearby as well, and she lists a number of other crime-related institutions in the neighborhood, all of which she speaks of as "a law-and-order ghetto."

These kinds of institutions, she concedes, do generate some jobs. "The trouble is that jobs like these depend upon the concentration of the poor within 'the service area.' It's like—one portion of the population generates the crime to keep the other part employed. So it's an investment in perpetuation of the ghetto, a guarantee of endless misery that services like these may partially alleviate but also need in order to be justified.

"When I was a young person," she goes on, "I did not believe that we would ever come to this. A good society had been defined as one in which the segregation of the races was abhorrent. Even conservatives were saying this by 1968. Today, at least here in New York, this is no longer so. The notion of the ghetto as a 'sin' committed by society is not confronted. You will never see this word in the newspapers. The abolition of this sin is simply not on the agenda. I don't think we should accept this, but I also think the powers that be are stronger now than any counterforce that we can build.

"Yes," she says, "there *is* real heroism everywhere within the neighborhood. I think of a woman, Charlotte Smith, who this morning buried her fourth child but remains a fighter, upright and unbroken. But, good Lord! The miseries around her are so vast!"

Later, as the sun goes down, I search the faces of the people that I pass, many of them tired-looking and some seeming scared. A man who may be in his early twenties, and who looks as if he has been crying, stands on 141st Street, staring into space. As far as the eye can see on Beekman Avenue are uncollected piles of trash.

*　　*　　*

"We know the killer," says a black musician in response to those who say that it is violent rap music that is
spawning death and rage. "The killer is not a song. The
killer is the street in which we live like rats."

Still, as the woman who directs the center that ex-
changes needles in the park has noted, there is a "life force"
that persists amid the ruins. Mothers decorate the doors of
their apartments with bright-colored cards and little bells
and sometimes hearts drawn by their children. Those who
can, buy Christmas trees. The crowds on 138th Street
throng the store that sells cheap clothing at steep discount,
the vegetable store that sells fresh carrots, oranges, and bat-
tered-looking beets, the fish store in whose windows trays
of oysters, mussels, and whole scaly fishes are displayed and
piled high. The homes of many people such as Charlayne
Washington and Cliffie's mother, no matter how besieged,
are nonetheless kept spotless and sometimes even look
cheerful. The force of life keeps pressing against the dismal
barriers in which it is contained; and finally, even in a tar-
nished corner lot on St. Ann's Avenue, a park evolves and
teddy bears take their places in the branches of a tree, and
destitute men who live in the streets and eat at the soup
kitchen just next door or the soup kitchen in the basement
of St. Ann's, and heroin addicts who use "Dynamite,"
"Black Sabbath," and "Black Death" and other name
brands of the needle drug their bodies need do not harm
the bears or try to tear them down but treat them with a
certain tenderness and speak of them protectively.

The snapshots of disaster that one sees in television
news reports on the South Bronx rarely seem to capture
these realities of ordinary life. There *is* a poetry about this
and, strange though it may sound to say, something often
of real beauty. But the poetry can also seem macabre: at
one end of the park, bears in a tree and, at the other, a
memorial to the drug dealer, dead at 35 after dealing
death to many. The bears, rain-sodden now and looking
quite forlorn, have seen it all.

At night, beneath a reproduction of a painting of the
Last Supper in a book-lined living room on St. Ann's

Avenue, I learn more about the park from a neighborhood historian and poet, Juan Bautista Castro, who has lived in the South Bronx for nearly 50 years and in this building seven years.

"A man named Frenchie did much of the work," he says, "but if he was the only one I do not know. He died since. He was murdered on the roof of an adjacent building.

"Every time a branch was cut out of the tree of life, somebody would add another bear. The last bear, and the biggest one, I'm told, was put up in the tree after the druglord died, but this may be one of those myths that have grown up over the course of time."

Reverend Overall, who has arranged this meeting and is with me in the poet's home, tells me she performed the service at the druglord's burial. "His coffin," she says, "was truly something splendid. It cost $7,000. After it was lowered in the ground, one of his brothers lifted a huge boulder and threw it down on top to dent the coffin. They were afraid that, otherwise, somebody would dig it up in order to resell it."

Behind Mr. Castro's back is a bookshelf packed, two-deep, with rows of old hardcover books, many leather-bound, and a set of the *Encyclopaedia Britannica*. In this room, during a period of three years that concluded in the spring of 1991, the poet, who tells me he was born in Puerto Rico, translated his favorite work, *Paradise Lost*, into Spanish—*El Paraíso Perdido*, as it says on the cover of the 156-page volume, *"Version en Rima, Al Idioma Español."*

After coming to New York in 1946, he says, he taught himself English by reading poets of the nineteenth century—first Longfellow, then Whittier and Whitman. "Soon I was drawn to the English poets. Edmund Spenser was at first my favorite, then John Donne, George Herbert, and then Milton. When I first read *Paradise Lost*, I said, 'Oh Milton! You are another of my pack!' I read him again and again over the years. During this time I was working in a bakery and a dry cleaner. Later, I played the accordion and worked in Spanish theater. Meanwhile, I was always thinking about Milton."

The only previous Spanish translations of *Paradise Lost,* he says, were mechanistic, literal, prosaic—or in prose. "All of the richness and the texture had been lost. I decided at last that I would try my own translation. So I used the royal stanza, *octava rima.* Oh, that was a long, long time! The strain was such that many days I felt that I had been within a trance. I was entirely overcome.

"All of these years I have written poetry. I used to go and read to children in the schools. Once a child comes to me out in the street. 'Sir,' he says, 'I heard you are a poet. Will you teach me how to write?' I told him, 'No, young man. I am just a versifier. Whether I am a poet too is something others must decide.' It was in my mind that I should not encourage him in a career with so much disappointment. Then I thought, 'What the hell! I am a masochist. Maybe he is also!' So I tried to teach him what I knew."

Interrupting himself to urge some wine on Reverend Overall and me, he rises with the bottle in his hand, goes to the bookcase, and pulls out a copy of *The Faerie Queene.* "I found this in a junkstore in the Bronx," he says, stroking the cover.

As I remember this experience, it occurs to me that it may strike a reader as a bit incongruous that we would be sitting here within one of the poorest urban neighborhoods of the United States, and one of the most diseased blocks of New York, and be speaking of John Milton's epic poem and Edmund Spenser's *Faerie Queene.* At the time, however, the anachronism did not come to mind. Speaking with a poet of the banishment from Eden in this building in Mott Haven has, perhaps, a certain logic of its own.

"I see New York as a symbolic city," Mr. Castro says. "These buildings are our concrete prisons piled up like Babel. A satanic technology surrounds us. What we see is apparatus, not humanity." Speaking of the simulated flower pots and curtains painted on abandoned buildings next to Featherbed Lane, he says, "The people downtown"—he calls them "the big roosters"—"they wanted passersby to think it was inhabited: an Eden. But when you're backstage you know the tricks. The people who live in the neighborhood are not deceived. They know their

banishment has been accomplished. Happiness is the for-
bidden fruit. They get a slice or two, but not the pie. The
roosters get the pie."

He speaks very little of politics. In one rare departure,
however, he says this: "The evil we are learning now will
serve us well when we are on the opposite shore."

I ask him if he means after we die.

"No. I mean when the minorities have power."

In a sudden shift, he says, "I meant to tell you, sir. In
your next book I would like it if you said something about
the manners of our children. They are God's spies on earth,
His specialized creation, but their manners need to be corrected.

"I call them spies because they are so vigilant and so
observant. They measure us constantly. They try to find out
what the hell we think of them. . . .

"Mostly," he adds, "they specialize in making us give
them more attention."

Of the druglord Calderon he says, "This is what happened: The man was addicted to heroin when he was ten
years old. Then, logically, he came to be a dealer. Since the
mother couldn't control her children, she made up her
mind to join them. So it became a family of Godfathers. I
knew this woman. My wife was acquainted with her also.
They knew each other from when they were senoritas. She
was a devil even then. People lived in terror of the mother
and the sister *and* the son.

"Still, when he died, he was deeply mourned. His
funeral was well attended. The great hero of *Paradise Lost,*
of course, is Satan. He is much more interesting than the
angels."

He hands me a poem in blank verse he has written
for me as a Christmas present. "Instead of toys," the poem
says in speaking of the children in the neighborhood,
"they wrote to Santa Claus to bring them food before it was
too late."

Standing by the door before I leave, he says, "To tell
the truth, sir, I have been a failure all my life." He tells me
that his translation of Milton, although photocopied and
distributed to friends, has not found a publisher. Only one

small volume of his poems has been in print. And, he adds, "I had to pay for that book to be published."

In wire-rim glasses, his mustache and receding hair turning from black to gray, slightly inebriated from the wine we have been drinking but still courtly and relaxed, he tells me he will soon be 70 years old. "I was born in 1924 and baptized in the Cathedral of San Juan." The last lines of the poem that he has given me recapture the years before he came to the United States.

> *I remember well my vivant boyhood*
> *A way of innocence*
> *It now seems like a dream.*

Outside the building I tell Reverend Overall that the entire evening had a dreamlike feeling for me. "The sense of danger was completely absent there. It felt like we were in a college class."

"The danger is still here," she says. "Three boys were murdered in this building." She tells me she has heard it was "an execution," which had been arranged by Calderon or by one of his rivals.

I ask her where she heard this.

"A woman who used to run our kitchen at the church," she says, "who had been in prison and was out on 'mercy leave,' had been a bodyguard for one of the dealers. She told me how this execution was arranged." The boys, however, as the priest later observes, may have been unintended victims of an execution meant for someone else.

At Children's Park, the bright blue letters on the Calderon memorial are visible in the streetlight just behind the rusted barrels in the back. Two small white doves are painted on a simulated sky above his name. "Calderon. Sugar. Rest in peace." Deliver us from evil.

In the park it is colder on December 24. A 12-year-old named Anthony, who is a friend of Reverend Overall and Mr. Castro, tells me he is a writer of "novels" and he makes a date to meet me in the afternoon. He mentions that he is "an acolyte" for Reverend Overall, whom he, like other children in the neighborhood, calls "Mother Martha."

I ask if he's made any wishes for the things he'd like for Christmas. Touching his sleeve, he says, "I have my Christmas present." He tells me that his coat, which his mother had promised him and given him early because of the windy and wet weather, is "the present I desired," which, as I wrote in my notes after he left, is an unusual way of speaking for a child of his age.

Saddened by the streets, I am repeatedly attracted into churches. I search them out, and although some of the pastors speak of politics and strategies of change, it is not their politics that I am really seeking, but their company. Many, in their conversations, cite the gospels. When I mention I am Jewish, they have often gone out of their way to draw upon Isaiah and Ezekiel and the other prophets. Meeting these men and women is a stirring experience for me. They are among the most unselfish people I have ever known. Many really do see Jesus in the faces of the poorest people whom they serve.

Father Glenworth Miles, pastor of the church that burned to the ground two months before—a church that also was his home—speaks, not surprisingly perhaps, with empathy for homeless people, many of whom wander in his neighborhood. "In the Middle Ages," he says, "the lepers were differentiated from the healthy by the wearing of bells. Someone would run in front of them and say, 'Unclean! Unclean!' We have no need of bells today but we still say 'unclean.'

"Many here are a great deal more devout than people you would meet in wealthy neighborhoods. Those who have everything they want or need have often the least feeling for religion. The rich are very busy storing everything they can accumulate: wealth, power, or prestige. The gospel said, 'Fool, tonight your soul will be required of you.'"

He does not wish, he says, to be judgmental. "Still, I think it grieves the heart of God when human beings created in His image treat other human beings like filthy rags."

He speaks of the words that Handel used in *The Messiah*—"He was despised and rejected, a man of sorrows . . . and acquainted with grief"—and tells me that these words, which make him think of many people in the streets of the South Bronx, are from Isaiah. "Much of the gospel has its origin in Hebrew texts," he says with hospitable sweetness. St. Paul's second letter to the Corinthians, which contains the admonition not to turn "the stranger" from our door—because many who welcome strangers have "thereby entertained an angel unaware"—also draws upon the Hebrew Bible, he informs me. "It's in Leviticus and also in Isaiah. Because *you* were sojourners once in a foreign land, therefore do not be unmerciful to those who ask to sojourn with you in the present times. . . ." Although some of these statements bear a sense of warning, he does not speak wrathfully. His British accent, he tells me, is a consequence of his upbringing in Jamaica.

Later in the day in Hunts Point, at Bright Temple A.M.E., a handsome structure built in the early 1860s, Reverend Gregory Groover, who studied at Union Theological Seminary under Cornel West, tells me that, since the closing of the only hospital in the community, the nearest place his parishioners can go for care is Lincoln Hospital. "Ten thousand people live here in Hunts Point but we do not have one private doctor."

More than 20,000 people work at Hunts Point Market, he reports—"the largest center for food produce on the East Coast"—but "the market is a separate world with virtually no payoff to our residents other than a perverse payoff in the form of clients for the prostitution trade. Almost nobody who works there lives here in the neighborhood."

Some people in Hunts Point, he says, support themselves by stripping cars or scavenging old buildings to collect and sell the brass and copper wire and the beautiful old bricks, which, I later learn, are frequently recycled into patios and fireplaces in the suburbs. The pastor compares the scavengers to "the gleaners" in the Bible. "Instead of fruit or grain, they gather brass or brick."

In winter, some of the prostitutes who stroll the area close to the produce stands use dumpsters as their beds to keep from freezing. But prostitution, he says, is not restricted to the market area. It also takes place in the residential neighborhood close to the church. "I'm constantly being stopped by women, even though I have the 'clergy' indication on my car.

"Some of the prostitutes pray at our altar. We feed the hungry three times every week, 600 meals. They do not stand on line. They sit down in our dining room. We serve them as our guests.

"If I were to ask one of these women, 'Is your life worth living?'—well, to tell the truth, I'd be afraid to ask. I think that I'd be scared of the response. All the reasons she could give to justify her feelings of depression—I could not counter these and tell her that they are not realistic."

Although Mott Haven is routinely called the deadliest neighborhood in New York City, he tells me that the homicide rate may be as high, or higher, in Hunts Point. "I remember a young couple in my congregation with a teenage son and two young daughters. They joined our church for Easter and rededicated their existence to the Lord. Two weeks later, the son came home and found his father in the living room, his mother in the laundry room down in the basement, both shot dead. What message do I give these three young people? I know that no words I can speak will ease their pain."

I ask him how he understands his mission as a pastor in this neighborhood.

"We are not literal fundamentalists here at Bright Temple," he replies. "We see God as a liberating force who calls us to deliver people from oppression. The apparent consensus of the powerful is that the ghetto is to be preserved as a perpetual catch-basin for the poor. It's not about annihilating segregation or even about a transformation of the ghetto, but setting up 'programs' to teach people to 'adjust' to it, to show a 'functional' adaptation to an evil institution. That is pretty much the good behavior that the segregator asks for in the segregated.

"As a religious man, I see it as my obligation to speak out against this, not to bend the poor to be accommodated to injustice but to empower them to fight it and to try to tear it down. We are not about amelioration here. As a church, we speak prophetically. We speak not of 'misfortune' but 'injustice.' We also look at the unjust."

"Do people in the neighborhood," I ask, "use language like 'injustice'?"

He presses his hands flat on his desk. "How often do you speak about the air? If something touches every aspect of existence, every minute of each hour of your life, it needn't often be spelled out. But it is always there, a quiet understanding."

When I ask, however, if these understandings hold the seeds of possible political resistance, he says, "No. People protest specific actions of the city. They protested the waste burner. But there's a sense of powerlessness that makes it hard to keep up a momentum. The reality of the streets is a continuing reminder and compelling reenactment of despair.

"When you walk in the neighborhood you may be mindful of Ezekiel's vision of the valley of the dry bones. God asked Ezekiel, 'Can these bones live again?' And the spirit of the Lord breathed into the bones, and breath came into them, and they did live. . . . Sometimes, though, to tell the truth, you have to wonder."

I tell him of the speculation of the priest who wondered what the children of the South Bronx feel when they look in the windows of expensive stores down on Fifth Avenue. His take on it is different, however, from that of the priest. "It's so far removed from them," he says, "so far from anything they dream of, that they don't resent its absence. Things like that aren't on their map. Many of them never go into Manhattan. Some have never traveled as far as 125th Street, which is close to us, in Harlem.

"One particular teenager—his name is Luis. We call him Danny. He was 16 before he ever went across the bridge into New Jersey when I took him with me on a trip I had to make. He told me, 'I thought New Jersey was this state out there near California.' I told him, 'Danny, this is New Jersey.' He said, 'No! How could it be?'

"Another boy, I used to ask him, 'Where do you want to go to eat?' He always said, 'McDonald's.' One time, when

81

he was 12, I took him to a Burger King in Queens. I later learned from his teacher that he wrote an essay on our lunch, 'My Trip to Burger King'—the way that wealthy kids might write about a trip to Florida." Although a trip to Burger King may strike some people as quite ordinary, which indeed it is, his voice trembles as he tells this story.

Reverend Groover asks me if I know the song "Amazing Grace." I tell him that I do.

"When we sing the song in church," he says, "I look at the eyes of the women in my congregation. The first three verses are well known and they belong to everyone, even to the wealthy. But when we come to the fourth verse I have always said, 'This verse belongs to us,' because it speaks to our unique experience."

When I say that I don't know that verse, he reaches behind him for a song book and shows me the words.

Through many dangers, toils, and snares
I have already come;
'Tis grace hath brought me safe thus far
And grace will lead me home.

"When we come to those words, the deepest feelings stir. Then I see tears in the eyes of the youngest and the oldest, the eyes of the 16-year-old prostitute and of the 60-year-old great-grandmother." He cautions me, "Be careful of those prophesies of 'the last days' that you may hear. Remember where they come from. Some of the blood-and-thunder churches overdo this emphasis. Although I believe that there will be a 'last day,' the church should not be preaching this. We should not be speaking of apocalypse but of the words of Jesus: 'I came that you might have life and,'" he says with deepest emphasis, "'that you might have it abundantly.'"

Anthony is waiting for me at St. Ann's, where he is playing with a furry dog who sleeps outside the front door of the church except on freezing winter nights, when Reverend Overall brings him in to sleep inside her office. "Mother Martha does not have a heart of stone. She has a heart of gold," says this remarkable boy.

We walk to Children's Park and then, because there are too many addicts there and it is growing very cold, we walk another block and find a sandwich shop where we can sit inside and talk.

He tells me of "a nervous feeling" that he gets when he is walking by the little park and sees the dealers selling drugs. "I feel angry when I see this, but when I told Mother Martha of my anger, she said that I should not bring my anger into church. But I still bring my anger into church."

Mr. Castro has referred to Anthony as one of the children in the neighborhood who sometimes visit him and ask him questions about writing poems. Perhaps it is the influence of the poet that explains the rather formal and sometimes inverted syntax that he uses, although his bilingualism may partly explain the latter too.

When I ask him, "Anthony, do you have a happy life?" he answers, "Mr. Jonathan, my life is like the life of Edgar Allan Poe."

I ask him how he knows of Edgar Allan Poe.

"Because I have read his books," he says. "Did you know he lived here in the Bronx?"

"No," I say. "I didn't."

"Yes. It's true. He lived here in a cottage with his wife."

I ask him what he's read of Poe and he replies, " 'The Masque of the Red Death'—and many other stories."

"Why is your life like his?"

"Because he had not a very happy life. He always began a job but for some reason never finished it, which is my problem too." He adds, "His wife had tuberculosis, but he loved her anyway. After she died, he had a breakdown he could never get out of."

I ask about "The Masque of the Red Death," which I have never read.

"It's about a plague that stalks the earth," he says. "For many, many days has it been on the earth. But a man decides to hold a party because he is not afraid. He thinks the plague will never come to him if he can make things very safe. So he closes all the windows, all the gates, and all the doors, even the little peepholes in the doors. 'Seal them!' he said. And they sealed them." Then he says, "This was because he didn't want the plague to get inside."

"What was this plague like?" I ask.

"Little sharp pins, like tuberculosis," he replies. "Or else like AIDS, because of the disease that gets into the blood, but maybe more like cancer. There was not AIDS in those days. I know that there was cancer."

I press him a bit and ask, "What is the meaning of this 'plague'?"

"A plague is an evil in one way," he says, "but not an evil in another way, because it could have a purpose." He then launches into a brief lecture on the history of plagues. "Now there was also the plague of Egypt where the firstborn died. The plague of Egypt is, of course, not over. It's over in Egypt but it could have gone to other places. Plagues are never really over. They can move from place to place.

"Sadness is one plague today. Desperate would be a plague. Drugs are a plague also, but the one who gets it does not have to be the firstborn. It can be the second son. It could be the youngest."

"Anthony, what should we do to end this plague?"

"Mr. Jonathan," he answers, "only God can do that. I cannot be God."

I ask him when he thinks this plague will end "or else go some place else."

"Mr. Jonathan," he says again, "I don't know when. I think it will only happen in the Kingdom of Heaven, but even the angels do not know when that will come. I only know that this is not His kingdom."

"How can you be sure of that?" I ask.

"This," he says with a gesture out the window that seems to take in many things beyond the dealers on the sidewalk and the tawdry-looking storefront medical office just across the street, "this out here is not God's kingdom. A kingdom is a place of glory. This is a place of pain."

I ask him how he started reading Edgar Allan Poe.

"I saw the cover of his book and I was interested by the

cover." The cover, he explains, was "gory," which, he says, appealed to him, adding that he is writing "a novel about Dracula."

But where, I ask, did he find this book of Edgar Allan Poe?

"I found it in a thrift shop."

"How much did it cost?"

"A quarter," he replies. "Many good things have I found in little stores."

He seems so knowledgeable that I attempt to get him to explain a little more about the bears in Children's Park, the presence of which continues to intrigue me, but he brushes off my question. "No interest have I in bears," he answers.

"Anthony, how do you do in school? How are your grades?"

"Not good," he answers. "Not even excellent."

At the church, after he gives Reverend Overall a Puerto Rican biscuit he has bought for her in a bakery we passed, he talks more like the 12-year-old he is, telling me he still likes *Sesame Street* because "I like Kermit the Frog," but that his favorite program now is *Carmen Sandiego,* a show on public television that teaches geography. He says his mother lets him watch the TV news at ten before he has to go to sleep. His bed, he says, is "on the sofa in the living room" of his apartment, which, he adds, with a funny face, "is not too good of a place."

Before the Christmas service begins, we go outside and he gives the dog the meat and cheese from half his sandwich, which he brought back for this purpose. While we are there, he tells me that he went to Rockefeller Center with the group of kids from St. Ann's Church two days before.

I ask if he enjoyed it.

"Very much so." In front of what he calls "the television building," a reference to NBC, he says, "I noticed it was very clean and beautiful. There were no drug addicts or drug dealers. This neighborhood *wants* to be clean also but we have not enough cops, so there are always people who need drugs out in the streets."

He speaks of people who, he says, "go like this,"

cupping his hands over his face and making the sound of sniffing.

"What are they sniffing?"

"Something called cocaine, I think. A kind of chemical. . . .

"Then, in the alleys sometimes, you see addicts with their needles and the rope around their arm. It looks like a bracelet. If they see me, they say, 'Go away!'

"I know one of these men," he says. "His name is Mr. Mongo. Many times has he been put into a police car. For two weeks is he away. In two weeks is he back. I like this man. I don't know what can cure him. Very sad is the face of this man, Mr. Mongo. Full of tears sometimes are his eyes."

"I cry in the daytime, but you do not answer," read the words of the psalmist in the Book of Common Prayer; "by night as well, but find no rest."

A six-piece Puerto Rican band plays Christmas music as the people take their places in the sanctuary of the oldest church in the South Bronx. The youngest parishioner, as the service starts, is a six-year-old; the oldest is her great-grandmother. After about 50 people have been seated, the priest enters with Anthony and three other children, who are her acolytes, and with two other adults. All are dressed in long white robes. One of the acolytes swings a censer as they walk in a procession up one aisle, behind the backs of the congregants, and down the other aisle to the altar.

As the procession ends, three black teenagers who look tough and shy at the same time enter the sanctuary from the rear, then another young black man approximately 25 years old, a young Puerto Rican woman in a rakish velvet hat, and an elderly Hispanic man in a straw hat with a red band, who sits next to me. Seated in almost the last row, I feel both part of the congregation and a privileged observer.

As Reverend Overall reads one of the Psalms in Spanish, three more people enter the church: a tall black woman with a tiny baby and an older woman wearing a beret, who may be the child's grandmother.

"In those days," the priest begins the reading from St. Luke after the last people to arrive have settled in their seats, "a decree went out from Caesar Augustus that all the world should be taxed." Speaking in a clear and natural voice ("not preacherlike," I noted on the program), she looks young and vulnerable beneath the cross. A graduate of Radcliffe College, 45 years old but looking hardly more than 25 or 30, a former attorney dealing in high finance for a leading New York firm, she gave up the law after her brother died of AIDS, and subsequently entered the church. "What is it like," I ask myself, "to come from the world of Harvard University and Wall Street to a congregation of the poorest people in New York? Does she fear that she may be unable to sustain the meaning of this obligation?" If she has such worries, they are not apparent.

"There were in the same country shepherds abiding in the field," she reads, "keeping watch over their flock by night. And, lo, the angel of the Lord appeared . . . and they were sore afraid. . . . But the angel said unto them, fear not; for, behold, I bring you good tidings of great joy."

In alternating passages, first in English, next in Spanish, she then begins the sermon that she has been working on for several days. The text for the sermon is from the passage she has just read: "The angel said . . . fear not."

The fear that the shepherds felt, she says, is a fear that all of us know well in our own lives. "It was not the 40th Precinct. It was not a drug bust. There was no helicopter like the one we saw last week on Beekman Avenue. But people were afraid."

The words of the angel to the shepherds, she goes on, are like the words of God to Abraham when he was asked to sacrifice his son: "Fear not, Abraham." And "when Hagar was in the wilderness with Ishmael, God spoke to her in the same words: 'What troubles you, Hagar? Fear not.' The message is the one we learn in the 23rd Psalm: 'Though I walk through the valley of the shadow of death, I will fear no evil, for Thou art with me.' "

She stresses the simplicity of God's message at Christmas: "The kingdom comes to us in the form of a baby. This little child was born to a poor family. They lived among the cast-offs of society. Because of Herod's ruling that the first-born must be slain, the child was at risk of death from the beginning."

I think of Anthony's reminder that it is not only the firstborn who may have to die these days. "It can be the second son," he had explained to me. "It could be the youngest."

"Look at the children who are here with us tonight," the pastor says. She nods at the acolytes beside her. "Joey dreams of becoming a priest. Anthony wants to be a writer. Every child among us has a precious life and holds a precious dream." No matter how terrifying life may seem, she says, we need to hold fast to the words of the angel and those of the psalmist: "I will fear no evil."

The unassuming character of the sermon seems to touch the people deeply. When it is over, a credo is sung, a prayer is recited, and then the acolytes kneel at the altar while the people in the congregation rise or kneel before their pews and join together in confession. During the time that this is taking place, the six-year-old who is here with her great-grandmother squirms in her seat, then turns around completely to make faces at the people in the pew behind her. With lovely cornrows in her hair and a smile of sweet mischief in her eyes, she finally disappears beneath the pew, emerging only when her great-grandmother rises from her knees and takes her seat again.

After confession, the priest absolves the people of their sins and then concludes this portion of the service. "The peace of the Lord be always with you," she says to the congregation.

But peace does not come swiftly, even at a pastor's invitation, on this Christmas Eve in the South Bronx. At that moment, two bullet shots ring out behind my back.

They are so close—and come so close together—it sounds like someone striking on the church door with a power-drill or a jackhammer. The pastor pauses. Two of the elders of the church rush to the door. After a moment they return and nod. The man beside me says in his accented English, "Not automatic fire." The incident seems to be dismissed as quickly as it happened. The congregation sings a song in English.

> Yet in Thy dark streets shineth
> The everlasting light;
> The hopes and fears of all the years. . . .

The priest offers communion. About two thirds of the people in the church, including the three shy-looking adolescents and the six-year-old in cornrows, kneel at the railing of the altar and receive wafers and wine. When communion is over and the service complete, the band strikes up a Puerto Rican song. People stand and shake hands with each other.

The six-year-old now undergoes the somewhat ferocious ministrations of her great-grandmother, who wraps her in a red wool scarf, a red wool hat, red mittens, and a heavy, padded jacket with a hood, so that the child, when she tries to shake hands with her great-grandmother's friends, can barely move her arms.

The child, who volunteers to me, "I go to school," says that her name is "Kia."

I ask, "Who made your pretty cornrows?"

She replies, "My mommy."

As her great-grandmother tugs her past me to the door, the child also volunteers, "I know how to do the dishes," at which her great-grandmother nods, as if she's heard this claim before, and looks at me and huffs a bit, and laughs.

Kia and her great-grandmother disappear into the night beyond the lighted doorway of the church. Twelve years from now, where will this pleasant little person be? Will she be on her way to Harvard University, where Reverend Overall received her education, or to another university or college, or will she be scrubbing floors for someone in Manhattan or climbing into trucks by an expressway?

On the sidewalk next to the entrance to the subway on

Brook Avenue, a solitary man wearing a hooded sweatshirt stamps about to keep his feet from freezing, saying again and again to nobody at all, "Okay, check it out. . . ." When I get close to him, to my surprise, he comes out of his recitation and he smiles and tells me, "Have yourself a very merry Christmas."

A message at the hotel from Mrs. Washington instructs me, "Turn on the news and call me."

I gather some newspapers I have bought but haven't yet had time to read, and turn on the TV.

"A few hours ago," a local news announcer says, "a fire roared through an apartment building in the Bronx. It burned so fiercely and so fast that 18 people are without homes." Among the people who have lost their homes, all of whom are black, are two young children, caught by a TV camera as they huddle in a van.

"It happens every Christmas to some family here," says Mrs. Washington when I call her back a little before midnight, and she mentions another fire the preceding night, in which, she says, a two-year-old was killed. "A Puerto Rican boy. His sister was burned too, but she's alive.

"I called Charlayne to make sure she's all right. She didn't go to church. She says the children were afraid to leave the house. I'll see them in the morning.

"Let's hope something good will happen in 1994," she says, a modest prayer that will be partly disappointed one week later when the city's first homicide of the new year will take place in the South Bronx, near East Tremont Avenue. A week after that, a former acolyte at St. Ann's Church will be arrested by police, charged with the killing of a woman working at a social service agency, murdered with a bullet to the brain. The 16-year-old boy, who had been a track star at the junior high that Anthony attends, had been living with his grandmother in a building just behind the Calderon memorial at Children's Park.

After speaking with Mrs. Washington, I watch part of the midnight mass on TV from St. Patrick's, then turn out the lights but find it hard to sleep. I get up around four

A.M., get dressed again, and go out for a walk. I get as far as Rockefeller Center. Christmas lights are glittering in the tree behind the statue of Prometheus above the skating rink. Feeling the effects of sleeplessness, I go back up Fifth Avenue, across to Lexington, and back to the hotel.

At seven A.M., I leave for the airport, persuading the taxi-driver first to detour to Mott Haven and to stop at St. Ann's Avenue, where I get out in front of Children's Park. A teenager in an army coat stands beneath the shelter in the back. Most of the children in the nearby buildings, I assume, are sleeping still. The bears look like they're sleeping too. Then to La Guardia and to the plane that brings me back to Boston and then up the highway on this snowless Christmas morning to the town in which I live, where people soon will wake to unwrap presents and to lead their customary lives, which sometimes are sad and sometimes happy, but usually are industrious and challenging and peaceful, and who often feel quite bad about those many people who do not have lives like ours, and speak of this sometimes in church or synagogue, and frequently write checks, which sometimes are quite generous, to various good charities, particularly during this season of mercy, which is winter in our land.

Chapter Four

S now blankets New York during the second half of January. Very cold weather finally arrives. Mrs. Washington's voice, when we speak a few times on the phone, is hoarse and lacks the energy it had when I was with her at Charlayne's apartment.

David calls me late one night when both New York and Boston have been hit by one of the worst storms in many years. I ask him how his mother feels.

"That's why I called. She's spitting blood. I went in the bathroom last night after she'd been coughing and I saw the toilet filled with blood."

I mention that she seemed to have been feeling better before Christmas.

"That's what it's like. She can be fine today. A few days later, she starts spitting blood and having fevers." Even on good days, he says, "she throws up every morning for ten minutes."

I ask if she's been eating.

"Only once a day. At night. Around ten-thirty. Even then, she isn't eating much. She nibbles a little." Still, he says, "she spends the whole day cleaning up the house. When I come home, my bed is made. I tell her, 'Leave it. I can make my bed.' She does it anyway. It seems like it's important to her to make sure that nothing changes.

"After I saw my mother's blood, my mind was there with her all day. I couldn't think of anything else. I had to do a paper for my English teacher. Usually I get A's in English but this time I couldn't concentrate. My teacher asked me what was wrong. I told her I was worried about my mother, but I was afraid to tell her why."

"Why were you afraid?"

"It's hard to explain. My teacher's spoken of friends of hers with AIDS. She's smart, a New York person. She knows what's going on. I don't think she'd treat me any different."

I tell him I agree with him.

"There are a lot of people who do treat you different after you say AIDS," he says. "Yes. Even doctors sometimes do. Even nurses. If the nurses and doctors feel that way, why wouldn't other people too?

"It shouldn't be different from other diseases, but it *is*. It seems like something different when they talk about it on TV. People speak of it as if it has to do with sin, as if it is God's punishment."

"You don't believe that."

"No," he says. "I don't believe this has to do with God. I think it's something done by men."

When I ask him what he means, his answer is somewhat oblique. "I think they fear that people of color are becoming the majority in the United States. I think that's why they want to change the immigration laws. I think that's why they stop the Haitian people on their boats."

I ask how he's connecting these events with AIDS.

"I don't know exactly how. I think that it might be a way to make sure the minorities do not become majorities. That would be an evil thing to do, but I have learned in school that history repeats itself. I've read about Tuskegee."

"You once told me, 'Evil exists.' "

"Evil exists? Yes, I said that. People who let other people be destroyed do evil. People who know but do not act do evil too. I don't know if I would call them evil but they're certainly not thinking about heaven."

Noting that it's past twelve-thirty, I ask if he's sleepy.

"No. I'm not. I've gotten used to staying up. I try to stay awake until my mother falls asleep."

"After you fall asleep, do you sleep through the night?"

"Not often. Very seldom. When I wake up in the morning sometimes I'm worn out and feel more tired than before I went to bed. Sometimes sleeping makes you tired.

You wake up feeling strange and shaky. So you're scared to go to sleep at all. Then, when I leave for school, I worry whether she's okay. So I keep calling home."

"Where do you call from?"

"The school office," he replies.

The school he attends is a so-called "pilot school"—a term used sometimes in New York and elsewhere to describe an innovative school that gives its students individual attention in small classes. Only a few children from his neighborhood attend the school, he says, perhaps because, like similar schools in other cities, it tends to enroll the children of the parents who know how to work the system and to cut through the red tape.

He mentions that, the week before, his English section had to do an essay on the homeless. "We had to stand and read it to the class."

"What did you write about?"

"I wrote about my mother," he replies. "I told about her being beaten by my father and the first hotel we stayed in, which was near Times Square—the one there was no water and we had to bring the buckets to the bar and grill across the street."

"How old were you at that time?"

"I was eight or nine."

"What floor were you on?"

"The seventh floor," he says.

"Who gave you the buckets?"

"The hotel did. It was their responsibility."

"That's amazing."

"Yes, it is," he answers. "Shameful and amazing."

Not knowing what to say, I ask, "How do you explain it?"

"I don't know how. There must have been hotels there in Manhattan that had water. My mother says the only way she can explain it is that people thought they had to punish us for being poor."

"Do you believe that?"

"I'm not sure. I think it also has to do with who we were. We were almost all black people and Hispanic people in that building. There were little children in the building.

97

If they were white children, I don't think it would have been permitted."

"Why do you say that?"

"I don't know. I just don't think white people could have done that to their children. I think it would have been unbearable for them to see."

"Was the owner of the hotel a white man?"

"No. He was from India, I think."

I ask him how his class reacted to the paper when he read it.

"Everyone seemed kind of speechless."

"Did they believe that what you wrote was true?"

"I think that they believed it but they did not *comprehend* it. They didn't understand how this could happen in our country."

David's mother goes into the hospital again in February. This time, she's held for four nights in a downstairs corridor before a bed is free.

"I took her there on Monday," David tells me on the phone. "It was one of those bad nights. We got there at seven, but it was so crowded there was no place to lie down. She sat up for five hours. Then at midnight I went to a nurse and said she needed to lie down.

"The nurse got mad and snapped at me. She said, 'I can't grant your request.' My mother had to sit there until three A.M. At three they put her on a stretcher and a doctor looked at her. He said she needed X-rays but he said that there was no one free to do them. She didn't get the X-ray for two days.

"She spent another three nights down there on the stretcher in the hallway. When they finally found a room for her, she suddenly began to shiver and her hands were cold. They didn't have no blankets. They ran out. I took a blanket to her today. No curtains. So they put a sheet over the window.

"They said the diagnosis was pneumonia and a blood clot in her lungs. She's on oxygen and an IV. It's six days since she went in."

Alone at home, he mentions it's his birthday.

I ask him if she finally got approved for SSI.

"No, she was turned down again," he says. "Her doctor said he was surprised."

"What was the reason that they gave?"

"They say she isn't sick enough," he answers.

The following week, when his mother has regained her appetite, David and his sister take turns cooking food for her because, as he explains, "the meals served in the hospital are not too good."

"You bring her food?"

"I wrap it in foil so that it stays hot," he says. "I have to make sure that she eats."

In March, when she's been home for a few weeks, she sends me a long letter. She doesn't speak of her health or of herself at all but tells me of a child's accidental death near St. Ann's Church.

"A little boy, an eight-year-old, who lived right near Charlayne, fell in the elevator shaft of his apartment building. This was a month or so ago. The little boy died. I think his mother is in jail. Charlayne says he lived with his grandmother."

In her letter, which comes in an envelope with pictures of blue geraniums and yellow daisies just over her name in the left corner, she says that the death of the eight-year-old is being attributed to a broken elevator door that opened when he leaned against it while he had been playing in the hallway. "The city is blaming the family," she writes, "for letting an eight-year-old go in the hallway. But they got to go out *somewhere*." Going outside for youngsters in the building, she explains, means "going in the hallway" since "the real outside, where they could get some air, is just too dangerous."

She encloses a clipping from the *Daily News* that speaks of "garbage piled five feet high in an airshaft" of the building where the child died and notes that the telephone company has come to the building "ten times," in the words of a woman who lives there with three children, because rats have "eaten through the walls" and "chewed through the phone lines." In another apartment, the clipping says, the ceiling has fallen in upon a child's bedroom.

Mrs. Washington also tells me that there have been warnings in the papers that Mayor Rudolph Giuliani, who took office two months earlier, intends to cut back sanitation and inspection services and programs for children and teenagers, the early stages in what soon will prove to be wide-sweeping cuts in a variety of services relied on by poor people, as a consequence of the most drastic cutbacks in the city's budget since the Great Depression.

Subsequent announcements warn the public to expect reductions in drug-rehabilitation programs—which already have a six-month waiting list and offer care to only one in ten of the half-million heroin and cocaine addicts in New York, turning away tens of thousands of addicted people every year—as well as reductions in lead-poisoning prevention programs and in the control of rats, elimination of programs that help hungry families in obtaining food stamps, the cancellation of AIDS services to 600 children and to 16,000 adults, and reductions in the numbers of orderlies, janitors, security guards, and lab technicians at the medical facilities that serve the poor, which, says the head of the city's public hospitals, is going to mean "more frequent" delays in care and "dirtier hospitals" and longer stays in "waiting areas."

Some people, says the *Times*, wonder why the city is planning "to cut services, which would hurt the . . . poorest residents," while once again planning to cut taxes, "which would help the city's richest." The paper notes that the AIDS services the mayor intends to cancel were created to spare the dying from being forced to "wait in long lines." In a strong editorial, it calls the threatened cancellation of these services "intolerable" and "inhumane."

A deputy mayor, however, says that these reductions in municipal expenditures will be "a victory for everybody," and, notes the *Times*, on Wall Street the reaction to the mayor's plans is "generally favorable."

In all, the city intends to lay off 15,000 workers, nearly 5,000 of them in the agencies that offer social services, which, says a political analyst in *Newsday*, "lends an unavoidable racial tincture" to the mayor's decisions, since the majority of those to be laid off in social service agencies are black and Hispanic women. Caseloads of social workers, already as large as 200 children to one worker in some instances, are certain to grow larger, the newspapers say. Meanwhile, nearly half the cuts in taxes will, according to Manhattan borough president Ruth Messinger, benefit only the five percent of the population who have incomes higher than $100,000.

The mayor tells a group of children from a segregated high school that they'll have to learn to manage without public help. "I think largely you have to help yourself. . . . Look at what is there and take advantage of it," he advises them, but cancels 11,000 city jobs for children of their age, as well as afterschool programs in which younger children can be safe while mothers work. He also announces that he wants to fingerprint welfare recipients in order to be sure they do not file double applications (which some do) but also, some observers feel, in order to comply with the desire of conservatives to add a greater stigma to dependence.

One of the mayor's top deputies proposes that people on welfare in New York—all "one million, two hundred thousand" of them, he insists, which includes dependent children—be made to wear "green uniforms" and sent out on the streets "to pick up papers" and "clean up graf-fiti"—a plan, as Mrs. Washington observes, that would place most of the people of Mott Haven in the same position as the prison inmates who already do some of these jobs in the South Bronx.

"It's going to make a lot of people feel like they are criminals," she says, in reference to the plans for uniforms and fingerprinting, both of which have been reported widely in the news. Speaking of the promised cuts in hospital funds, she adds, "There's going to be a lot more blood-stained beds."

In a postscript to her letter, she says that the grandmother of the boy who died in the elevator shaft, whose name was Bernardo Rodriguez, Jr., has been "inconsolable," a strong word, which she follows with this statement, written in her slanted script: "I don't think New York is poor, do you?"

In a phone conversation two nights after I receive her letter, she says that the family lived in a building two blocks from her daughter. Speaking of a photograph of the child's family in the clipping from the *Daily News,* she says, "There's three women in the picture. The one with short hair is the boy's grandmother. The others are her daughters. There's one daughter missing. She's the one in prison."

"Is that the child's mother?" I ask.

"It *was* his mother. Now she doesn't have her son no more. I feel sorry for her but, to tell the truth, I feel a little worse for the grandmother."

"Have you seen her since the child died?"

"I seen her twice—once from a distance across the street, then at the check-cashing place where Charlayne pays her bills. Charlayne said, 'That's the lady whose grandson fell into the elevator shaft.'

"When I saw her, she had just been comin' back from church. I think it's a Catholic church but I'm not sure which one. She had one of her daughters and some friends with her, some friends from church, so she's not all alone. Still, your friends can't bring your grandson back to life.

"You could tell from lookin' at her face that she'd been crying. Maybe she feels guilty that she let the little boy go outside in the hall to play.

"Charlayne says this woman's organizing a petition. Goin' around and gettin' everyone to sign. Holdin' meetings. Has a lot of energy. She speaks good English. Never went to school but taught herself and speaks it well. She says she's goin' to bring the city to accounts. Her anger's strong. It just pours out of her. I hope that she succeeds.

"This woman isn't a violent person but she says before she dies she's goin' to make somebody pay. I don't know what she means. She don't look like the type to take revenge but these days in New York you never know. What *does* that type of person look like? Could she just walk into city hall holding a gun, or into a housing office, or some other place, and shoot somebody in the face? I hope she don't. I don't want to see more people killed.

"Anyway she's stirrin' up the neighborhood and gettin' everybody to complain. . . .

"I was thinkin', maybe all this anger is her way of dealing with her grief. Someone knocks at your door one day and says, 'Your grandson's dead'—out of the blue. 'Fell in the elevator. It's a shame.' What do you do? I guess it's easier to give in to your anger than to cry."

On Good Friday, a procession makes its way through the streets of the East Tremont section of the Bronx in commemoration of Jesus' walk to Calvary. Parishioners, according to the *Times,* take the roles of Mary, Jesus, and the Roman soldiers. At the end of the procession, the man who plays Jesus is placed upon a cross. An 18-year-old musician who plays in a rock band called Driven By Hatred has the part of Jesus this year. To avoid the risk of violence, however, the crucifixion, which has taken place in a neighborhood park for over 20 years, has to be moved indoors.

Late on Good Friday afternoon, the courtyard of the building where Bernardo Rodriguez lived and died is filled with many idle-looking and not very friendly men. When I get no answer pressing at the bell, however, one of the men comes over with his key and lets me in.

The inside of the elevator, which is made of steel, is pocked with bullet indentations. At one point, roughly chest-high, there is a raw-looking hole where a large-caliber bullet must have ripped right through the steel. The boy, I later learn, fell four stories through the open shaft and struck the elevator roof above me. His fate was not discovered until his blood began to drip on passengers.

The boy's grandmother isn't home when I arrive. It turns out she has gone to church with her granddaughter and another grandson. Bernardo's aunt, however, is expecting me and she invites me to sit down.

My meeting with Bernardo's aunt, as I wrote in my notebook later, has "an other-worldly feeling." She is, to start with, an ethereally pale and thin and pretty woman who looks fragile but whose voice is silvery and strong.

When she speaks she looks right in my eyes. Her gaze is so direct that I look down sometimes in order to avoid her eyes.

She begins by telling me that the elevator in the building had been broken for a long time. "Something was wrong with it and people had complained. There had always been some blackish grease that dripped down from the ceiling. My mother had asked the management to fix it but I don't think anything was done.

"The day he died, it was six-thirty in the afternoon. The evening. I was sitting with my mother here in the apartment. A neighbor came up and knocked on the door and said, 'There's something wrong. There's something sticky dripping from the elevator.'

"My mother said, 'It's only grease.' But the woman said, 'It looks like blood.' So then my mother was afraid and went downstairs to check, and it was blood, and it was coming through the ceiling of the elevator, which was on the second floor.

"So then my mother came upstairs to make sure that the children were all right. We found the other children but we could not find Bernardo.

"So, basically, that's when security was called. And then police. They found his body down there on the elevator roof. We couldn't believe. He was alive. Now he was gone, like that. It takes a while for a bad thing to sink in. Even to this day I don't accept."

"Does your mother accept?"

"No. She does not accept."

I ask her where the funeral took place.

"It was at a funeral home," she answers, "but the mass was at my mother's church, St. Luke's."

Her sister, she says, is still away in prison. I ask if she was brought here for the funeral and mass.

"Yes, she was here. She had to come in handcuffs but they took them off outside the church so that the children wouldn't see them."

"Did Bernardo visit her in prison?"

"No. He never had the chance."

"How long has she been in prison?"

"Seven years."

"Have you seen her since the funeral?"

"Yes. I took the other children there two weeks ago." In August, she adds, she will take them again "because they're going to have a children's day, with picnics."

"How much longer does she have to serve?"

"Maybe three more years," she says, but sounds unsure.

"What was Bernardo like?"

"Serious," she answers. "He did his lessons. He loved his teacher and he never missed a day of school. He passed his tests. His last test he passed with an 85—in mathematics. All his papers he brought home to let us see. My mother kept them all, here in this album."

Over the chair in which she's sitting there is a communion photo of the boy, dressed in a black suit and necktie. Taking another picture of Bernardo from the album where she also keeps his last arithmetic exam and various other documents from school, she says, "This one I took on Christmas morning." The photograph shows Bernardo in pajamas with a lighted tree behind him. "We had a beautiful Christmas day. Before our dinner Bernardo stood up on a chair and said our prayer."

"Was he religious?"

"Yes," she says. "He knew all of his prayers. He went to his religion class on Saturdays. He went to mass on Sunday. He had been baptized and had had his first communion. He did not yet finish his first penance. He did not know sin."

"Are you religious too?"

"I am," she says.

Although I am afraid of pressing her too far, I ask a question that has been in my mind since she began to speak. "I don't understand. I need to ask. How do you handle this? It seems as if it ought to be unbearable. How do you remain so calm? What gives you strength?"

"I pray."

"Does praying really ease the pain?"

"Yes. It does." She gazes at the Christmas photo of the boy in his pajamas. "I am 19. Bernardo could have been my brother. But he was more like my child. If God has taken him, I know it must be for a reason. He must have needed him in heaven. He must have wanted him. He must have said, 'This boy is better off with me in my own kingdom.' So He took the name of Bernardo to be with Him."

I have heard statements like this often in Mott Haven, and although I know that words like these give people consolation, I have often wondered if they come from absolute conviction or are more like recitations of enforced convention. I have also wondered many times, "If God is a good power, why would He want to take a little kid before he's had a chance to live?" I pose this question to Bernardo's aunt, but phrase it somewhat indirectly. "You said you don't 'accept.' Yet, in a way, it also seems you do."

She looks for a time at his picture. "In one way I don't accept," she answers finally, "and in another way I do. I have to believe God picks a person when his work on earth is done."

"At eight years old?" I ask, and then regret my question.

"You can be eight years old and still your work is done."

Then, in that silvery voice again that seems to come out of a different place from where we are, she says, "God knows when somebody has suffered long enough. When it is enough, He takes us to His kingdom. In heaven there is no sickness. Here, there is sickness. In heaven there is love. Here, there is hate. On earth you grow old or else you die in pain. In heaven you are young forever."

The spell cast by her voice and by the piercing look within her eyes subdues my inclination to ask her more questions. After a few moments, I get up and thank her for her willingness to talk.

"I wanted to talk," she says. "You can come back and visit me again if you would like. My mother can tell you more about the elevator." Touching my shoulder with her hand, she says, "We have had troubles. But please say we are not a bad family." It seems important to her to see me write this down before I leave.

In the hallway I notice that the elevator door still seems quite loose, and although it doesn't open when I press it, I decide to walk down to the street. The stairway smells and its walls are smeared with something greenish. This is where Bernardo played for eight and a half years. This is the best New York could do for him. The kennel where I leave my dog while I am in New York is cleaner and smells better. The kennel also has a place where dogs can go outside and have some fun in the fresh air. I hold my breath, then breathe through my mouth, until I get down to the lobby.

On the corner of Cypress Avenue a number of children are standing in front of a woman with a small cart, waiting to buy "icies" from her, which is what the children call *coquitos*. Not having eaten since the morning, I get in line and buy a cherry icie, then walk to Brook Avenue to get the train.

On the day after Easter, another little boy who lives in Bernardo's neighborhood is killed, this time by a fire that consumes his home.

Mrs. Washington connects the deaths of both these children with the cutbacks in inspection services and other public services that have now begun in earnest. But the cutbacks she refers to are, in fact, not really new. In one form or another, these reductions in the programs that defend the life and health and safety of poor children have been taking place for over 20 years in New York City. In 1970, for example, 400 physicians tended to the health of children in the city's public schools. By the spring of 1993, the number of school physicians had been cut to only 23, most of them part-time. Where once there had been 30 rat exterminators on the city's payroll, says the *Times*, "now there are only ten," only two of them in all of the South Bronx. Housing inspectors, whose job it is to check on matters such as broken elevator doors or five-foot piles of garbage, have also been cut back repeatedly over these years—from 700 in the 1970s to 213 at the time

Bernardo died. Now, in early 1994, the city announces plans to cut their ranks again, this time in a way particularly likely to be felt in places like Mott Haven.

Up to now, building inspectors, fearful of going into certain buildings all alone, have been able to request permission to go out in teams of two in the South Bronx. Henceforth, according to the city, "solo code enforcement inspectors" will go into areas previously served by teams of two, and in "daylight . . . only"—allowing taxpayers "a reduction of 20 inspectors."

What's going to happen, says an official of the inspectors' union, is that inspectors, who have the right to refuse to enter a building where their lives may be endangered, will simply write, "No access to building" on inspection sheets, which means that hundreds of broken elevators, trash heaps in which rats may thrive, and serious fire hazards like illegally barred windows or illegally obstructed doors will be added to those other hazards that already have gone undetected.

"It means more kids are goin' to die," says Mrs. Washington. "I just wish that when the papers talk about these 'cuts,' they'd put some pictures in of all the children who got burned in fires or got killed in accidents, show some pictures of the hallways in these buildings, so that folks would understand what it's about."

"You don't think that they already know?"

"They know and they don't know," she replies. "What can I say?"

As with many fatal accidents and fires in Mott Haven, it is impossible to know for sure if better inspection and enforcement would have saved Bernardo's life or that of the boy incinerated in the fire; and city officials are at times reluctant to release such information even when it is available. But, as Mrs. Washington observes, if the function of inspectors is to save lives by detecting dangers, then cutting their numbers by two thirds seems to assure that you've increased those dangers severalfold. "If that's not so, then why have *any* inspectors?" she quite reasonably asks. "Why not just fire them all?

"Drug dealers aren't the only people killing children,"

she remarks, the sort of statement one hears often in the South Bronx and which sometimes causes great offense among the affluent because it speaks so clearly of incendiary feelings of which most of us would just as soon not hear. But it may be important that we hear these words because they make it absolutely clear that what some financiers and politicians see as nothing more than fiscal prudence, other people see as social homicide; and every time another bit of mercy is subtracted from the public treasury, feelings of this nature are compounded.

The mayor insists that "all the people of the city" will be shouldering the human costs of his decisions; but this is obviously not so. The costs of cuts in sanitation, for example, are incurred and felt almost immediately in the South Bronx. Their consequences are significantly diluted in those neighborhoods where sanitation, like so many other basic services, is being purchased more and more through private means by local business and homeowners' groups, which have been granted semi-governmental taxing powers to raise money locally and spend it locally, another stage in the secession of the fortunate from common areas of shared democracy.

In midtown neighborhoods, privately purchased sanitation services have made "a stunning difference," says the president of the Times Square Improvement District, one of several dozen of such districts, which have also hired private guards in order to discourage beggars and drive out the homeless, sometimes gently, sometimes forcibly, and have also paid for better lighting, additional street signs, even cleaner trash cans. "When districts feel clean, they feel orderly. . . . When they feel orderly, they feel safer," the head of the Times Square district notes.

Calling this development an example of "reinvented government," an assistant to the mayor tells a reporter that "his goal is to see Manhattan . . . blanketed with such improvement districts"—"at least south of 96th Street," which is the point at which the Harlem ghetto starts on the East Side.

Mrs. Washington asks me, as she will do many times this spring, why there is so much pressure to cut taxes. I repeat to her the arguments I hear downtown: Taxes are already viewed as very high in New York City. If they are reduced somewhat, it is believed that this may spur investment, which might generate some jobs. If taxes, on the other hand, were to increase, it is feared that wealthy people may abandon New York City.

"But," she says, "it seems, in a way, like they've abandoned it already. Their kids don't go to the same schools our children go to. They don't use the subways much. They have their private cars and limousines. Most of them don't use the hospitals we use. Now, if they have their own street-cleaning and their own police, it isn't like they're really living in New York. How much more could they abandon it than they have done already?"

I have had talks like this with friends in the financial world and with some journalists, but never before with someone who is truly poor. I carry the argument along, as I have often heard it stated. "The fear is that they could abandon it completely and go somewhere else that might have lower taxes."

"Where would they go?" she asks.

"I don't know. Connecticut? New Jersey?"

She sweeps away the argument impatiently. "All this is a game the politicians play. People in New Jersey and Connecticut could say the same until they cut us down to nothing. If you want to solve the problem, raise the taxes everywhere in the United States. Then the millionaires won't have no place to hide."

"That's a good idea," I say, "but I don't think it's going to happen."

I tell her of the comment of a lawyer in New York, who told me that a further flight of business from the city is quite probable if taxes aren't reduced. "They're being killed by personal income taxes," he had said, in speaking of some of his business colleagues.

"There's killing and there's killing," Mrs. Washington replies when I repeat this to her. "I don't think the man you talked to knows what 'killing' means."

"Do you want me to say that?"

"Write it down."

The year before I had this talk with Mrs. Washington, a Wall Street money manager who had been extremely lucky, or had made some very shrewd decisions, had had earnings of more than $1 billion, which was just about five times the total income of the 18,000 households of Mott Haven. An extra 20 percent tax on his earnings, if redistributed in the South Bronx, would have lifted 48,000 human beings—every child and every parent in every family of Mott Haven—out of poverty, with enough left over, I imagine, to buy many safe new elevator doors and hire several good physicians for the public schools that serve the neighborhood. Dozens of other investors in New York, according to financial publications, were making annual earnings of between $10 million and $400 million during 1992 and 1993.

When the newspapers speak of New York City's lack of money, clearly, they are referring not to private wealth but to the public treasury. Still, the statements Mrs. Washington has made stick in my mind. Ever since that time, when I have seen news stories about "fiscal shortages" in New York City, I have read those words with complicated feelings.

On the phone a few nights later, David spells out another consequence that he foresees from cuts in public services. "It means we're going to see more rats in the South Bronx. I think we have enough already."

"Where do you see rats?" I ask.

"You can't miss them," he replies.

"Rats or mice?"

"Rats," he answers. "Ugly rats. They're almost everywhere. They come out even in the daytime."

I ask, "Where do they come from?"

"The biggest ones, the water rats, come out of the Bronx River. At four P.M. or five P.M., when it's beginning to get dark, you see them coming out in hordes. Very large rats. You see them right here in the street outside our building. I don't like to see them. I feel nausea when I see them.

"A supermarket close to the train station had to be

shut down because there were so many rats. They were tearing open the food boxes. There used to be a Kentucky Fried Chicken on the corner but they had to close it because it was rat-infested too. They didn't reopen. There's nothing left there now except an empty store."

He speaks of the threatened cuts in children's programs and AIDS services. "The mayor says that he needs to take these things away from us, but *we* don't need to have these things taken away from us. Once they're gone, a lot of us are going to go with them."

His distrust of the mayor is visceral, intense. "I don't like him. I don't like his ways. I don't like the way he speaks about poor people. I don't like his eyes. I watch his eyes. There's too much coldness there."

I ask him if he thinks the mayor is ignorant of how poor people view him and of what they're going through.

"I don't think he's ignorant. He seems to be well educated, though you can be educated and still be ignorant, but I don't think he's ignorant. I think he's cruel."

I say to him something that has frequently been said to me. "There's always been unfairness in the world. There has always been selfishness. This isn't something new to the United States, or to New York."

"I don't think it's always been this way," he·says. "I don't believe it. I don't think that there was this much selfishness in olden times, in Bible days. I think there was more kindness and that people helped each other more. I would like to see it again but I don't think it's going to happen. Not any time soon."

I tell him about Cliffie, whom I met last summer at St. Ann's, and Cliffie's anecdote about the slice of pizza that he handed to a man who asked for it, because "God told us, 'Share!' "

"That's right. God did say that," he says. "That little boy knows more about the way to get to heaven than most grown-ups do."

"Do you believe the Bible is the word of God?"

"I think it's God's beliefs and His commandments. But He gave to man the wisdom and intelligence to write it."

I ask him if the teenagers he knows speak about God or heaven in this way.

"Some do. But some are too embarrassed. They're afraid to sound like children. But it isn't bad to sound like children. Children sometimes understand things that most grown-ups do not see.

"I like to look at children on the train. You don't see many people who look friendly on the train. But children do. Some of them do. Some of them look joyful. Some of them say hello to you, even to strangers. No one else does. They want to be loved."

David's troubled reactions to the cutbacks taking place now in New York and his belief that they are linked to self-ishness or to a wish for punishment, as much as to necessity, stand in contrast to the mood apparent in the words of many downtown financiers and politicians when they comment on these shifts in social policy.

"In some ways this is a bit of a grand experiment," says the director of the state Municipal Assistance Corporation, a powerful financial organization that has pushed hard for the fiscal cuts that have, in turn, led to these cuts in public services. New Yorkers are going to have to learn "to make more bricks with less straw," says another official of the corporation, an investment banker formerly at Lazard Freres.

The biblical experiment of which they speak does not seem particularly grand, or wise, or in the long run even cost-efficient, from the point of view of those who work among the poor; but the reduction in taxes that the mayor has promised seems to be appealing to the middle class and affluent, and he is, it seems, reading the mood of the electorate adeptly.

"All right," concedes Anne Roiphe, a columnist in the *New York Observer*. "Out there, someone is sleeping on a grate. . . . Somewhere in the parts of town where white powders are served in contaminated needles, someone is daring fate . . . and the emergency rooms are full of people. . . ." Still, she says, "cruelty is as natural to the city as fresh air is to the country. . . . I used to feel this cruelty was wrong, immoral. . . . Now I don't know. Maybe it's the fuel that powers the palace."

Encouraged by this state of mind, she says, "I like the wicked clink of glasses, the light bouncing off the rhinestone clasp . . . , the chandeliers glinting against the dark. . . . Cruelty is part of the energy, part of the delight. . . . I want to . . . eat good food till the millennium. . . . I am feeling full of nerve. Nerve is what you need to get through. . . . What you must decide is that shame is bearable."

The author, who calls herself "a cold old liberal" in search of a fur coat, may be right in calling cruelty "the fuel that powers the palace" of our satisfactions. Perhaps this has been true in all societies. Tolstoi described a number of people in St. Petersburg and Moscow who said things like this 100 years ago. Still, the note of self-congratulation in her voice takes one aback. It sounds as if she views her new-found power to feel comfortable with shame as therapeutic. If this is what a person who regards herself as liberal is thinking, what do conservative New Yorkers feel? What will this mean for children in the Bronx?

David's description of the rats that come up out of the Bronx River in late afternoon is what I remember longest from our conversation. I repeat it to his mother the next time I see her, in mid-April.

"You see them earlier than afternoon," she says. "These rats are fearless. Light don't scare them. Noise don't scare them. You can see them in the park at noon." Shaking her head slightly and holding her fingers to her breast, touching her throat, she adds, "Any time you see the rats at noon, it's time for people to move out."

She tells me of a seven-month-old boy who was attacked three blocks away from here a month before by several rats that climbed into his crib. "Doctor said he hadn't seen bite marks like that in years. The baby's fingers were all bloody. I think it was the third time that this baby was attacked. His mother's terrified but can't move out. The city put her in this building and she don't have any money to move somewhere else.

"The day before Easter, one of the Puerto Rican families that I know was over there next to the park. The baby wanted an Easter bunny and his mother said, 'We don't need no bunnies. We got our own brand of bunnies. They live rent-free in our walls and they're called rats.' "

The city, she says, has posted signs about the rats in schools and stores. "It says don't try to kill them. Call the Board of Health. You see these signs all over. We got one posted right here in this building. Says that they're Norwegian rats. I don't know how they got here all the way from Norway.

"Something's happened. They're resistant to the poison that the Board of Health lays down. They get swollen with the poison but it doesn't seem to kill them. They live in dirty water. They look like they're all blown up, like if you pricked them they'd explode. Sharp little claws. I've seen them walk right up a tree like they were walkin' on the ground.

"A month ago, I was tryin' to sleep. It was early mornin', but still dark. I heard these screeching sounds and thought it was a rat fighting a cat. My granddaughter was at my house. Sometime around six o'clock she came into my room. 'Nanny, look outside,' she said. 'There's a big rat fightin' with a squirrel.' I looked out the window and I seen this rat. Squirrel was dead. Rat sittin' on him, eatin' from his back. When he was done, he went back down the tree. Sara said, 'He killed the squirrel and he ate him for his breakfast and he went back to his hole.' Nothin' was left except the hair that must have been the squirrel's tail."

The rats, she says, have a frightening meaning for some of the more religious people in the neighborhood. "This Puerto Rican lady says that rats are s'posed to come before Armageddon. You hear a lot of people talkin' of Armageddon. Bible says that there will be 10,000 rats for every person."

I ask, "Do you believe that?"

"I ain't sayin' I believe it. I'm just sayin' what the Bible says . . . 10,000 rats per person." Smiling, she adds, "If that's the truth, we must be gettin' close."

The sign in the lobby of the building, which she takes

me out to photograph, has had a heightening effect upon the fears of residents. "It's like—you know the rats are there because you see them, and you hear them in the walls. But, when the Board of Health puts up these signs, it's like it's telling you that something else is goin' on. You wonder what it is. You want to know."

"What do you mean—'something else'?"

"I can't explain. It makes you think there's something there that you don't know about."

Speaking of Mayor Giuliani, who has just announced his plan to terminate the agency that offers services to people who have AIDS, she says, "I don't know if this man knows what he is doin'. People say he isn't wrapped too tight." She glances at a pack of Salems on the table, reaches out her hand, then draws it back.

"Me and my friend was talking yesterday—what we would do if he came to our neighborhood. She said, 'He better not even think about it 'cause I'm sure his life would be endangered. Even with all the guards he's got, they can only stop one bullet at a time.' "

"Do you think she's right?"

"It could happen. Plenty of people here hate him enough to kill him."

"If it happened, how would you react?"

"I don't know. I hate to say this. I'd feel bad but I don't think I'd cry. You can only cry so many times." She turns it around into a question: "Do you know how tired people get? You mourn for someone's little girl who's murdered. You mourn for someone's little boy who's burned to death. At some point you feel you're done with mournin'. You feel so beaten down. Then, if the person who's been beatin' you comes in his limousine to tour your neighborhood, you're all worn out from mournin'. You don't have nothin' left. You wouldn't feel glad if somebody was hurt. You just might not feel nothin'."

"Do you think it's really come to that?"

"I don't know. I'm just not sure," she answers.

Despite these speculations and despite the ugly image of the swollen rats resistant to the poison laid down by the Board of Health, which, she says, "is like the TB that we got

116

now—it's resistant too," there is still amusement in her voice. When I ask, for instance, how the Board of Health knows that the rats have come from Norway, she says, "Search me! I don't think these rats have passports!"

Then, in a really cheerful voice, she adds, "I like to watch the squirrels from my window. I like the way they leap from tree to tree. Life is interesting, isn't it?"

David is at his sister's house. So Mrs. Washington insists on walking with me to the train. At a bodega opposite the station, she says that she needs some milk and asks me to go in with her. As we enter the store, however, a man comes in behind us, shouting at the owner, who is seated on a stool behind a counter, partly separated from the customers by a protective shield. The man, who shoves past Mrs. Washington and me, pulls out a length of pipe and swings it at the counter, yelling something in Spanish I can't understand. The store-owner leans down, then rises with a shotgun. Customers scatter. Mrs. Washington grabs me by the arm and shoves me out the door. She buys a token at the subway station so that she can go up on the platform with me. The train comes rattling from the north. She stands alone on the platform waving to me as the train moves from the station.

"Bulldozers leveled Children's Park last week," says Reverend Overall when I telephone her during April. "The trees are gone. The bears are gone. All the things the people did, the brickwork, everything, has been destroyed." Even the graffiti that memorialized the druglord Calderon, she says, has been effaced.

"They came in with a tremendous show of force. Four or five police cars. Ten or 20 officers. I'm not sure what they expected. They had to close the street off for six hours."

She also tells me that she and Anthony went out for lunch a few days earlier. "We went to a restaurant where I have been with him before. Before we got there, he kept asking, 'Do you think the waitress will remember me?'

"He ordered two pieces of bread with cottage cheese,

which doesn't seem too nourishing to me, but he says that he loves cottage cheese. They offered to toast the bread for him but he insisted that he likes it cold. I bet the waitress will remember him the next time he comes in!

"Whenever I feel afraid that he is being overwhelmed by things, he seems to sense that I am worried and he says something he thinks will cheer me up. Not long ago, he announced, 'I'm going to try to write more cheerful stories from now on. I'm not going to dwell so much on the macabre.' When I asked him how he came to that decision, he took on a grown-up look. 'You have to remember,' he explained, 'I'm a kid from the dark side and I'm just beginning to come out of it.' I thought that was a wonderfully pretentious thing to say."

She adds, however, that his school attendance has been faltering. "Last week he didn't go to school at all. He says he has lost interest but he's promised me he'll go tomorrow and will do his best to keep up his attendance. I think he's simply hungry in the morning but is too embarrassed to admit it.

"I'm also sure he doesn't sleep enough. The sofa he uses for a bed is barely five feet long. Sometimes I find him with his forehead on the radiator in my office, sound asleep.

"His birthday was in January. He's 13, and starting to get tall. I'm going to try to talk with his school principal next week.

"I wish he had a bed to sleep on."

Back in Mott Haven for a weekend, I have no luck in finding Anthony but spend an evening with a Puerto Rican woman who was one of the politically active leaders in the neighborhood until ten years ago. The demolition of the park has saddened her, she says, because she and her husband helped to build it.

"Frenchie, Stevie, Tony, me, my husband. . . . It had been a vacant lot. We were in the Young Lords," she explains, referring to a militant Puerto Rican organization modeled in certain ways on the Black Panthers. "The people fought to get the lot. We planted trees and laid the bricks and got the jungle gym and built the benches and the shelter. This was in the last years of the 1970s, maybe even 1980. There were drugs on the corner, but it was conservative and not like now."

It wasn't until the Young Lords splintered—or, as she believes, were broken up at the instigation of the government—that drug addiction took control. Calderon, she says, did not move in to take over the block until approximately seven years after the Young Lords had fragmented.

"What was he like?" I ask.

"With his intelligence," she says, "he could have been successful in an honest occupation. But he had nothing in his life but drugs. He was a good-looking man and women liked him. He was friendly but I wouldn't call him flashy. He had a nice car but he didn't show it off unless he had to come down to the block to settle something. He could be very polite. He'd come into the place I worked and say, 'Please tell me if somebody gives you trouble.'

"He had the neighborhood under complete control. I remember one day I came along and saw this crowd at Children's Park. I mean, the place was packed! It must have been 300 people. I said to myself, 'Hey! All these people are drug dealers!' Next day, I asked a dealer that I know what had been going on. He said that Calderon had been upset that dealing had been taking place in front of children. So he called a 'conference' and he said, 'Don't come with drugs and come unarmed.' Then he got up and lectured them: No dealing in front of certain stores. No selling drugs to kids. He laid down penalties and I can tell you that they were enforced."

"Is it true," I ask, "that he shut down the sale of drugs when kids were coming home from school?"

"That is the honest truth. They'd stop. Then they'd start later."

The "conference" she describes suggests the corporate sophistication and internal rationality of the druglord's operation, which many others in the neighborhood have also spoken of. "Still," she says, "this was the end of everything we'd fought for." Her husband had long since succumbed to drugs and alcohol and later died in the hospital of AIDS and of cirrhosis of the liver. "Frenchie died. Tony died.

He's buried out there on the island. Most of the men that I was working with are gone, some from AIDS, some from shootings. More than half of the grown men that I knew have gone to prison. Those who are still in the streets are using heroin.

"Take Sandra," she says, speaking of a woman who was active with her in the Young Lords. "I see her in the street. I grab her hand. 'Sandra, look at yourself. What are you doing? We fought together. We've gone a long way for the things we battled for. Why do you need to use this needle?' She's afraid to look up at my eyes. She looks down at the ground. For her, the battle's over.

"Sometimes I think it was the end of the sense of political hope that finally broke her spirit, but I just don't really know."

The mention of Calderon's name, I find, still sets off complicated and ambivalent reactions. A man who lives a block and a half from Children's Park and was once a "corner manager" for Calderon speaks of the druglord as "evil personified" but nonetheless reveals enormous admiration for his business skills and offers me a detailed picture of the way the operation worked.

"My territory was exactly four squares on the concrete of that sidewalk down there on the corner of Brook Avenue," he says as we are sitting in his living room. "You can't see the lines in the cement from here, but those were my borders.

"Technically, I did not work for Calderon. I rented space from him. I rented the right to *use* those four squares on the corner. Every Sunday his collector came around and I would pay $500 as my rent for selling heroin. If I sold coke, it was $300 more.

"I was allowed to sell one brand of heroin only—DOA—and five-dollar caps of coke. Not snorting coke but shooting coke. If I had wanted to sell crack, there would have been another rental fee for that. I didn't see Calderon. I dealt with his subordinates."

The breakdown of the block into discrete sales areas brings to mind the regionalization that takes place among food dealers, booksellers' representatives, and others who supply the retail businesses of our society. The retailers, in this instance, were the dealers he assigned to stand out on the corner. "I had seven dealers who worked on a staggered schedule, so there was someone out there at all times except when school let out in the midafternoon. I kept the coke and heroin and cash in my apartment."

"What if you didn't have the money to pay Calderon the day that it was due?"

"If you were late one time," he says, "you'd get a warning. Second time, they'd take your drugs and throw you off the block one week and you would probably get a beating. If it happened a third time, it was serious."

Serious punishment for the failure to pay debts to Calderon, he says, was carried out in the cellar of a house across the street from Children's Park. The basement room, which was under a corner store, was used for questioning and torture sessions and to settle scores with rival dealers, in one notable case by cutting off a dealer's ears.

"They used two rooms above the store as their headquarters. I'd see them bringing out the shopping bags of cash on Mondays."

I ask how much he thinks the corner where he rented space was worth.

"I had four squares. Ten other managers had other squares on the same corner or close to the same corner. In all, he was getting about $4,000 every Sunday." Calderon's total income from the rental of this corner was, he estimates, at least $200,000 yearly. Since Calderon's organization had control of more than seven corners, and since he also got a cut on sales of DOA, his total yearly income might have been about $2 million.

The man who shares this information with me was, himself, an IV heroin user. He is now HIV-infected. His wife, who had been an IV user also since she was 18, died of AIDS six years ago. Today, after a stretch at Rikers Island and a period in drug-withdrawal treatment, which, he says, was painful but successful, he earns his living in a bakery near Yankee Stadium. He walks to his job each morning, then returns in time to see his kids as they get home from school. On weekends he takes his children on the train to

SoHo to buy health foods. The window ledge in his living room is crowded with the medicines he needs to stay alive. He is healthy for now but does not know how many years he has. He has no nostalgic feelings about Calderon.

"Do you still have any fear?" I ask.

"I do—to a degree."

"Even though he's dead?"

"His mother's still alive."

I ask how he feels about the demolition of the park.

"It's better that it's gone, but I felt sad, I had mixed feelings, when they came and knocked it down. There are many memories associated with that corner."

A month after this conversation, Calderon's mother is arrested in a massive sweep that federal agents hope will put an end to the activities of his former colleagues and subordinates. The druglord's mother, who is 63 years old, is penniless; after all the money that allegedly passed through the family's hands, she can't make bail. The press subsequently reports a marked decline in murders in the area. Drug sales, however, do not seem to be affected by the 17 indictments. The market, I'm told, may be chaotic and disorganized until another druglord rises from the streets to take control.

"What are these holes in our window?" asks a fourth grade teacher at P.S. 65 in a rapid drill that, I imagine, few of those who read this will recall from their own days in school.

"Bullet shots!" the children chant in unison.

"How do police patrol our neighborhood?" the teacher asks.

"By helicopter!" say the children.

"What do we do when we hear shooting?"

"Lie down on the floor!"

In the lunchroom I talk with a serious-looking boy in the sixth grade, named Damian, who tells me he does not live with his parents. I ask him who takes care of him.

"My grandma," he replies.

"Where does your mother live?"

"She lives in Harlem."

"Why don't you live with her?"

"She gave me to my father."

"Why don't you live with your father then?"

"My father is in prison."

A teacher has told me that Damian is considered the top student in his class. I ask him if he knows what he would like to do when he grows up.

"X-ray technician," he replies without conviction.

When I ask him where he lives, he names the street and block on which Bernardo Rodriguez lived.

"Did you know Bernardo?"

"I used to play with him," he says. "He was my friend."

After lunch, I ask the children in his sixth grade class to tell me what they hate or fear the most in life.

Several children answer, "Dying." One boy says, "The rats that have red eyes." A small girl with curly hair and large round plastic glasses says she is most afraid "of growing up," but when I ask her why, she says, "I don't know why." The only white boy in the class and in the school, an immigrant from Russia, says, "What I hate most is the unfairness on this earth."

I ask the children to tell me something they consider beautiful.

Virtually every child answers, "Heaven."

"What," I ask, "is heaven like?"

"A peaceful place with only the innocent," one child says.

"Where is heaven?"

Rolling her eyes and pointing above her at the ceiling, a child with a ponytail, named Anabelle, replies, "Upstairs."

"How far upstairs?"

"Oh very far!" she answers.

"Where is the other place?"

"Downstairs," she replies, pointing with her finger at the floor.

I ask again, "How far downstairs?"

"All the way down!" she says, like someone giving orders to an elevator operator.

Before I leave the class, I ask the children if they'd speak of something wonderful or beautiful, not in the afterlife but here on earth. Several girls say, "Flowers." One of them says, "My mother," and another says, "My baby brother." One child says, "Myself." Anabelle, one of the smallest children in the sixth grade, answers, "My pet mouse." The boy from Russia answers, "Life itself. Being alive is wonderful."

The affirmation heard in certain of these voices, and the merriment in others, are, however, anything but universal in this school, which serves not only children from the Continental Wingate complex but also those from several homeless shelters, and which ranks 627th out of 628 New York City elementary schools in reading scores.

"So many of our children," says one teacher, "walk with their fists clenched and with scowls on their faces. I see a boy come in. I say, 'Good morning,' but he walks right by. I think, 'What can we teach this boy today?'

"One boy named Alexander looks down at the floor and mutters when his father's name is mentioned. He seems ashamed of him. There's so much bitterness within his eyes."

At the same time, the teacher says, despite this bitterness or shame, many of the children also seem to love their fathers. "There was gunfire last week during recess. When it stopped, we saw the man who had been shot. He was face-down across the street, covered with blood. Several of the children said, 'Oh God! It's my daddy! Is it my daddy?' It wasn't anybody's father that I know of, but you can see from this why children you've been meeting speak so frequently of heaven."

The notion of "trauma" as an individual event, he and other teachers say, does not really get at what they feel is taking place, because these things are happening so often. "'Traumatization' as an ordinary state of mind is closer to the fact of things for many children here," another teacher says. "They lead the life most people only read about. A little one speaks to me, and I have tears in my eyes."

I ask if she makes referrals to a clinic or a hospital in cases where a child's state of mind particularly alarms her.

She sighs and says, "We do. But every place is overbooked. You make the referral. Then you wait for months.

"A 13-year-old boy," she says, "came in one day during the winter in a despondent state of mind. I've never come across a child more depressed. He sat here and he said, 'I want to die.' We reached his mother. She took him to Lincoln Hospital. They did a brief assessment, then turned him right around."

I ask, "What does that mean?"

"It means that they did nothing for him," says the principal, who is sitting with us in the teacher's room.

"A week later," says the school psychologist, "the mother took him back. This time, he got a blood test, whatever that was for, and was released again. They told the mother she would hear. But she heard nothing.

"Eight weeks after we referred him, he had still received no medication and no treatment. I told the hospital, 'This boy has suicidal ideation. He's in crisis.' But this is the way it is. They say, 'We'll see him in four weeks or so.' Then—nothing."

I mention Damian, the boy who said he wanted to be an X-ray technician when he grows up, although he had said it with a shrug. I tell the psychologist that I had wondered why, if he's one of the best students, he would not have had in mind at least the possibility that he'd become a doctor.

"Many of the ambitions of the children," she replies, "are locked-in at a level that suburban kids would scorn. It's as if the very possibilities of life have been scaled back. Boys who are doing well in school will tell me, 'I would like to be a sanitation man.' I have to guard my words and not say anything to indicate my sense of disappointment. In this neighborhood, a sanitation job is something to be longed for."

At two P.M., a terrific, rhythmic sound of clapping fills the gym of P.S. 65, as 18 girls in fourth, fifth, and sixth grade go through a cheerleading routine. A few of the girls are fairly tall and look grown-up. Others, like Anabelle, who spoke of her pet mouse during the class discussion, still look like little kids. Small and skinny, full of pep, her big white T-shirt hanging down over her jeans, she snaps her fingers, stamps her feet, swings her ponytail back and forth, then claps her hands with a live-wire frenzy and a big, bright smile in her eyes. "If all this energy could be stored up somehow," a teacher says, "and used in just exactly the right way, I bet these little girls could lick the world."

The same energy is still there later in the schoolyard as the girls do double dutch and other jump-rope games.

> *Grandma, grandma*
> *Sick in bed*
> *Called the doctor*
> *And the doctor said:*
> *Get the rhythm in the hands!*
> *Get the rhythm in the head!*

A number of teachers and some parent volunteers are standing by the side to supervise the children as they swing the ropes and chant the rhymes, some of them passed down for six or seven generations from grandmothers to their children and grandchildren.

> *Shake it to the east!*
> *Shake it to the west!*
> *Shake it to the one*
> *that you love best!*

The rhymes, combining mischief, challenge, and flirtation, fill the pleasant air of afternoon with innocence and fun.

> *I can do the hoochie coochie*
> *I can do the split*
> *Bet you five dollars*
> *You can't do this!*

Ten or 12 boys in the schoolyard, attracted by my tape recorder, seem overly eager to tell me of some recent murders they have seen.

"A man over there in front of the church shot another man," a nine-year-old announces. "The man he shot was a teenager. I guess he knew him, so he shot him."

"How many times did he shoot him?"

"Seven times," he answers.

"How close were you when this happened?"

"He did it to him right in front of my face," the boy replies.

"My friend's mother was killed," reports another boy. "She uses cocaine. She overdosed and died. It happened in his house."

"Where is his house?"

"On St. Ann's Avenue," he says.

"His father died of a shot in the heart," he adds.

"Where did his father die?"

"On Cypress Avenue."

There isn't much emotion in their voices. They speak of these events the way that people speak of things they've seen on television. I ask the boys to lift their hands if any of them have asthma. Three of their hands go up.

"Do you have someone in your family who has asthma?"

Half the hands go up.

"What do they do," I ask, "when they can't breathe?"

"Go to the hospital, get some shots," one boy replies.

A small boy eyes me mysteriously and says in a half-whisper, "I got three quarters in my pocket." He squeezes his hand into his pocket and brings out the coins to show me. His mother, he says, gives him a quarter every morning. "When I get another quarter, I will have a dollar."

"What are you going to do with the dollar?"

"I'm going to buy a hot dog."

A blaring voice from a police car, which is moving slowly past the school, temporarily drowns out the voices of the children. "We are trying to locate a 14-month-old infant who is missing from her home," the magnified voice from the patrol car says. "If you have any information on this child, please telephone the following number. . . ." The patrol car moves on toward a modern-looking homeless shelter in the block behind the school.

As class lets out at three P.M., the sidewalk in front of P.S. 65 is filled with mothers and grandmothers waiting to escort their children and grandchildren to their homes. Some of the older children slip loose from the other kids and enter a bodega on the corner of the street. A toddler with a canvas backpack that looks almost as big as he is says goodbye to another toddler, hugs her awkwardly, then reaches up to take his grandmother's hand.

As long as I have visited in inner-city schools like P.S. 65, I have always found the sight of children coming out at three o'clock, their mothers and grandmothers waiting to collect them, tremendously exciting and upsetting at the same time. The sheer numbers of the children, the determination of the older women to protect them, and the knowledge that they cannot really be protected in the face of all the dangers that surround them fill a visitor with foreboding. You wish that while they were in class, someone with magic powers had appeared and waved a wand and turned the world outside the building into fields of flowers.

Sympathy for these children, though movingly expressed in some news stories, is not of the magnitude one would expect within a richly cultivated city. One of the radio talk-show hosts who broadcasts on the ABC affiliate in New York City, who refers to African blacks as "savages" and advocates eugenics in America, recently wondered aloud, during a monologue about black people, "how they multiply like that," then answered, "It's like maggots on a hot day. You look one minute and there are so many there. . . . You look again and wow! they've tripled." These are not unusual statements these days on the radio in New York City. It often seems as if the hatred for black women in particular is so intense that there is no longer any sense of prohibition about venting the same hatred on their children.

"I didn't breed them. . . . I don't want to feed them," says a woman cited in the *Times*. The woman, who lives in

Arizona, is speaking of Mexican children who enter border towns illegally; but the sentiment is not unlike the one you hear repeatedly in New York City from a number of the talk-show hosts whose scorn for children of black and Hispanic people, frequently conveyed with searing humor, seems to stir the deepest, most responsive chords among white listeners.

The sparklingly happy little girl, named Anabelle, who had explained to me where heaven is ("upstairs"), sees me opposite the school and walks right up and tells me, "Hi! Do you remember me?"

I ask her where she lives, and when she says, "Two blocks away," I ask if I can walk her home, so we can talk a little more. As we walk, I ask her to tell me more about her images of heaven. "Tell me everything. Who gets to go there? What's it like? What happens to the ones who don't get in?"

She seems more than willing to comply.

"People who are good go up to heaven," she begins in a singsong voice, as if this part is obvious. "People who are bad go down to where the Devil lives. They have to wear red suits, which look like red pajamas. People who go to heaven wear a nightgown, white, because they're angels. All little children who die when they are young will go to heaven. Dogs and kittens go to animal heaven. But if you loved an animal who died, you can go and visit with each other on the weekend. In heaven you don't pay for things with money. You pay for things you need with smiles."

I ask her, "Can a pet mouse go to heaven too?"

"I don't know about a mouse," she answers. "He's quite small."

She tells me that she also has a dog and cat and parakeet. "If I had my own house, I would have nine animals. Cats in one room. Dogs in another. I would have a room for every animal and I'd put pillows for them on the floor. My mother will not let me do it."

I tell her I'm not surprised by that.

"If I had my own house I would do it."

I ask the names and ages of her animals. When she gets to her parakeet, she says, "He's 59."

"How old are you?"

"I'm only 11," she replies.

She adds that she had another bird before she got the parakeet but that he died the year before. "When he died," she says, cupping her hands and looking into them, "he died in my hands." She smiles, however, as she says this, and does not look sad.

I ask if she says prayers at night.

"I do."

"Who do you pray for?"

"I pray for my dog and cat."

"What do you pray?"

"I pray for them to stay right next to me all night and wake me up if I have a bad dream."

"Do you have many bad dreams?"

"Many!" she replies.

"How do you know when you are in heaven?" I ask her, finally.

"You'll see an archway made of gold," she answers.

I meet Anabelle again a few days later. She has two quarters in her hand to buy a pineapple *coquito*. I go to the corner with her and I get a pineapple *coquito* too. It's a beautiful day. She stands with me eating her icie and chatters about nothing of importance for a while.

Being treated as a friend this way by children in the neighborhood feels like a special privilege. It seems like something you just wouldn't have the right to hope for. Why should these children trust a stranger who can come into their world at will and leave it any time he likes? Why should they be so generous and open? Yet many of them are. In the drabness of the neighborhood, the friendliness and openness of little kids like Anabelle seem like the sunshine that has not been seen in New York City during many months of snow and storm and meanness.

Anabelle's images of heaven give me a delightful feeling that I rarely have in New York City. I speak of these kinds of things as often as I can, and of the feelings children voice for animals they love, because I think they show us something very different from the customary picture we are given of a generation of young thugs and future whores. There is a golden moment here that our society has chosen not to seize. We have not nourished this part of the hearts of children, not in New York, not really anywhere.

Anabelle is, by any odds, one of the most joyful children I have ever met. There is seldom any hint of sorrow in her voice. Only once, when she told me of children at her school whose mothers or fathers or older sisters had died recently of AIDS, did she become quite solemn. I asked her how the children who are orphaned seem to handle what they have gone through.

"They cry. They suffer. People die. They pray," she answered softly.

A block from P.S. 65, I run into Cliffie, the little boy who was concerned about the "burning bodies" in the medical waste incinerator built on Locust Avenue. He's sitting on a high brick wall as I come up the street.

As I approach, he shows no particular surprise at seeing me again after eight months but asks me, "Do you see that wall back there, behind this yard?"

I say I do.

"This man I saw, he buried another man back there. The man he buried was alive."

"Is that true?"

"The man was alive! And then, when I went back in there, I saw a dead dog and I saw this little, little bottle with a purple top. The man was moving. I saw his fingers sticking out. There was a crucifix and it was moving too."

I ask him, "Did you try to dig him out?"

"No!" he says. "It was too gross! I put more dirt on top of him so he would not get out. I asked him, 'Are you still alive?' But he said no."

He says this in a cheerful voice, adding, "People pee in there and bring their dogs to doodle on his grave."

"I think you're making this up," I say.

He doesn't contest my statement but slips down

adeptly from the wall and reaches up and takes my hand and walks with me in the direction I was heading.

"Long ago," his mother tells me later, "one of the hospitals used to use that plot of land to bury people who had nobody to claim their bodies. There used to be markers on the graves but they've been gone for years." She wonders if he may have heard this story and inflated it into his fable of the moving hand.

If it is true that children often make up fables to explain the things that trouble them or things they fear, then there is certainly sufficient reason for the many legends that some of the children have created in Mott Haven. Month after month, they witness shootings and police raids, hear of bodies found in trash chutes, other bodies found in elevator shafts, and always, and predictably, they see the consequences of life-taking fires.

The fires sometimes come so close together that the names and ages of the victims soon dissolve into a vague scenario of sadness that can seem uncomfortably abstract. "FIERY TOMB FOR TWO BRONX KIDS," reads a headline in the *Daily News*. "NO ESCAPE," reads a second headline. "TRAPPED TOT KILLED IN APARTMENT BLAZE," reads a headline one day later. "APARTMENT FIRE KILLS BRONX BOY," reads a headline on the next day. "BRONX APARTMENT BLAZE KILLS MOM AND SON," reads a fifth headline for another fire in Mott Haven.

The last of these fires, in which a mother and her child died together, took place in a building I have often passed in walking from the train to St. Ann's Church. The building is across an airshaft from another building, where the child's uncle and grandmother lived. The grandmother and uncle, awakened by the fire, watched the flames consume the mother and the boy. The mother, according to one account, was last seen with the child at a third-floor window, screaming, "Mami! Mami! I can't get out!"

"The fire got bigger," says the uncle of the boy. Then "they became quiet," and then "we couldn't see them anymore." A photograph under the story in the *Daily News* shows a thin Hispanic man standing in the street outside the building, cradling a beagle puppy in his arms and looking upward with dark, shadowed eyes.

132

The boy who died, a ten-year-old, was, like his mother, believed to be somewhat retarded. A woman who works in a hardware store one block from where he lived tells me he used to come into her store to say hello. "He had a round face, like a Mexican boy," she says. "He'd pick up a key chain or some other little thing that didn't cost a lot and he might ask me, 'Can I have it?' I would tell him, 'Take it!' His mother watched him like a hawk. She'd stand outside the door and wait 'til he came out.

"On the day before the fire, he came in and handed me a dollar bill. He asked me, 'Would you change it for five dollars?' I told him, 'I can't do that, Papi!' He looked up at me as if he was confused. 'Why can't you do it?' I explained, 'One dollar and five dollars aren't the same.' He gave me a look that made me laugh, as if he thought that I was fooling him. I asked him, 'Papi, what do you need five dollars for?' He said he wanted to buy a baseball at the store across the street.

"The store got crowded then. I couldn't talk. He gave me another look and went back out the door. Later, I learned that he went up the line of all the other stores and asked them all the same thing: Would they change one dollar for five dollars? That's when I knew that there was something wrong. Two days later, when I learned that he was dead, I wished that I had gone and bought the baseball for him. I wish that I could go and buy him 20 baseballs. A baseball's not a big thing for a boy who has so little."

"The boy who burned to death," a third grade teacher at P.S. 65 recalls, "was sitting right there, right in that chair, the afternoon before he died."

I ask if it's true that the boy and his mother were retarded.

"No," she says. "That was the 138th Street fire. This is the boy who died on 140th Street. This boy was a little one. That boy there was older."

In order to keep these different children clear in my own mind, I finally had to make a map of the South Bronx and put it on the wall over my desk, placing a marker on each block in which a child died, using one symbol for death by fire, one for death by accident, and one for death by gunshot.

"This little boy was in a special class because he had a learning disability," the teacher says. "His regular teacher had to go to a meeting after lunch that afternoon, so I was asked to keep him here until the end of school.

"One of the things that makes me sad is that I didn't spend as much time with him as I would have liked. It was one of those hectic afternoons. I never had a chance to stop and just sit down with him and chat. The only thing that I recall is that this boy right here"—she gestures at a fat boy sitting near the door—"kept teasing him and I finally had to interfere.

"One of the other boys, a sensitive child named Domingo, had befriended him. He made a date to visit him and play with him that afternoon. But Domingo had to stay late for some reason. By the time he got there to the house, he saw the child's body carried out."

"How old was this boy?" I ask.

"Eight years old," the teacher says.

"Was he the only victim?"

"No," she says. "His mother's in a coma at Jacobi Hospital. Another child, a five-year-old, is dead. Two of the other children are in critical care." She then lifts one hand over her face and starts to cry.

Leaving the school, I walk three blocks to see the apartment building where this child died. A garbage bag is billowing from one of the upper windows, charred and open. It isn't apparent if the family has moved out. With the mother and two children in the hospital, however, that does not seem likely.

A few doors away, my attention is arrested by one of the most unusual memorials that I have seen in the South Bronx. In bright white paint against a soft beige background is a painting of a large and friendly-looking dog, his tail erect, his ears alert for danger. Above, in yellow letters, I read "MOONDOG," which appears to be the nickname of the person who has died. "Gone is the face. . . . Silent is the voice. . . . In our hearts we'll remember," reads the epitaph.

As I am standing on the sidewalk copying these words, a plump Hispanic woman rises from the stoop nearby and comes up to my side.

"Is this where he died?" I ask.

"Yes," she answers. "He was shot right there, inside the door."

"Why was he killed?"

"He was protecting a woman who was pregnant."

"Did the woman live?"

"The woman lived. She's fine."

"Did the baby live?"

"The baby's doing fine."

"How old was the man who died?"

"He was almost 21."

I ask her how he got his nickname.

"He loved dogs. He used to bring them home." Her voice is jovial and pleasant.

"Did you know him well?"

"He was my son," she says.

Nearby, in the afternoon sun, dozens of children are playing in a playground flecked with broken glass. Puerto Rican music with a pounding salsa rhythm fills the air. In the distance is the jingling melody from an ice cream truck, parked at the corner of Brook Avenue. Under a basketball hoop without a net, a number of teenage boys are warming up before a game.

At five P.M., I stand at the corner of East 139th Street and St. Ann's Avenue. Tall iron bars have been installed around the space where Children's Park once stood. There is no one enjoying the space inside the bars, which will remain an antiseptic fortress, walled off from the public for most of the year to come; but it is, for now at least, defensible against drug dealers. At some of the local bodegas, store-owners are installing stronger, more protective barriers to fend off bullets; bulletproof vests are also becoming part of their work uniforms. So the bodegas soon will be a little more defensible as well.

All the strategies and agencies and institutions needed to contain, control, and normalize a social plague—some of them severe, others exploitative, and some benign—are, it

135

seems, being assembled: defensible stores, defensible parks, defensible entrances to housing projects, defensible schools where weapons-detectors are installed at the front doors and guards are posted, "drug-free zones" in front of the schools, "safety corridors" between the schools and nearby subway stations, "grieving rooms" in some of the schools where students have a place to mourn the friends who do not make it safely through the "safety corridors," a large and crowded criminal court and the enormous new court complex now under construction, an old reform school (Spofford) and the new, much larger juvenile prison being built on St. Ann's Avenue, an adult prison, a prison barge, a projected kitchen to prepackage prison meals, a projected high school to train kids to work in prisons and in other crime-related areas, the two symmetrical prostitute strolls, one to the east, one to the west, and counseling and condom distribution to protect the prostitutes from spreading or contracting AIDS, services for grown-ups who already have contracted AIDS, services for children who have AIDS, services for children who have seen their mothers die of AIDS, services for men and women coming out of prison, services for children of the men and women who are still in prison, a welfare office to determine who is eligible for checks and check-cashing stores where residents can cash the checks, food stamp distribution and bodegas that accept the stamps at discount to enable mothers to buy cigarettes or diapers, 13 shelters, 12 soup kitchens, 11 free food pantries, perhaps someday an "empowerment zone," or "enterprise zone," or some other kind of business zone to generate some jobs for a small fraction of the people who reside here: all the pieces of the perfectible ghetto, the modernized and sometimes even well-served urban lazaretto, with civic-minded CEOs who come up from Manhattan maybe once a week to serve as mentors or "role models" to the children in the schools while some of their spouses organize benefit balls to pay for dinners in the shelters.

All these strategies and services are needed—all these and hundreds more—if our society intends to keep on placing those it sees as unclean in the unclean places. "In reality, it *is* a form of quarantine," says Ana Oliveira, who directs an agency that serves ex-prison inmates who have AIDS, "not just of people who have AIDS but of people who have *everything* we fear, sickness, color, destitution— but it has been carried out in ways that seem compatible with humane principles.

"We don't have 'pass cards' in New York. Black women who have AIDS don't have to clip a photo ID to their dress. You don't need a permit to cross over at the magic line of 96th Street. We just tell you the apartment that's available is in Mott Haven, or East Tremont, or Hunts Point. 'That's where we can serve you best. Here's a referral number. Call this agency. They'll help you to get settled. . . .' That's what I mean by 'humane principles.' For those who work within these agencies, as I do, it appears benevolent. And, of course, once you accept the preconditions, all these things are absolutely critical."

One of the humane principles of which she speaks is present, it appears, here at the former site of Children's Park. The city has apparently tried hard to make this into a "good" corner. By smashing the benches and the shelter where drug needles once were given out, and flushing out the last remaining symbols of the age of Calderon, it has created something clean and modern-looking, metal, geometric, which will someday be transformed into a pleasant place for children. The part of the drug trade that once flourished here has moved both up and down the street, a number of blocks in each direction. The needle exchange is now in a new location, just four doors from P.S. 65.

A few of the people who once frequented the park, however, are standing on the sidewalk looking through the bars. A woman I have seen here several times and who, I am told, is HIV-infected holds a pack of Winstons in one hand, a single cigarette in the other. In a voice that is a bit peremptory and gruff, she asks me for a match.

Lighting the match and holding it for her as she cups her hands, I ask her something that, I realize, even as I say it, must strike her as somewhat strange. "What do you call this kind of place?"

She looks perplexed. "What do I call *what* place?" she asks.

"This place here—what do you call it?"

"This place here?" She shrugs. "This here is the ghetto."

When she sees me taking out my pen, she says it louder, "GHETTO," and then spells it.

I ask, "Why do you live here?"

She looks around her at the street and shrugs again. "This is where poor peoples *lives,*" she says. "Where else you think poor peoples goin' to be? You a professor? You wants to meet poor peoples, you come to the ghetto."

She seems frustrated by my question, no doubt with good reason. She walks away, repeating my words in a sarcastic voice, and heads for St. Benedict the Moor, a residence for people in drug treatment, with a soup kitchen on its ground floor, which is just next door.

After she leaves, I leave the corner also and walk to St. Ann's, where vespers have begun. The pastor's clear and calming voice fills the chapel of the church, in which six people from the neighborhood have come to pray. It isn't my religion, but it lends a sense of blessed peace and sanity to evening.

Chapter Five

Despite the fact that the just are dying with the unjust, wrote Cyprian, the bishop of Carthage, at the time of an epidemic there in 251 A.D., "it is not for you to think that the destruction is a common one for both the evil and the good. The just are called to refreshment, the unjust are carried off to torture." The plague, he wrote, "examines the mind of the human race" and "searches out the justice of each and every one."

Consolations of this nature, however, have not always been persuasive to the victims of a plague. "God's justice" often seems "far to seek" in the way that a plague spares some and kills others, notes William McNeill, a distinguished historian at the University of Chicago whose classic study of this subject, written 20 years ago, was brought to my attention by a woman in New York who works with adolescents who have AIDS.

In speaking of the Black Death of the fourteenth century and similar periods of pestilence across the centuries, McNeill remarks on "the disruptive effect" of an epidemic, which, he says, is "likely to be greater than . . . mere loss of life." Particularly when the highest toll is taken upon young adults, survivors often "lose all faith in inherited custom and belief."

Population losses "within the 20 to 40 age bracket," he believes, are "far more damaging" in this respect than "destruction of either the very young or the very old." Indeed, he writes, "any community that loses a substantial percentage of its young adults . . . finds it hard to maintain itself materially" or "spiritually." These words were written in the middle of the 1970s, about ten years before the full effects of AIDS and crack-cocaine addiction had been seen among black and Hispanic men and women in New York and just before the vast expansion in the city's prison population had begun. We may wonder what McNeill would say about these matters now if he were to visit in Mott Haven or go out to spend a day with inmates on the prison island that is clearly visible from many rooftops here.

Rikers Island—"a 415-acre Alcatraz in the East River" where, says the *Times*, "92 percent of the captive population is black or Hispanic"—was erected largely on compacted trash and stands less than 1,000 yards across the water from the Hunts Point Sewage Treatment Plant and about two miles north and east of the narrow water passageway called Hell Gate. Passengers departing La Guardia for Boston on the Delta shuttle get a good view of the island if they're sitting on the left side of the plane, though few may know that what they see beneath them is the largest penal institution in the world, serving some of the most damaged human products of the largest ghetto population in America.

The city spends $58,000 yearly on each adult inmate, $70,000 on each juvenile—nearly ten times what it spends to educate a child in its public schools.

"The cost is justified," says a woman who runs an education program on the island, "in terms that go beyond financial calculations. Without this island, the attractive lives some of us lead in the nice sections of New York would simply not be possible. If you want to get your outcasts out of sight, first you need a ghetto and then you need a prison to take pressure off the ghetto. The fact that it doesn't make financial sense is not the point. Short-term terror and revulsion are more powerful than long-term wisdom or self-interest. That's why corrections is one of the few growth industries in New York City now.

"Think of it in 'entrepreneurial' terms," she says. "Our biggest 'area of opportunity' is the South Bronx, Harlem second, and then Brooklyn. That may sound insensitive but that's the way things really are. Guys who grow up in some of those neighborhoods have two real choices: either to be our clients or else our employees.

"Well," she adds, "obviously they have some other op-

142

tions. But those are certainly two of the big ones. We employ more than 10,000 people, 8,000 of them guards. That's a huge employment opportunity in a downsized economy."

As jobs have fled the city in the past 12 years, putting hundreds of thousands of idle people on street corners, while stronger and stronger drugs have been imported into the poor neighborhoods and drug laws have grown more severe, the population of the prison island has skyrocketed. There were 6,000 inmates there in 1982. There are 18,000 in the spring of 1994 while I am visiting Mott Haven—a number that will rise to 20,000 one year later. This number, however, which records the population of the ten jails on the island at a given moment, fails to reflect the vast number of inmates who enter or leave the system in the course of any year. In all, about 130,000 men and women are incarcerated on the island and within the city's other jails in any 12-month period. Most are in pretrial detention because they do not have the money to make bail.

After trial and conviction, those with lengthy sentences are transferred to one of the 69 state prisons, in which another 68,000 inmates now are held—more than a fivefold increase over 1973, when the prison system held only 12,500 inmates.

Nearly three quarters of the inmates of state prisons in New York come from the same seven neighborhoods of New York City: the South Bronx, Harlem, Brownsville, Bedford-Stuyvesant, South Jamaica, East New York, and the Lower East Side of Manhattan, all but the last of which are deeply segregated ghetto neighborhoods. Twice as many black men in New York are under control of the criminal justice system as are enrolled full-time in all the colleges within the state. In the city itself, they are 14 times more likely than white men to be incarcerated—Hispanic men 12 times more likely. Of children imprisoned in "secure detention" in the city, 97 percent are black or Hispanic.

The national statistics parallel those of New York State in most of these respects. Only 23,000 black men earned degrees from colleges and universities in the United States in 1990. In the same year, 2.3 million black men and black juveniles passed through the nation's jail and prison systems.

I asked a question about Rikers Island once when Anthony and I and Reverend Overall were riding in her car. I can't remember where we were heading or how the subject of the island happened to come up. But I remember turning in my seat and seeing a dark look in Anthony's eyes.

Reverend Overall later told me that he has an uncle who has been there several times. "It's a part of life here," she observed. "Some children in the neighborhood were born to women there."

"Where were they born?" I asked.

"They're born in a hospital. Then they go back to prison with their mother."

"The babies stay behind bars?"

"Yes," she said. "They have a nursery there."

A few days later, I went out to spend a morning in the women's prison, which is named the Rose M. Singer Center but is known to the women there as "Rosie's Place" and held some 1,600 inmates on the day I visited. Walking through the corridors of Rosie's Place was a surreal experience. Seeing hundreds of dark-skinned women, some on methadone, others on antipsychotic medication, filing past me, many with subdued expressions—a few of them saying "Hi" or "How you doin'?" but most of them with eyes fixed to the ground—I felt I was back in a high school in the Bronx but one where, for some reason, no one smiled and the students were required to wear uniforms.

Talking later with some inmates who were waiting to be transferred to another prison, one of them wearing shackles, I knew, even before I asked, how many must have been the former students of some of the schools I've visited, which, in an awful sense, have come to be their preparation for life on this island and in many ways resemble prison buildings, although the facilities on Rikers Island are, in general, in better shape than most school buildings in New York. It's an ugly thing to see, and it feels even uglier to be there as a white observer.

The nursery, however, to which only a handful of the

inmates are admitted, was a humane place and was attractively arranged. The inmates' cells, some of which were decorated with the photographs of children, some with stuffed animals or dolls that had been tucked beneath the blankets of their beds, surrounded a central area walled off by Plexiglas. Behind the Plexiglas were 16 cribs. Each crib had a tag that gave the name of a baby and cell number of a mother. Twelve of the babies were asleep.

"About 70 percent of women in this building are drug users," said a nurse who stood beside me, looking through the Plexiglas. "One in five tests positive for TB, one in four for HIV. The oldest baby we have today is four months old, although some babies stay here for 12 months."

"We've had three sets of twins!" she said with pride.

In an adjacent area that looked like a day care center, a young mother showed me her baby, eight days old. When I asked the baby's name, she said, "Juan Carlos."

"How much does he weigh?"

"Six pounds," she said. "He's 18 inches long."

The infant, dressed in a bunny suit, had a head the size of a large navel orange and a lot of black hair, which his mother had been brushing.

"Does he make any sounds?"

"Hiccups!" she replied.

"Can I hold him?"

She carefully put him in my arms: a new life, warm and sleepy. She let me hold him for only a few moments. Everything about this seemed so normal that I temporarily forgot that I was in a jail.

All of the stories, however, weren't so happy. Another mother with a history of drug use, whom I did not meet but whose face, distorted by pain, I later saw in documentary footage filmed here in the building, held up a piece of paper that recorded her baby's death and showed his footprint. "They gave me a certificate," she said through tears. The certificate indicated that the baby weighed "one pound, 11 ounces."

"He died in me two weeks ago," she said. "He's in the morgue but he can't stay there but so long. I don't know what they goin' to do. . . . I can't bury him."

In these cases, I am told, the city buries the infant in a plain box costing $27 in a grave at Potters Field, situated on another island, which was formerly a missile base and is now owned and managed by the Department of Corrections. "Inmates do the burials," said a teacher I met on the prison island. "In this way, when a baby is born dead to an inmate and is taken to the other island to be buried, everything, in a sense, is self-contained."

The same documentary footage shows an inmate who was born in prison and is now dying here of AIDS, even though the judge who sentenced him reduced his sentence of 25 years by 18 months to give him credit for "time served as an infant." Transported in chains to a courtroom where he has appealed for mercy release, he sits in court while his lawyer tells the judge, "I don't believe I've ever had a client before who was born in jail and is likely to die in jail if the court doesn't take action." Because of frequent delays and canceled hearings, this is the thirty-second time he has been brought here. After he's turned down, he is returned in chains to the AIDS unit on the island, where he's working in the laundry but needs frequent naps because he is so weak.

"Born in here . . . addicted to drugs," the inmate says. "Now I'm going to die here in this motherfucker."

Nationwide, 50,000 men and women who are HIV-infected or have AIDS are now behind bars. About 8,000 of them are incarcerated in New York, where, as of 1992, nearly 1,400 prisoners had died of AIDS while still imprisoned, with about 200 more fatalities projected for each subsequent year. "New York's prison system," notes the *Times,* "is now apparently the largest AIDS care provider in the state."

Some women from New York's poor neighborhoods, however, may get better care in prison than they can obtain on the outside. If they are pregnant, they receive prenatal and perinatal care, parenting classes, and addiction therapy, in addition to the services of nurseries. A woman from the South Bronx, says a nun who works with female inmates, "begged us not to take her out of prison . . . until her baby was delivered, because there was a four-month waiting list for prenatal care at Lincoln Hospital."

The nun wonders, "Is that what we do? Incarcerate people so they can get the services they need?"

Her words suggest the possibility that, at some future time, a state or federal government under control of a tough-minded politician of the kind now in ascendance in the U.S. Congress and in some of the state capitals may decide that it is logical to extend this strategy to women who have *not* committed crimes but who are simply seen as unfit parents because their addictions or lifestyles pose a danger to their unborn babies. Standing in the nursery at Rosie's Place, a visitor may wonder whether he is looking at a vision of the future.

What is it like to be born in prison and to know that you may die there?

"I'm not sure that it's too different," Reverend Overall once said, "from being born in any other ghetto if you know it's where you'll probably die. The racial makeup of the island and that of the city's poorest neighborhoods are virtually the same." Prisons, schools, and churches, many religious leaders have observed, are probably the three most segregated institutions in our nation, although the schools in New York City are quite frequently more segregated even than the prisons.

Racial segregation, as a governing fact of life in New York City, seldom surfaces in public dialogue about the problems faced by children in poor neighborhoods. Even the word "segregation" is not often used in local press discussions of the city's schools and neighborhoods—or, if used at all, is handled gingerly. References to "ghettos" or to "ghetto neighborhoods" are generally circumvented too, although these terms are sometimes used in writing about other sections of the nation. Semantic somersaults are often undertaken to avoid the use of clear words on a matter in which clarity is badly needed. One hears of "underserved" communities in New York City, of "low-income neighborhoods" inhabited by people called "minorities," of "gritty," "bleak," "distressed," "hard-bitten," or "impacted" neighborhoods—rarely of "segregated neighborhoods," an apparently intentional omission that seems to confirm Lee Stuart's feeling that the issue is no longer part of the agenda.

How segregated are the New York City schools?

For Hispanic children, according to a study carried out at Harvard University in 1993, New York's public schools are the most segregated in the nation. For black children, New York's schools come third after the schools of Illinois and Michigan. A new term, "hypersegregation," has been introduced to speak of schools like these, where there are simply no white children, or not more than token numbers; and similar schools are to be found, of course, in almost every city of the nation. "Two thirds of America's black children," notes the *Times,* "know few, if any, white people." The civil rights momentum of the 1960s, says Professor Gary Orfield, one of the authors of the Harvard study, "is dead in the water and the ship is floating backward."

School segregation in New York, moreover, notes a teacher there, is not merely the result of housing segregation. "Even when black and Latino children ride the bus or take the train to go to school in a white area, white families often vacate schools in their own neighborhoods." One of the classically segregated high schools in New York, he says, is named for Justice Louis Brandeis—"right in the middle of the liberal West Side."

Bigotry, he concedes, is not the only factor in the flight of some white children from these schools. "Many of their parents simply don't believe these schools are good for *any* child, theirs or anybody else's. So they put their own kids into private schools and try to raise some scholarships to pay for black kids to attend them too. But it tends to be a triage operation. The black kids who get into private schools like these are screened quite carefully. So, in one sense, it simply makes things worse in public school by pulling out the children that a teacher counts on to keep class discussions going and to spur the others to succeed.

"Sometimes," he adds, "I walk by Brandeis High

School and I think of Justice Brandeis and I shake my head. I mean—God help us! If you can't have racial integration at a school in *this* community, where can you ever hope to have it?

"Many of the people in this neighborhood," he says, "were in the protest movements of the 1960s. They sang the songs. Some of them did more than sing. Some were in the integration struggles in the South. They risked their lives. Now they feel they have to flee poor children at a school in their own neighborhood. They're not even being asked to put their children on a bus. The children of color ride the bus into *their* neighborhood! And still they flee. What does this say about New York today? What does this say about America?

"A dream," he says, "does not die on its own. A dream is vanquished by the choices ordinary people make about real things in their own lives. The choices that some of your friends on the West Side have made may seem benign and innocent and, in the short run, even logical. But the net effects are very much the same as those we saw in Alabama and Virginia when white people left the public schools after the first court orders. The motive may be different, and I'm sure it often is; the consequence is not."

Some of the West Side people he describes still hold to the convictions of their youth; some tell me that they feel a sense of disappointment—in themselves, in our society— when they withdraw their children from the public schools, which guarantees their segregation. Others have retired into a severe conservatism, masked frequently by over-stated references to youthful episodes of activism, which are sometimes used like amulets to ward off any possibilities of self-reproach. "I was on the bridge at Selma" is a state-ment heard quite often from late-middle-aged conser-vatives today in New York City, a claim that, whether it is true or not, stirs caustic comments from some of the black adults I know.

"You see," says the teacher, "to the very poor black children that I teach, who suffer more than any kids should suffer in a country like America, it doesn't matter much what bridge you might have stood on 30 years ago. They want to know what bridge you stand on now. And, every time they walk into a hospital, or school, or simply ride the train, they see the answer; and it isn't a good answer."

The view of the United States that children get in looking out the window of a school in Harlem or the Bronx, he says, "is not one that is likely to affirm a sense of confidence in human goodness."

P.S. 65, the elementary school on Cypress Avenue, with one white child in a student population of 800, is, in its near-total segregation, indistinguishable from almost any other public school in the South Bronx, where racial isolation is nearly as absolute as anything one might have seen in Mississippi 40 years ago. Six months after the events described within this book, when I am in the neighborhood and stop to visit at the school again, the Russian boy who was the sole white student here when I first visited will have gone on to junior high, but there will be a new white student in the school, a German boy, also an immigrant. His third grade teacher will point him out to me. "I've been at this school for 18 years," the teacher says. "This is the first white student I have ever had!"

Despite its racial isolation and the destitution of its children, nonetheless, P.S. 65 is still sometimes a cheerful place in certain ways. The "atrophy of childhood by physical and spiritual night," of which Victor Hugo wrote in 1862, has not yet destroyed the playfulness and trusting innocence of many of the younger children, who may not yet be aware of what is happening to them. Even in the older grades, some of the children, like Anabelle, do not seem to lose their willingness to trust.

It is at the secondary level—in junior high and, more dramatically, in high school—that the sense of human ruin on a vast scale becomes unmistakable. Numbers cannot convey the mood of desolation that pervades some of these secondary schools; but certain statistics, even when you think that you already understand some of the problems of poor children in New York, jump off the page and strike you with astonishment.

"I count the graduating class," writes City University professor Michelle Fine, in speaking of one of these segregated high schools—"a total of 200 in a school of approximately 3,200." Almost a thousand students out of these 3,200 are officially "discharged" for poor attendance or a number of other reasons, including violent behavior, every year. Studying the fate of 1,436 children enrolled in the ninth grade during one academic year, she finds that, six years later, a full 87 percent have been "discharged"—the term used by the school—and that 80 percent of the original ninth graders have yet to receive a degree from any other academic institution.

"My job is like a pilot on a hijacked plane," a school official tells her, "and my job is to throw the hijacker off, even if it means bodily" and even if, as the visitor observes, more than 80 percent of children in a given class are seen as the hijackers.

"From inside the school," she says, the discharge process seems "inevitable" and "necessary." The overcrowding of the school and the "disincentives" of teaching kids who don't show up for class or cannot understand their work compel the school to carry out "this transfer of bodies." But would it appear inevitable or necessary, she asks, "if almost a third" of a middle-class white school "were to disappear between September and June?"

In order to make the rate of failure less apparent, or to placate students who have failed to learn enough to graduate, officials at some schools have been prepared to make unusual concessions to their pupils. At one Brooklyn high school, for example, where only one in six of those who enter graduates in four years, the principal allows the kids who cannot graduate, but who at least have not dropped out or been ejected, to participate in the commencement exercises if they pay $200—an arrangement, says a teacher, that is known as "pay to appear."

Many of the schools with the most devastating academic records are also physically offensive places. At Morris High School, where less than 70 of the 1,700 children in the building qualified for graduation in the spring of 1993, barrels were filling up with rain in several rooms the last time I was there. Green fungus molds were growing in the corners of the room in which the guidance counselor met kids who were depressed. Many of these schools quite literally stink. Girls tell me they won't use the toilets. They rush home the minute school is over. If they need to use the bathroom sooner, they leave sooner.

At Taft High School in the Bronx, one of the grimmest schools in the United States, the self-esteem of children has been crushed to the degree that students ridicule themselves, as David Washington has told me, by making a bitter joke out of the letters of the school's name. "Taft," they say, means "Training Animals For Tomorrow." The area around the school is heavily patrolled so students can get from the subway to the school unharmed. But the greatest harm that faces the 4,000 boys and girls who go here may be what is done to them inside the building after they arrive.

A few of the children from poor neighborhoods like Hunts Point and Mott Haven, but not nearly enough, defy all expectations by obtaining entrance to selective high schools, such as Stuyvesant High, one of the city's two top secondary schools. To say that not nearly enough succeed in doing this, however, is to understate the matter. In a city where black and Hispanic children make up 75 percent of students in the public high schools, only 9 percent of kids at Stuyvesant are black or Hispanic. Of the 32 elementary districts of the New York City public schools, District 7, in which P.S. 65 is situated, has the fewest students who get into Stuyvesant and similar selective schools. The district serving the children of Manhattan's Upper East Side has the highest number.

Admissions to Stuyvesant are based upon a child's score on an exam. The numbers therefore testify to something far more troubling than the potential bias that may skew admissions to some other schools. They tell us of hundreds of thousands of black and Hispanic kids whose power to compete with other children for the high rewards that a good education might make possible has been demolished at a very early age and in some coldly measurable ways.

"Everything these kids touch turns to gold," says the principal of Stuyvesant with the normal pride that any principal of such a school would voice, a statement I have *never* heard, and can't imagine hearing, from a principal in the South Bronx.

The school is housed in a handsome, new, ten-story building in Manhattan with 12 science labs, five gyms, an Olympic swimming pool, an elegant theater, a rooftop satellite dish that captures data for meteorologic computations, 450 IBM and Macintosh computers, "a dignified two-story library . . . furnished in warm woods" that holds some 40,000 books, and "a penthouse cafeteria" that offers students "peerless riverviews," according to a story in the *Times*. The school's "sturdy masonry walls, devoid of graffiti," says the writer, "refresh the idea that the public school is among the finest flowers of America's Enlightenment."

"While a billion dollars was cut from the city's school budget between 1989 and 1992," *Technos* magazine reports, and while 1,300 children in a school I visited in one Bronx neighborhood did not even have a school but had been housed in an abandoned skating rink that had no windows, affording its segregated kids no chance at all of riverviews nor any view at all, "Stuyvesant got almost everything it asked for. . . ."

The $150 million spent to build the dazzling new structure, which opened its doors in 1992, is almost exactly the same as what the city spent in the same year to purchase the massive prison barge that it has moored at Hunts Point in the South Bronx, where it accommodates the graduates and dropouts of much less attractive high schools on six floating floors of prison cells, one of them under water.

"Through both public and private channels," says former governor Mario Cuomo of the students attending Stuyvesant, "we are serving this elite group rather well." The "quality of these facilities speaks eloquently to the students" of New York's "respect" for both "their work and their ideas—a priceless boost."

"We deserve it," says a 17-year-old at Stuyvesant. "We're supposed to be the best kids . . . ," and, he adds, "there may be something to that." A *Times* reporter describes the students as a "brainy bunch" that "deserves every bit of indulgence a cash-strapped city can muster."

No one who spends time with kids from Stuyvesant, a

school whose graduates are said to earn more Ph.D.'s than those of any other high school in America, can doubt that they deserve this splendid school. The question that one wants to ask is: What do *other* kids deserve and how is the whole idea of a "deserving" or an "undeserving" person used to mask some of the cumulative consequences of injustice?

"Some people are better than others," wrote conservative social scientist Charles Murray several years ago. "They deserve more of society's rewards." The coldness of this statement offended many people at the time that it was published. But Murray's views are not entirely different from what politicians, business leaders, and the school board of New York seem to believe and have embodied in providing the "best" kids with the best building and best vista not just of the harbor, but of their own future.

"I went to Stuyvesant once to visit," David told me when we spoke of the conditions in the schools he sees within his neighborhood. "My teacher took us for a student conference. They say that it's a very good school. There weren't too many black kids there—or Puerto Ricans. . . . Hardly any."

Then he said, "I think that's wrong."

I asked if he could be precise in saying just exactly *what* he thought was wrong.

"Many of us are trying to change history," he said. "It seemed like something from the past."

I reminded him that admissions there are by exams.

"I know they are," he said.

"Doesn't that guarantee it's fair?"

"Not really," he replied. "In certain ways it makes it worse."

David's comment left a stubborn silence in the air. Why *is* it that so few black and Hispanic children in New York or elsewhere get into top-rated schools like Stuyvesant?

Some advocates for children in poor neighborhoods emphasize the cultural bias they believe to be inherent in

154

some of the standardized exams and also note that affluent parents often pay for private "coaching classes" for their children in the weeks before admissions tests are given. Others point to the initial damage done to many of the poorest children by the virtual absence of good preschool education in their neighborhoods. Less than ten percent of children at P.S. 65, for instance, are accommodated by the Head Start programs in the area or by any comparable programs—"probably much less than that," according to the principal.

Advocates for children in the South Bronx also speak about the many elementary schools and junior high schools in which students seldom see a certified teacher but are instructed, for the most part, by "provisionals," or permanent subs, while more experienced teachers are assigned to schools in less abandoned neighborhoods. At one junior high school in the South Bronx, for example, in which money was so scarce in 1994 that girls were using pieces of TV cable as their jump ropes at the time I visited the area, only 15 teachers in a faculty of 54 were certified. The overcrowding of children in these schools compounds the chaos caused by staffing difficulties. At some schools in the South Bronx, in the same year, classes were taking place in settings like stair-landings, bathrooms, and coat closets, because the population of poor children was increasing but there was, according to the press, no money to build schools for them.

Many of the children who attend these schools also suffer the emotional and physical attrition that results from chronic illnesses like asthma and anxiety, as well as the steady and low-level misery of rotting teeth, infected gums, and festering, untreated sores. Many, like Anthony, have no bedroom of their own but sleep on sofas if they're lucky, mattresses thrown down on the floor if they are not.

It is also recognized that many children in poor neighborhoods such as Mott Haven have been neurologically impaired, some because of low-weight prematurity at birth, some because of drug ingestion while in utero, and many from lead poison in their homes and also, shockingly enough, within their schools. Although New York officially banned the use of lead in residential paint in 1960, this prohibition was unevenly enforced in ghetto neighborhoods and never energetically enforced in city-owned apartments. And, notes the *Times,* the city "continued to apply 'industrial grade' lead paint" in public classrooms until 1980. John Rosen, a well-known pediatrician and lead-poison specialist at Montefiore Medical Center in the Bronx, warned officials in 1987 that schools in the area were "dangerously loaded with lead."

Between the apartments in which the city places them and the schools to which the city has assigned them, thousands of poor children, it appears, are sacrificing parts of their intelligence to city fiscal policies and losing some of the capacity for abstract thinking that might otherwise have rendered them sophisticated critics of such policies. The damage done to the brain cells of lead-poisoned children is, according to researchers, not reversible.

In the light of all these socially created injuries to intellect, most of which could be corrected by a fair-minded society, it may seem surprising that scarce research funds should be diverted to investigations of "genetic links" between the IQ deficits of certain children and their racial origins. There is something wrong with a society where money is available to do this kind of research but not to remove lead poison from the homes and schools of children in the Bronx.

Many of the liberal intellectuals I know who are concerned with questions of unequal access to good secondary schools tend to focus more on inequalities that may be caused by our selection systems than on those that are engendered by environmental forces and are neurological in nature. In human terms, it's understandable that people would prefer to speak about examinations than about brain damage. There is a natural fear of the irrevocable in almost all of us; and, if we know some of the children in these neighborhoods and also know that they have lived in lead-infested buildings, in an atmosphere where poisons of many different kinds, both physical and spiritual, are in the air, we do our best to shut these darker matters from our minds. It is less painful to speak of an unfair test than of brain damage since a test can someday be revised and given to a child again, but childhood cannot.

"Anthony, would you like a glass of orange juice?" asks Mr. Castro.

"Yes, please," Anthony replies.

"Jonathan, would you like a glass?"

"Yes," I say. "I'd like some too."

Mr. Castro is in a wonderful mood when Anthony and I stop in to visit him one warm and sunny afternoon, because, he says, he "was on a rampage" the preceding night and wrote for 14 hours. He shows me 18 closely written longhand pages, which, he says, he wrote "to please myself" and not with the thought of publication. "The Vulgar As Culture" is the title of the essay that he wrote, which examines the varieties of slang used in past times and in the present day.

I ask if he's familiar with the slang expressions used by rap musicians, but he says that he is not. "I do not know this kind of music." He says that his musical preference is for "operatic songs," and he speaks enthusiastically of "a beautiful soprano" who was singing Mozart arias on television two nights earlier.

"This woman!" he says, bringing a forefinger and thumb up to his mouth and making an appreciative sound. At the words "beautiful soprano," Anthony looks down and makes an awkward face.

Seeing Anthony's reaction, Mr. Castro smiles slightly, goes into the kitchen, and comes back with two glasses of juice. Sitting with us in the living room, he talks for a time about some of the books he read when he was growing up in Puerto Rico. "The first adult book that I read was Fénelon's *Telemachus*," he says. "I was 13, Anthony's age. It was the first great book to come into my hands!"

When I mention that, although I have read Fénelon, I can't remember who Telemachus was, he reminds me, "He was the son of Odysseus."

"Yes!" says Anthony, pleased, it seems, to make his contribution to the conversation. "The one who tricked the Cyclops!"

"Yes, that is exactly right," says Mr. Castro.

Later, while we speak of something else, Anthony goes to Mr. Castro's bookshelf and pulls out a book about the Greek and Roman myths with which he seems to be familiar. Seating himself again on Mr. Castro's sofa, he thumbs through the pages of the book until he finds what he is looking for, then moves his finger slowly as he reads.

"After I read Fénelon," says Mr. Castro, "I became a maddened bibliophile. I once even stole a book out of the library because I wanted to complete that book at home. I read and read but I ignored my studies. It was a miracle when I was graduated from eighth grade."

His saddest memory from his early years, he says, is of a time when he was forced to leave his book collection with his aunt when he came to New York. "I put my books in a big box and I buried them beneath her house. Three years later, I wrote to her and said, 'I have the money now. Please send my books.' 'Oh bambino!' she replied. 'Your cousins found your books under the house and they have made the tails for a *chiringa* from them!' "

I ask him, "What is a *chiringa?*"

"It's a local Puerto Rican word," he says. "It means a kite. My little cousins had ripped up the pages for their kite." Laughing at this now, despite the pain it caused him at the time, he says, "At least some of my books soared high and maybe reached the upper spheres. The ones I write stay down here on the ground."

Years later, he says, after the end of World War II, he still remembered all the books he'd lost. "I knew by heart the titles so I went to Greenwich Village and replaced them. There were many stores at that time where you could obtain old books."

"There still are many stores like that," says Anthony.

"Yes, that's right," says Mr. Castro, "but not quite as many as before."

It turns out to be a literary afternoon, congenial and enjoyable in all respects. Perhaps because of Anthony, perhaps simply to satisfy himself, the poet manages to weave a thread of intellectual or didactic value into almost every subject that comes up. Even topics that would seem to have no possible connection with the literary life appear to be enhanced in interest for him if he can associate them somehow with a book that he has read. When I mention something Reverend Overall has told me about Lincoln Hospital, for instance, he shifts the matter effortlessly into his own preferred domain by saying, "Mother Martha! Yes!"—then asking, "Did you know that she is a descendant of the Russian poet Alexander Pushkin?"

"Who is Alexander Pushkin?" Anthony asks.

"Ah!" says Mr. Castro, his eyes glowing. "The great Pushkin! Someday you will read him. You will know."

On a visit to New York many months later, I will not be in the least surprised when Anthony asks me, "Have you read the Russian writer Alexander Pushkin?" Without a word about the content of the writer's work, Mr. Castro manages to lend an aura of excitement to the name that Anthony will not forget. Mr. Castro has told me more than once since then that Mother Martha is related to the Russian poet, an association, I suspect, that may command more reverence in him than the fact that she's the pastor of his church.

On one wall of the living room, above a collection of volumes on philosophy and history, there is a framed quotation from Flaubert in Spanish.

*Un modo de tolerar la existencia es
perderse uno en la literatura en
una perpetua orgía.*

He translates it for me in these words: "One way of tolerating existence is to lose oneself in literature in a perpetual orgy."

Anthony asks him what "perpetual orgy" means and seems impressed when Mr. Castro tells him "endless pleasure." As Mr. Castro continues to share his stories, however, Anthony gets drowsy, and before another 15 minutes have gone by, he's closed his eyes and is asleep on Mr. Castro's sofa. Mr. Castro places a cushion underneath his head, comes back to the table where he has been sitting, lights a cigarette, and seems at peace.

Anthony's relationship to Reverend Overall and his discipleship to Mr. Castro have a reassuring quality that is not present in most stories that one hears about the lives of children in the South Bronx. Some preachers speak of situations of this kind as "little miracles," which happen now and then in poor communities and testify to the ability of certain children to create a safe space for themselves and, in this way, transcend some of the grimness of the places where they live.

The trouble with miracles, however, is that they don't happen for most children; and a good society cannot be built on miracles or on the likelihood that they will keep occurring. There is also a degree of danger that, in emphasizing these unusual relationships and holding up for praise the very special children who can take advantage of them, without making clear how rare these situations are, we may seem to be condemning those who don't have opportunities like these or, if they do, cannot respond to them.

It is true that there are many little miracles and thousands of heroic people in Mott Haven, and not all of them are children who like Edgar Allan Poe or adults who write poetry. Many are simply strong, resilient mothers and grandmothers, some of them devout black women, in whom Cornel West has rightly said one often finds a spiritual strength unknown to most other Americans. I think of my friend Elizabeth in Roxbury, for instance, whom I cite in many of my books because her words so frequently convey the liberating energy heard also in much of the language of Sojourner Truth—what Henry Louis Gates has called "a voice of deliverance from the . . . discursive silence," utterly pure, transcendent, deeply wise, and also wisely funny in the face of the unspeakable. Mrs. Washington too, for all the bludgeonings she has received, seems virtually unbreakable and proud. When she dies, I am convinced, her death will be from an infection of the chest or brain, not from a loss of courage.

Each of these women wins hundreds of small victories each day. Countless other women I have met in homeless shelters and AIDS hospices, sometimes cooking meals for others in the basement feeding-centers of small churches in New York and Houston, Cleveland and Los Angeles, Chicago and St. Paul, and all over the nation, strike me as authentically heroic figures, instruments of moral transformation and of spiritual salvation, if only for the few who know them, and every one of them, no doubt, deserves a monument in fitting and respectful prose, though many die with no memorial at all.

"Before she died," says Reverend Overall, in speaking of a woman in the neighborhood whose name was Mrs. Blue, "during a time when she was dying of breast cancer, she mustered all her strength to cook a last Thanksgiving dinner for her son out of donated food. Mother and son had their first Thanksgiving in three years outside of a soup kitchen. In December she summoned all of her last energies to go through the lines at the Salvation Army so that he would get a Christmas present. She wanted him to have these memories when she was gone. That woman reminded me of Hagar in the wilderness. I believe that the wilderness is where God is found."

One could write forever of such women, and of many men as well, who work together to create a genuinely "beloved community" on St. Ann's Avenue, one that is at once political and spiritual, joyful and prophetic. Again, however, I worry about speaking too much of the triumphs that such people and communities achieve without positioning these stories in a realistic context.

I have, after all, seen hundreds of small victories like these over the years, and have been involved in some of them in Roxbury, New York, and elsewhere, but I have also seen them—almost all, with few exceptions—washed away in time by larger losses. I've also seen heroic and ephemeral victories of individuals used by conservative sectors of the press to militate against the larger changes it would take to win enduring victories for their communities. If only enough children, we are told, would act the way the heroes do, say no to drugs and sex and gold chains and TV and yes to homework, values, church, and abstinence, and if only enough good parents, preachers, teachers, volunteers, and civic-minded business leaders would assist them in these efforts, we could "turn this thing around" and wouldn't need to speak about dark, messy matters such as race, despisal, and injustice.

I am afraid these stories, if they are not qualified, can leave the misimpression that sufficient levels of intrinsic heroism, reinforced perhaps by charitable help from outside groups, perhaps at some point by an "enterprise zone" or "site-based school" with textbooks "sensitive" and "relevant" to inner-city children's needs, and other innovations of this kind, are all that is required for the evolution, in due time, of what might be referred to as "good ghettos."

I guess that I do not believe there are good ghettos and I get quite nervous about seeing stories of this kind in the newspapers, generally signaled by a standard set of headlines ("FROM THE ASHES: A FLAME OF HOPE") that seem to be recycled periodically, because I believe that they inflate exceptionality into a myth of progress that is not based in reality. They do console us, but I think they may permit us also to congratulate ourselves too easily about the "bootstrap" possibilities for individual endeavor or for localized renewal efforts in an atmosphere where the toxicity of life is nearly universal.

So long as the most vulnerable people in our population are consigned to places that the rest of us will always shun and flee and view with fear, I am afraid that educational denial, medical and economic devastation, and aesthetic degradation will be virtually inevitable; and this, I am afraid, will be the case no matter what the individual or even shared achievements of small numbers of good human beings who are infused with the essential heroism of the people whom I have described. So long as there are ghetto neighborhoods and ghetto hospitals and ghetto schools, I am convinced there will be ghetto desperation, ghetto violence, and ghetto fear because a ghetto is itself an evil and unnatural construction.

I do not think these many self-help efforts, as important as they are, can conceivably prevent these outcomes on more than a very limited scale and always in quite special situations, and I even feel a bit bewildered that a point like this needs to be made in the United States in 1995. That it *does* need to be made, however, may be one more added piece of evidence of just how far the nation has regressed during the quarter-century that has transpired since the death of Dr. King and of the dream that seems to have died with him.

Some government officials argue that the violence and devastation seen in places like Mott Haven are caused by only a small fraction of the population, "maybe five to ten percent," and that if these individuals, the bloodiest murderers, the top drug dealers, the most ruthless of gang-leaders, could somehow be "weeded out"—"subtracted"—from the larger population, those who remain could lead good, normal, peaceful, and productive lives. Many residents of these neighborhoods are understandably attracted to such strategies. The scenario, as it is usually laid out, is to remove these men and boys from streets and schools and place them in what would amount to ghettos-within-ghettos, so-called "boot camps," "shock-incarceration centers," to use two of the widely circulated terms.

One would like to believe that this might work; but I do not. After one group of criminals is gone, as the experience of countless neighborhoods makes clear, another group of lower-level dealers and apprentice pimps and killers generally emerges very soon to take their place, because the market of tormented people who need drugs, or think they do, to face the pain of living, still remains. Where, then, would the "weeding" process stop? How many boys—and girls too, for that matter—would we ultimately need to "weed out" from the poisoned fields before we end up with a happy ghetto?

Exactly 30 years ago, in an influential work, *Dark Ghetto,* Dr. Kenneth Clark spoke of the ways in which a segregated population may be induced to satisfy the wishes of the white society by claiming to desire, even to enjoy, a caged condition that it has not chosen but knows no way to

escape. "A most cruel . . . consequence of enforced segregation," he wrote, "is that its victims can be made to accom-
modate to their victimized status and under certain
circumstances to state that it is their desire to be set apart,
or to agree that subjugation is not really detrimental. . . ."
The fact remains, he said, that these forms of isolation "are
not voluntary states." Segregation, he concluded, "is neither sought nor imposed by healthy . . . human beings."

Many of my white friends who live in New York City, I
believe, would probably agree but might insist that they are
personally "imposing" nothing on the people we have met
within this book. They might say that they have simply
come to New York City, found a job, and found a home,
and settled in to lead their lives within the city as it is. That
is the great luxury of long-existing and accepted segregation in New York and almost every other major city of our
nation nowadays. Nothing needs to be imposed on anyone.
The evil is already set in stone. We just move in.

A friend of Reverend Overall, whose name is Shirley
Flowers, lives on Beekman Avenue, two blocks from P.S.
65, in one of the 38 buildings owned by Continental Wingate, the company that also owns the house where Anabelle
lives, the one where Mrs. Washington's daughter, Charlayne, lives, and the one in which Bernardo Rodriguez
died. Reverend Overall has told me that Mrs. Flowers,
whom her neighbors call "Miss Shirley," sits for several
hours every day at a table in the lobby of her building to
keep out drug dealers.

On the night I visit, her mood is clouded by concern
about her daughter, who is 29 years old and is in misery
from asthma. When I arrive, her daughter's resting in one
of the bedrooms.

"She's been coughing up her guts," her mother says.
"The ambulance had to take her to the hospital from work
today. Doctor says she might have ruptured her insides.
She spits up blood."

I ask what medication she's been using.

"She used to use the pump but now she's getting

164

shots," says Mrs. Flowers. "To tell the truth, I'm not too thrilled about the pump. When she uses it, it makes her heart beat fast."

On the living room table I see a "dispossess," one of those same routine eviction orders Mrs. Washington receives from time to time.

"I pay all my bills on time," she says. "I keep all of my receipts. Still, when this happens, you have to go to court. I've been through this before."

"What court do you go to?"

"Housing court. The line is long. It's like a cheese line. It goes down into the basement. You go at nine. You don't get a court date sometimes until four P.M.

"I go alone," she says. "Think what it's like if you got children. You see little mothers there with infants in their arms. They have to drag along the older kids sometimes. It isn't nice to see. It's something pitiful to behold."

Her son-in-law, a handsome man of 33 with a short Afro and trimmed beard and mustache, comes in from work soon after I arrive and joins us in the living room. His wife comes out of the bedroom and sits by her mother on a kitchen chair. I ask her how she's feeling.

"Not good," she says, her hand pressed up against her heart.

"What happened at the hospital?"

"They gave me shots." The doctor, she says, has also made arrangements for an oxygen machine—"two oxygen machines," she adds.

"Why two?"

"One for me. One for my son."

"Your son has asthma too?"

"He has it worse than me."

"Where do you take him?"

"Lincoln Hospital," she says. "When you're there you only pray that you don't need to use the bathroom."

"Why?" I ask. "Because it's dangerous?"

"No. It isn't dangerous. It's just disgusting. *Very* disgusting," she emphasizes. "Waste spread all over the floor. Very disgusting for a hospital."

"Do you have to wait a long time when you go there?"

"Usually you do," she says. "Only thing they'll rush you through for is if you can't breathe. They're good if you have asthma."

I ask what medicine her son takes for his asthma.

"He uses liquid and he has his pump." She adds, however, that she worries when he takes the pump "because it makes him nervous and he trembles."

"Is that the effect it has on you?"

"It gives me an uneasy feeling."

"Can you sleep when you have asthma?"

"When it's like this? No. I don't sleep. I'm scared of lying down. Need to sit up."

I ask her husband, who grew up in Mississippi, if he can compare their lives here in New York to life as he recalls it in the South. He answers that he and his wife have spoken of this often. "She thinks it's better here. I disagree."

"Down south," says Mrs. Flowers, who has relatives in Alabama, "people let you know exactly where you stand. Here in New York they smile and smile and pat you on the head and then they send you back where you belong."

Her son-in-law speaks of going downtown with his wife to buy her a gift at Saks Fifth Avenue. "You get a feeling of emergency as soon as you go in. It's like you're 'guarded,' like you've got an escort service. Other customers walk along and pull out something that they want. They take a shirt or jacket from a rack and hold it up in front of them to see the way it looks. Me and my wife, the minute we enter, right away they're in your face. 'Excuse me. Can I help you?'"

"What's the message that that gives you?"

He leans forward on his knees so that his face is very close to mine. "'You can't afford the stuff we sell. Come on, nigger. Time to get your train. . . .'

"I was brought up very mannerable," he says, using a word my friend Elizabeth uses often, which seems to refer not just to being well-behaved, but also to behaving with a basic sense of rectitude and gentleness. "When I go in a store I act polite and I speak softly, as my mother taught me." In words that remind me of a comment that the 16-

year-old student Isabel had made when we were talking in the summer, he goes on, "It doesn't matter how you act or how you speak. They want you out. 'It's time to take off, nigger.'"

Despite his anger, he speaks softly in precise and measured syllables. His face, however, is deeply lined for somebody so young.

"You have to understand," he says in the same steady tone, "that if you're black or if you are a dark Latino man, they really do *not* want you. Not in that store. Not in that section of the city."

He makes explicit a connection that he sees between the way he has been treated in certain Manhattan stores and the recent rush to get the beggars from the subway trains, and the homeless and the "squeegee men" out of the streets. "Sure, they're annoying," he concedes. "They're a royal pain in the butt sometimes. Some of them, to be honest, are scam artists. But, after all, they're not stray dogs. Give me a break!"

I ask Mrs. Flowers's daughter if she gets upset the same way that her husband does when they go into a Manhattan store.

"Not really," she answers, holding her hand up hard against her chest. "It don't bother me as much. I don't get angry. Little things don't get to me the way they do to him."

In my notes: "She does not get angry. But she is the one who needs an oxygen machine. She is the one who cannot breathe."

We talk for a while of some of the children I have met at St. Ann's Church, almost all of whom have relatives in prison. Mrs. Flowers speaks of one of these kids, a 14-year-old boy who used to live here in this building and whose mother has since died of cancer.

"Is that Mrs. Blue?" I ask.

"Yes," she says. "The family lived upstairs. The daughter's out at Rikers Island. Been there several times. Had two of her babies there. Now a brother of hers is out there too. Another brother's dead."

"What happens to the kids," I ask, "when mothers are in prison?"

"Some of them, their relatives take them in. Others go in foster care. Other times, a neighbor takes the baby. To tell the truth, sometimes I wish that I could take them in. Rent a big house and make them a nice place to live. There's something that draws me to the little ones."

She speaks of toddlers in the streets who sometimes don't know where their mothers are. "If it's dinnertime I'll bring them in and feed them. If they're dirty I'll give them their bath." Many of the kids, she says, have little bugs all over them. *"Piojos* is the word the Puerto Rican children use. They get into their hair and skin. I say to them, 'Stay here with me. I'll keep you safe until your mama's home.' The children know me, so they know that they don't need to be afraid."

"My moms," says her daughter, smiling for the first time since I've seen her, "loves the little ones."

We speak of babies who are sometimes left by a young mother in a bundle of blankets or a cardboard box, often to be found by neighbors or police. Those who do not die end up sometimes in pediatric wards, where they remain for months, or even years, until they can be placed. "It brings to mind the baby Moses in the Nile," a black preacher told me once in speaking of these infants. When I repeat his words to Mrs. Flowers, she says, "Yes. It's there. It's in the Scriptures. It was written to be done."

Some months before, the press described a gang of murderers and dealers, based for the past seven years four doors from this apartment building, who sold crack in a distinctive vial with a red-and-orange cap and disciplined dishonest dealers by such terrifying means as mutilations. In one "midday mutilation," *Newsday* noted, gang enforcers punished a refractory gang member by taking him to St. Mary's Park, right at the end of Beekman Avenue, where "they hacked at him with machetes" and a "serrated" knife, "opening wounds so severe that some of his organs spilled out." A crowd including children from the nearby junior high school watched the killing.

The gang chose Mrs. Flowers's street for its headquarters, *Newsday* said, because there is a "narrow alley" in the back where drug transactions could be shielded from the observation of police and because there were so many neighborhood teenagers who could be recruited to peddle the gang's product. Beekman Avenue also offered easy access to the highways used by customers and certain well-located rooftops from which lookouts could keep track of the police while supervising dealers in the streets below. In one massacre that took place on the street two years before, a man and woman were shot dead for buying crack from the wrong dealer, the dealer was shot and killed as well, and a fourth person who had no drug involvement but was walking in the alley at the wrong time was chased down the street into St. Mary's Park and shot there 14 times.

I ask Mrs. Flowers, "Have you ever seen a shooting victim die before your eyes?"

"I've seen a *generation* die," she answers. "Some of them was killed with guns. Some lost their minds from drugs. Some from disease. Now we have AIDS, the great plague, the plague of AIDS, the plague that can't be cured. It's true. I've seen it. I've been there. I've been here in this building 24 years and I have seen it all."

"How," I ask her, "do you keep yourself composed?"

"I pray. I talk to God. I tell Him, 'Lord, it is your work. Put me to my rest at night and wake me in the morning.' "

"Do your children have the same belief in God that you do?"

"Yes," she says, nodding at her daughter and her son-in-law. "They do. This family talks to God."

Before I leave, she shows me a handful of photocopied clippings from newspapers that have sent reporters here to talk with her. It occurs to me that I must be one in a long line of people who have come to ask her questions. "Do you ever get sick," I ask, "of seeing all these people knocking at your door year after year to pick your brain?"

"No," she says, "I don't get sick of it because a lot of them have been nice people. The trouble is: You answer their questions and you give them your opinions. They collect your story from you. Then you see it and you read it. You think, 'Good.' But nothing happens. It's just 'there' and then it drops. It's like they put you in a bucket, like a wishing well. Only it's a wishing well where wishes don't come true."

I note, however, "That's not the wishing well that you believe in, is it?"

"No," she says, a little weary-sounding but rock-solid. "I put my wishes in another basket."

The asthma attack experienced by Mrs. Flowers's daughter on the night that I was visiting—particularly her hand pressed up against her chest and her brief answer, "Not good," when I asked her how she felt—reminds me of how many times in the South Bronx I've seen young children pull inhalers from their pockets. The brand that I have seen most frequently is Proventil, a yellow-and-orange plastic unit, which is almost as much a standard piece of "traveling equipment" for some of the little kids as beepers seem to be for some of the teenagers.

The longer I talk with children here, and then with doctors who work with asthmatics, the more I am convinced that what I first thought might be anecdotal accident, the sheer coincidence that writers learn to view with a degree of caution, is not mere coincidence but something painfully widespread. I can't remember ever being in another place in the United States in which so many children spoke of having difficulty breathing.

A woman whom Reverend Overall describes as "the great-grandmother of our church" tells me of the sickness of her great-granddaughter, three years old, who, she says, wheezes unendingly on many nights. She is convinced that this began only after the waste burner in the neighborhood went into operation.

I ask her what the child's mother does to counteract severe attacks.

"She uses the machine."

"A breathing machine?"

"Oh yes," she replies.

"How do you use it?"

"You put the mask over her face."

"Do you know other children who have asthma?"

"Of course."

"Are you sure that this is caused by the waste burner?"

"Oh yes," she says in a melodious voice, accented slightly, as I later learn, because she was born and grew up in Belize.

When, in response to several other questions that I ask, she replies repeatedly, "Oh yes," there is a slight sarcasm in her tone, an elegant edge of bitterness that seems to voice her doubt, her skepticism, as to whether an outsider can imagine, or has any real wish to imagine, what the children in her neighborhood must undergo.

According to a zip code breakdown of New York shown to me by Dr. Robert Massad, a family-practice specialist at Montefiore Medical Center in the Bronx, the rate of hospital admissions for asthma statewide in New York is 1.8 per 1,000 people. In New York City, it is 2.5 per 1,000, but in Mott Haven the rate rises to 6.0 in the St. Ann's neighborhood and 6.9 in the adjacent zip code. The lowest rate of pediatric asthma in the Bronx, according to this breakdown, is in Riverdale, a predominately white section; the highest rate, more than five times that of Riverdale, is in Mott Haven, where the rate of child pneumonia is also very high: ten times that of Riverdale. The asthma mortality rate for people in the Bronx, the borough with the highest concentration of black and Hispanic residents, is nearly nine times that of Staten Island, which is the whitest borough in the city.

One reason for the higher rates of death from asthma in poor neighborhoods like the South Bronx is the relative absence of preventive care. But the cost of asthma medication is a factor too. Inhalers cost between $15 and $40 each and often last only two weeks. Some children need three different kinds of medication simultaneously, and parents who aren't on Medicaid or who can't get refills of prescriptions at the proper times because of long lines at the hospitals may simply take a chance on using an inhaler past its date of expiration. A heroin user who lives close to the Grand Concourse tells me that one of the dealers he has known for years "peddles asthma inhalers on Third Avenue," where, he says, "they are more valuable than heroin," but, he adds, "nobody ever asks him if they are outdated."

Other asthmatics turn for urgent care to storefront medical offices, which the press calls "Medicaid mills" and where, according to one news account, doctors of unknown qualification "grind through dozens of patients" in an hour, often seeing each one for less than a minute, then writing prescriptions, often for strong drugs, which are dispensed at pharmacies owned by the Medicaid mills. "Eight of ten patients complain of asthma," notes a congressional subcommittee that has been able to obtain case records for some of the Medicaid mills of the South Bronx. "Almost all" are given drugs that "potentiate [i.e., intensify] the effects of cocaine."

Some of the Medicaid mills don't even bother with examining rooms, says Dr. Massad, who tells me of seeing a line of men out in the street one day and asking them what they were waiting for. "They said, 'To see the doctor.' I went to the front of the line and saw this guy behind a kind of bank-teller window. He was sitting behind a bulletproof glass just writing out prescriptions."

"You can't call what goes on in those places medicine," says another doctor, who supervises the professional conduct of physicians for the state Department of Health. "It's a continuous obscenity. . . . No real doctor would spend a day there."

Partly because of the hiring methods of the Medicaid mills, which advertise for doctors in "help wanted" columns in newspapers, less than 13 percent of the doctors practicing primary care in the Mott Haven area are certified by medical boards to practice—an astonishing statistic in a city with a surplus of well-qualified physicians in its wealthy neighborhoods. When you ride on the Number 6 train from East 59th Street to the racial cutoff point at 96th, you pass beneath an area in which 2,400 private doctors, most of them highly qualified, have their offices and in which the ratio of doctors to residents is approximately 60 to 1,000. When you leave the subway at Brook Avenue, you are in a neighborhood in which the ratio is two per 1,000.

A handful of good, publicly funded clinics, which are perennially overcrowded, try to compensate for the abandonment of New York City's poorest children by much of its medical establishment.

At one such clinic, on 162nd Street, overseen by Dr. Massad's staff, I meet a Puerto Rican boy, a nine-year-old asthmatic who has only recently begun to suffer from severe attacks. His mother says that overexertion or emotional distress brings on the worst attacks. "If you scold him or if anything upsets him, you can hear the noise: a roaring sound, then wheezing." The boy, she says, uses two drugs—Proventil and one other medicine, the name of which is unfamiliar to me. "He brings the pump with him to school. His younger brother has it too. Also, his father does, and his grandmother, and his uncle, and his aunt. I started getting asthma too, a year ago." She tells me that she uses "the pump" also.

"I saw him itching and I heard the wheezing. I brought him to Lincoln Hospital at four A.M. They took him right in, but when they sent him home, he was still wheezing. Two weeks after that, he caught a big attack at night. 'Mami, I can't breathe,' he said. That time, the hospital kept him for four days."

I walk home with them after their appointment. Their apartment is a fifth-floor walk-up. By the time we get to the top of the stairs, all three of us are out of breath. I ask the child's mother if I can use her telephone. "We don't have no phone," she says—a common situation in the Bronx, which, according to the 1990 census, has the highest percentage of households without telephones of any highly populated county in the nation.

Back on 141st Street in Mott Haven, Jesus Gilberto Sierra, who grew up here and now runs the only reputable primary health care center in the St. Ann's neighborhood, speaks of the factors that contribute to high rates of pediatric asthma. "Some of it is obviously environmental—housing infestation, pesticides, no heat in an apartment. But a great deal is emotional as well. Fear of violence can be a strong constrictive force. If you moved these families into a nice suburb, nine tenths of this feeling of constriction, I'm convinced, would be relieved.

"My secretary's father lives in a little town in Puerto Rico. Every time he comes here to the Bronx, he has attacks. He comes out of the subway at Brook Avenue—something hits him and he's wheezing." He mentions, "I have asthma also."

The clinic, he tells me, after running through a number of statistics on staff, finance, and admissions, "cannot meet the needs" of the community. "We serve Mott Haven, but we also get the overflow from Hunts Point since the city closed the only hospital in that area some years ago."

He says it has been hard to attract American physicians to the clinic. "Of the last 12 that I hired, nine were African or Haitian. So, with the Haitian doctors for example, you've got doctors who sometimes speak French or Creole or have very heavy accents, patients who speak Spanish or else black folks who speak English. So I try to find bilingual nurses." White American physicians, numerous studies seem to indicate, often evince a strong aversion to providing health care in such neighborhoods.

"What do you do with some of these realities?" Sierra asks me, or himself, in the last moments of our conversation. "Here is a city in which nine out of ten children born with AIDS are black kids or Latinos, many of their mothers or fathers IV users. You have 14-year-old girls who are crack users. If you don't believe in God and don't believe in family or society and don't believe you'll ever have a job, what *do* you have? Even when a good political leader speaks to them, his rhetoric has no effect. It's like walking into an intensive-care ward in a hospital and saying, 'Rise!' "

His words remind me of the tremendous sigh that Cliffie made as we were walking in the neighborhood nine months before, and of his ominous announcement: "The day is coming when the world will be destroyed." Whatever the culpability of New York City's health officials or its politicians in allowing the incinerator to be placed within this powerless and ravaged neighborhood—an installation to which radioactive waste has twice been brought, allegedly by accident, this year—the truth is that the concentrated and sequestered children of Mott Haven probably need no toxins stronger than despair and fear and isolation to constrict their bronchioles. The waste incinerator may, as many people here believe, contribute to the asthma suffered by so many children, or it may be little more than a slow-burning metaphor. But people in every era, as we know, want desperately to find a visible explanation for their suffering. These ugly installations—burners, sewage plants, and dump-sites—seem to offer one that many people in the South Bronx find persuasive.

The following day, during a conversation with a nurse who has been working in the South Bronx for five years, I ask a question that has come into my mind before but that I've never posed to anyone who knows the medical system from within.

"Why don't people in this neighborhood, when they get sick, take their Medicaid card, get on the train, get off in Manhattan, walk into the lobby of one of the nicest hospitals and ask for care? I make that trip quite often and it isn't a long ride."

"Ah!" she answers, as if, after a lengthy and meandering conversation, I have inadvertently come up with the right question. "You see, it wouldn't be the same ride that you take. Geographically it would, but not in other ways that matter more. For you, that ride means coming home. It brings you to a place where you belong. For them, it's more like heading out to sea. It's not 'coming home' at all. It's the reverse."

"But, if they're really sick," I ask, "how much would that matter?"

"It matters a lot. First of all, they don't feel welcome in some of those hospitals. As bad as Lincoln or Bronx-Lebanon may be, at least receptionists don't call a woman of color by her first name. And some of the nurses and housekeepers talk to you! If a woman's black, Hispanic, and on welfare, maybe a drug user, or has HIV, she knows she isn't welcome in a first-class hospital. This is not perception.

It's a fact. If they wouldn't want you as a neighbor, why do you think they'd want you in the next bed?

"People learn this lesson very fast. It's like, 'They're right. I don't belong in a nice hospital. My skin is black. I'm Puerto Rican. I'm on welfare. I belong in my own neighborhood. This is where I'm *supposed* to be.' In other words, they've learned what we have taught them."

As it turns out, this is not always true, however. Certain people refuse to learn these lessons and do not accept these arbitrary borders. Many women from the South Bronx, for example, knowing the problems of the hospitals that serve the area, do attempt to gain admission to prestigious hospitals that serve the affluent. Some are not successful in these efforts. Others, while they do obtain admission, run into some of the same uncomfortable situations that they face when they go into an expensive store and notice that reflexive "stepping back" that seems to indicate a fear of getting close to them.

A heavily marked collection of clippings from the *Daily News* that Mrs. Washington shows me one night in her home illustrates one of these painful situations. On the fifth floor of Mount Sinai Medical Center, a distinguished private hospital, according to the paper, 17 newborn babies are placed in a row in front of a window in the obstetric ward. All are white. One flight down, in the fourth-floor nursery, are 14 other babies—"all black or Latino." The fifth floor, supposedly reserved for private patients, offers "private and semiprivate rooms with bathrooms." On the fourth floor, black and Hispanic women are assigned, four each, to "overcrowded rooms" with "peeling paint" and "showers in the hallways."

Although officials of Mount Sinai claim that the segregation of the wards is not by race, but by method of payment—private patients on the fifth floor, Medicaid patients on the fourth—a reporter interviews a woman who is not on Medicaid, but Hispanic, who was placed on the segregated fourth floor even though she was a private patient. Nurses, meanwhile, tell reporters that they sometimes see white Medicaid patients on the fifth floor.

"The fifth floor," according to one of the patients, a

black woman on the segregated floor who had apparently walked upstairs to see what she was missing, "had plants . . . had pictures. . . . It was brighter. . . . Even the bathroom was different." When a white woman who was a friend of hers and had had her baby on the fifth floor came to visit, "she couldn't believe it was the same hospital."

Patients on the fifth floor are given classes in nutrition, exercise, breast-feeding, and infant care, which, says a nurse, are not provided to the patients on the fourth floor. On the fifth floor a nurse is instructed not to document the fact of alcohol abuse in making out a patient's record. On the fourth floor, in contrast, "nurses . . . note for the records a mother's drug or alcohol abuse" and notify welfare officials if a mother uses drugs.

When she first visited the hospital, says a black woman from the Bronx, she was with her husband, who is white, and was shown attractive rooms on the fifth floor. When she returned to have her baby, however, she was not with her husband and was placed on the segregated floor. "The whole attitude of people was different. . . . You'd think it was a different hospital," she says, describing the personal hurt she felt as "devastating."

"The de facto segregation" of the hospital, according to the *Daily News*, "apparently has been in existence for at least ten years."

"I didn't think you'd ever hear of something like that in this city," David says when I discuss the story with him and his mother in their kitchen. "Now I see that I was wrong. It isn't right to separate people in a hospital because of race"—one of those straightforward observations that well-educated people often find it hard to state with an equivalent simplicity. The hospital, he notes, says the issue is not race, but Medicaid. "But black ladies with insurance had to stay on the same floor as people who had Medicaid. So the hospital, it seems, was not telling the truth.

"I don't think that this was a mistake," he says. "White people must have known about it all along. They could look around them and see nothing but white women on their floor. Where did they think black women had their babies? Did they think that they were having babies in their homes like in the days of slavery? They must have seen black women sometimes in the lobby. Where did they think that they had gone? When I read this, I was thinking, 'Why did it take reporters ten years to discover this?' "

I ask him if he means that they were purposely ignoring it.

"That's what I think. I think that they agreed to keep this thing a secret to protect the reputation of the hospital. I feel upset about this. I think of my mother sitting up all night when she goes to Bronx-Lebanon. It makes me feel distrustful."

In a pointed reference to the name of the hospital, he adds, "Mount Sinai was a sacred place. That makes it worse. The Ten Commandments told us not to lie."

"Three years ago," says one of the grandmothers who prepare the meals for the soup kitchen at St. Ann's, "I was having bad pains in my breast and my right arm. I went to Mount Sinai because I had had a bad experience at Lincoln.

" 'You live in the South Bronx. Your catchment area is Lincoln Hospital,' they said. 'Why don't you go back there in your own zone?' I said, 'I have Medicaid.' They said, 'We can't help you.' "

"How far is the hospital from here?" I ask.

"Six stops on the subway," she replies. "You get off at 96th. It's right there in that area. . . ."

"Do you believe," I ask her, "that you would have been accepted if you were someone"—I hesitate because I don't know how to say this—"someone like Reverend Overall or me?"

"To tell the truth, I do. You see? They're *going* to be paid. So I don't know what else it could have been except the color of my skin. I don't like to think of that. I'm not a prejudiced person but I cannot understand why else they would not let me in."

The woman, who was born and educated in the Virgin Islands, suffers from depression and, the pastor says, cries easily. She had worked for years as a household maid for several families in Manhattan and had thought of going to Mount Sinai because one of her employers had routinely used that hospital and she had regarded it therefore with confidence.

"Were they polite to you?" I ask, a question I bring up because I'm told that these rejections generally are presented tactfully and with exaggerated friendliness that upsets people all the more.

"No," she says. "They weren't polite at all." Mimicking the voice of the intake person at Mount Sinai, she repeats the woman's words: " 'No, no! Oh no! You have to go back to your zone.' "

"How did you feel when she told you this?"

"How *would* you feel?" she says. "You feel ashamed. You feel inferior. You're angry. You feel tight inside your chest. It feels like somebody has got his fist around your heart and just keeps squeezing it. You do not want to think that this can be."

"Does it hurt when people look at you and see a 'colored woman,' not a human being?" Elizabeth once asked in reference to a similar moment of humiliation that she underwent in going to a hospital in Boston. "It does. It sinks right in. It stays with you. It eats you up inside. It stays and stays. You think of it for years."

At home in Massachusetts, when I think about my conversation with the woman who cooks for the children and the homeless people in the kitchen of St. Ann's and her reaction to the way she was turned down when she had asked for medical treatment at Mount Sinai, it is the aching weariness within her voice that stays the longest in my mind. Some of this weariness, I imagine, must reflect the cumulative effect of many years of difficult encounters like the one she has described; and some may be the consequence of many other pressures and humiliations in her life. But weariness among the adults in Mott Haven does not always call for complicated explanations. A lot of it is simply the sheer physical result of going for long periods of time with very little sleep because of the anxiety that seems so common, nearly chronic, among many people here.

"Every little thing you have to do is painful," Mrs.

179

Washington once said in speaking of the weariness she feels in periods of time when there is trouble in her building or her neighborhood and she is too scared to sleep. "You have to struggle to get through the afternoon. You drink a lot of coffee and you smoke too much to keep from crying or exploding at somebody. You feel nervous all the time and can't calm down."

There is a great deal of discussion in the papers and on television panels about "apathy" and "listlessness" and lack of good "decision-making skills" among the mothers of poor children. It seems that there is something like this almost every evening on one of the cable stations. I rarely hear the people on these TV panels talk about such ordinary things as never getting a night of good deep sleep because you're scared of bullets coming through the window from the street. In this respect and many others, the discussion of poor women and their children is divorced from any realistic context that includes the actual conditions of their lives.

The statement, for example, heard so often now as to assume the character of incantation, that embattled neighborhoods like the South Bronx have undergone a "breakdown of the family" upsets many women that I know, not because they think it is not true, but because those who repeat this phrase, often in an unkind and censorious way, do so with no reference to the absolute collapse of almost every other form of life-affirming institution in the same communities. "Nothin' works here in my neighborhood," Elizabeth says. "Keepin' a man is not the biggest problem. Keepin' from bein' killed is bigger. Keepin' your kids alive is bigger. If nothin' else works, why should a marriage work? I'd rather have a peaceful little life just with my kids than live with somebody who knows that he's a failure. Men like that make everyone feel rotten."

Perhaps this is one reason why so much of the debate about the "breakdown of the family" has a note of the unreal or incomplete. "Of course the family structure breaks down in a place like the South Bronx!" says a white minister who works in one of New York City's poorest neighborhoods. "Everything breaks down in a place like this. The pipes break down. The phone breaks down. The electricity and heat break down. The spirit breaks down. The body breaks down. The immune agents of the heart break down. Why wouldn't the family break down also?

"If we saw the people in these neighborhoods as part of the same human family to which we belong, we'd never put them in such places to begin with. But we do *not* think of them that way. That is one area of 'family breakdown' that the experts and newspapers seldom speak of. They speak about the failures of the mothers we have exiled to do well within their place of exile. They do not condemn the pharaoh.

"Do you ever turn on C-SPAN? You see these rather shallow but smart people, most of them young and obviously privileged, going on and on with perky overconfidence about the values and the failings of poor women and you want to grab them in your hands and *shake* them!"

Elizabeth made a similar comment once about a government official from the Reagan era, a particularly youthful-looking man who is often on TV and is severe in what he has to say about black women: "I'd like to take this little fellow on my knee sometimes and spank him. He reminds me of the boys I used to care for when I was a maid—pink and pretty, and too smart by half.

"Don't he remember," she asked, not with humor now, but with tremendous hurt and bitterness, "who it is who wiped his bottom when he was a baby?"

Mrs. Washington said it once in her own way. "I feel like somebody beat me up." She was speaking of the way that she was treated by welfare officials; but she and many other mothers in her neighborhood could say the same of the repeated verbal beatings they receive from less mature, less seasoned, and far less transcendent human beings, most of them white, most of them male, who sit on television panels from which people such as Mrs. Washington have been excluded and say many things that are not true, to which these women can't reply, and other things that are in part the truth but to which these critics often add an edge of venomous interpretation.

"Like Job," said the minister I have cited, with whom I spoke at length about the tone of public criticism of the poor, "many women could reply, 'What you know, the same do I know also. . . . I am not inferior unto you.' " I later looked up these words in Job and found them followed, in another passage, by a question many women that I know ask almost daily in one manner or another: "How long will you vex my soul and break me in pieces with words?"

"We haven't been fair," says Harvard professor David Elwood in speaking of the way we treat and talk about poor women and their children, "and we still don't understand what we've done to them." It's a beautifully quiet statement; but I'm just not sure that we don't understand. Many poor people think we understand these things extremely well but acquiesce in them without much personal discomfort. In other words, they don't see innocence in our behavior. They do not think that what is being done to them is a mistake.

Chapter Six

No matter how final a visit seems, I keep on going back to the same places—Beekman Avenue, and St. Ann's Avenue, and Cypress, and East Tremont, and the area around the Hunts Point Market, then to Featherbed Lane and Shakespeare Avenue, and back to St. Ann's Church. Thinking often of a teacher I had met some months before at P.S. 65, who had wondered whether the kinds of questions I was asking could be answered by a teacher and whether they were "better asked to priests or theologians," I go back again and again to talk with ministers and priests in neighborhoods I've visited before, to Gregory Groover in Hunts Point, to the priest of St. Luke's Church, near P.S. 65, in which Bernardo Rodriguez had been baptized and in which a memorial mass was held upon his death, and to the ministers of storefront churches on Brook Avenue and elsewhere in the area. I also talk with a number of the nuns from several different Catholic orders who work at the schools and clinics and food pantries in these neighborhoods.

Each time, the conversation starts with something quite specific—AIDS or education, welfare rules or housing or lead poison or the flight of jobs—but ends with talk of personal pain, anxiety about the future of the children, the search for faith in almost anyone or anything that offers strength, sometimes with talk of God.

The specifics of each issue—dump-sites, asthma, or waste burners, or whatever else—soon begin to seem almost beside the point. The search for explanations of the sadness heard in many of the voices of the people I have met is not answered by the factual questions one might ask about "environment" or "health care" or "the

185

public schools." The questions that need asking seem to go beyond these concrete matters. One wants instead to know how certain people hold up under terrible ordeal, how many more do not, how human beings devalue other people's lives, how numbness and destructiveness are universalized, how human pity is at length extinguished and the shunning of the vulnerable can come in time to be perceived as natural behavior. "The poor frighten me," a rich lady told St. Vincent. "The poor are frightening," he answered, "as frightening as God's justice." What do we do to those who frighten us? Do we put them off, as far away as possible, and hope, as one of the students said to me during the previous summer, that they'll either die or disappear? How does a nation deal with those whom it has cursed?

One day in the spring, when Reverend Overall is driving with me from Manhattan to the Bronx, she stops her car at 96th Street, then drives one block more to 97th Street, in order to enable me to see the cutoff point between the races in this section of New York.

The sharpness of the demarcation line, which I have never seen before at the street level, is more dramatic and extreme than I anticipated. To the south, along Park Avenue, impressive buildings stand on both sides of the street, pedestrian islands with well-tended grass and flower plantings in the center. In the other direction, to the north, a railroad line, submerged beneath Park Avenue up to this point, appears from under 97th Street and splits the avenue in two. The trains, from this point on, run along the street for several blocks until Park Avenue dips slightly and the tracks are elevated on a large stone viaduct that shadows children playing in the sun of afternoon.

The significance of 96th Street in New York is inescapable and comes up time and again in conversations and in the newspapers. Luxury grocers advertise their willingness to make deliveries only south of 96th Street, and even liberal papers such as the *Observer* print these ads. McDonald's announces "home delivery" from 40 of its outlets in New York, but none of them north of this point on the East Side.

Maps in tourist books and maps accompanying stories in the papers about leisure-time activities tend to stop at 96th Street too. A church in Harlem that attempts to forge religious links between the races calls the program it has started "Crossing 96th Street." But casual conversations with a sampling of people who reside just south of here, as well as a ride on the Number 6 or Number 4 train almost any hour of any day, will demonstrate to readers who may visit New York City just how little crossing by white people actually takes place.

"South of here, and over toward Fifth Avenue," says Reverend Overall, "is one of the wealthiest and whitest places in the world. It's known as Carnegie Hill. North of here are several of the poorest, most unhealthy places in America." The infant mortality rate on Carnegie Hill, where average annual income is $300,000, is, according to Ruth Messinger, the Manhattan borough president, one of the lowest anywhere on earth: seven children in 1,000. Just to the north and a little to the west, in Central Harlem, it is 28 per 1,000, higher than in many Third World nations.

After chatting for a while with some people on the bridge at 97th Street, we get back in the pastor's beat-up car and head north into Harlem, rattling over ruts and potholes, past the gloomy viaduct, past the boarded buildings and the small bodegas and the many groups of idle men in clusters at most corners. On street after street, there are exactly the same kinds of signs one sees all over the South Bronx, advertising beepers, Medicaid mills and pharmacies, check-cashing, social services of all varieties, and other enterprises of the kind Jane Jacobs once described as "the transactions of decline."

We drive a few blocks to the west, then north again along a boulevard named for Malcolm X, the heart of the drug traffic in this part of Harlem now, then to the Madison Avenue Bridge across the Harlem River, and back finally to Mott Haven. Crossing Morris Avenue, then Third Avenue and Alexander, then Willis, and then Brook, and heading for St. Ann's, the pastor stops her car before a burnt-out house. She tells me of a child, an unhappy 12-year-old, the granddaughter of a friend of hers, who rides

187

in the car with her sometimes when she is doing errands in Manhattan. "While we are in Manhattan, she seems care-free and excited. The minute we cross the line of 96th Street, you can see the cloud of deep depression settle over her. By the time I drop her off at her apartment here, she's frequently in tears.

"As many times as I have driven up Park Avenue," she says, "it has never ceased to puzzle me that anyone who lives south of that line would have the nerve to lecture people here on 'character' or 'values.' It has to take extraordinary self-deceit for people who plant flowers on Park Avenue but pump their sewage into Harlem and transport their medical waste, and every other kind of waste that you can think of, to Mott Haven, to imagine that they have the moral standing to be judges of the people they have segregated and concealed. Only a very glazed and clever culture in which social blindness is accepted as a normal state of mind could possibly permit itself this luxury."

I repeat to her Lee Stuart's words—that segregation as "a sin committed by society" is no longer of much interest to the press in New York City.

"They don't deny its presence," she replies. "They can't. What they do instead is to refer to it, in passing, in a way that makes it sound too obvious to warrant indignation.

"This is the way that certain things are handled in New York. The papers don't ignore realities like these. They cover them, the same way that they cover things like the waste burner, but they do it in a way that tends to neutralize their dangers almost instantly.

"A friend of mine from seminary says that suffering is 'wine.' I think that's the right image: sacred wine. If you water it, it isn't sacred anymore; but watering the wine of suffering is terribly important for the people who don't suffer. Some of the magazines and papers in New York are very good at this."

"Do you ever use strong words like that when you discuss this with white people? Do you speak of segregation as a sin?"

"I can say it, but it doesn't seem convincing to most

people. I can call it an 'injustice,' but that doesn't always sink in either. You have to understand the nature of the culture in New York. Words that are equal to the pain of the poor are pretty easily discredited. A quarter of the truth, stated with lots of indirection, is regarded as more seemly.

"Even when people do accept the idea of 'injustice,' there are ways to live with it without it causing you to change a great deal in your life. A mildly embarrassed toleration of injustice is an elemental part of cultural sophistication here. The style is, 'Oh yes. We know all that. So tell us something new.' There's a kind of cultivated weariness in this. Talking about injustice, I am told, is 'tiresome' unless you do it in a way that sounds amusing."

I note that I have never heard her speak with so much anger in her voice.

"Maybe I'm too harsh," she says, "but I don't see how you can work within a neighborhood like this and not feel anger in your heart."

"Anthony says you told him not to bring his anger into church."

"I did," she says. "I want the church to be a gentle place for children. But driving up Park Avenue, especially when I remember the effect it has on children, brings out these feelings in me every time."

Many of us who came of age during the 1960s thought that these most blatant forms of residential segregation, and the gross extremes of wealth and poverty, of cleanliness and filth, of health and sickness in our nation, would be utterly transformed within another generation. It was a confident, naive, and youthful expectation, characteristic of that era. Our confidence, we now know, was mistaken.

Every few years, amidst the news of murder and lead poison, drug addiction, toxic waste, dysfunctional hospitals, and overcrowded schools, a number of exciting stories about neighborhood renewal and construction of new housing in the South Bronx suddenly appear in several different magazines and papers almost simultaneously, often

189

with a certain number of familiar words that speak of architectural and other piecemeal physical improvements as the metaphors of cultural and spiritual rebirth. "Long written off as the ultimate bombed-out wasteland," says *New York* magazine in 1994, "New York's poorest quarter is now undergoing an almost astonishing recovery." A headline above the story promises "A SOUTH BRONX RENAISSANCE."

A similar, but better-balanced, story in the *Times* points to a number of town houses with "wrought iron" gates and the "suburban feel of vinyl siding" under construction, or already built, approximately 15 blocks north of the St. Ann's neighborhood, and speaks of a total of about 500 of such houses, which, says the writer, have already been sold "at prices from $90,000 to $165,000" to "qualified" homebuyers. An additional 4,500 houses are in planning stages or have already been built for working-class homeowners elsewhere in the South Bronx, says the paper.

The *Times* concedes that the area is not "a Garden of Eden," that it has "among the worst-rated public schools" and "highest crime rates" in New York, and that the Mott Haven section, where "the ravages of crime and drugs . . . have continued unabated," has been largely "left behind" by these renewal efforts. Still, the writer tries to offer a degree of hope. A priest says the feeling in the city toward the South Bronx used to be, "Just let it die. . . ." Now, he says, "Maybe we are on one knee."

Each time one reads one of these stories, a brief sense of optimism stirs. Sometimes it seems justified at first. If one has followed these events, however, over the course of 30 or more years, one tends to view these promises of neighborhood renewal through the medium of architecture and design with a degree of wariness. At least five times in my adult life, I have seen similar renewal efforts in the Roxbury ghetto heralded by the press in Boston, almost always in exactly the same kinds of headlines that we see now in New York. When I have gone to visit one year later, the buildings sometimes look quite nice. Four years, five years, six years later, they begin to look run-down and overgrown. Ten years later, as if the physical erosion process common everywhere is somehow expedited here, they have become another bleary section of the slum.

Perhaps this is one reason why so many older people in Mott Haven read these stories in the papers with a good deal of ironical detachment. It was, after all, only 20 years ago that the housing in which Anabelle and Mrs. Flowers live and where Bernardo died was being heralded by the New York City papers as "an innovation in urban planing," a symbol of "resurgence," and a "showpiece" of what was *then* known also as "the South Bronx renaissance." The Diego-Beekman buildings, said the *Times* in 1973, since being purchased by the Continental Wingate Company of Boston, "have been transformed into sparkling new apartment houses" with "elevators," "trash compactors," and new "plumbing, wiring, and heating systems."

"New hope" is "rising amid the desperation of this slum," said another *Times* reporter. "New public schools on concrete stilts," "the steel skeleton of a new Lincoln Hospital," and plans for "garden-style housing" are "signs of a vast program of public reconstruction that is giving a new look to the South Bronx."

"The next ten years will see a new South Bronx," said South Bronx congressman Herman Badillo in 1972, in reference to these and other signs of progress.

Visitors to Lincoln Hospital or Beekman Avenue today may have an opportunity to judge to what degree the optimism of those years was justified. The new public schools of the South Bronx, with stilts or without stilts, have proven, with a few remarkable exceptions, to be sad repositories for the disappointed dreams of children of dark skin. The newly built Lincoln Hospital has proven to be another poorly funded and chaotic monument to medical apartheid. The wiring in many of those "sparkling new apartment houses" along Beekman Avenue has long since been eaten through by rats. The new plumbing of 22 years ago sprays scalding steam at mothers and their infants. One of those brand-new elevators heralded by the press in 1973 turned out to be Bernardo's tomb.

"If there is one thing more destructive and demoralizing to poor people than to live in desolation," Reverend Overall observes, "it is to have these false hopes reawakened at these routine intervals. Do that to me enough times and I'll never hope again. It's like shooting someone up with drugs. This is how you turn poor people into zombies."

There is another, entirely different issue that is being raised about these promises of reconstruction and renewal. Even if the efforts under way today should prove, unlike those of the past, to be enduring, and even if they ever reach the St. Ann's neighborhood, many of the poorest residents believe that they are not the people who will benefit. They are convinced that those who benefit will be "the least poor of the poor," for whom the city or a nonprofit corporation may provide unusual security and private sanitation, so that the immediate environs may become an island of protected, if ephemeral, wholesomeness within a sea of suffering and sickness. And, if the South Bronx as a whole should ever become a truly pleasant place to live, many here feel certain that the very poor will simply be pushed off into another squalid quarter somewhere else, perhaps one of the deeply troubled, segregated suburbs that are now proliferating on all sides of New York City.

No one in New York, in any case, expects the racial isolation of these neighborhoods to lessen in the years ahead. A demographic forecast by the city's planning agency predicts that the population of the Bronx—both North and South—half of which was white in 1970, and nearly a quarter of which was white in 1990, will be entirely black and Hispanic by the early years of the next century, outside of a handful of de facto segregated enclaves of white people and a few essentially detached communities like parts of Riverdale. By that time, the Bronx and Harlem and Washington Heights will make up a vast and virtually uninterrupted ghetto with a population close to that of Houston, Texas, which is America's fourth-largest city.

Despite these demographic probabilities, the Bronx borough president, Fernando Ferrer, with whom I've talked at length about the health and education problems of the families here, manages to be contagiously enthusiastic. He is a likable person and seems genuinely dedicated to the people whom he represents; it is, of course, his job to be enthusiastic. I have met politicians equally dedicated and enthusiastic in Detroit and East St. Louis, but their energy and dedication could not bring back life-sustaining jobs or first-class schools or anything like modern health care to a population viewed as economically and socially superfluous; nor, of course, could they reverse the flight of most white people from those cities. There are neighborhoods with handsome houses in Detroit and East St. Louis too. Both these cities have their periodic episodes of neighborhood renewal also.

Perhaps something is truly different this time in the Bronx. Perhaps the skepticism of the people I have talked with in Mott Haven is misplaced. Perhaps the predictions of the city's planning agency will prove to be in error too. Perhaps the children of the children who are growing up today in the South Bronx will someday live in attractive houses on the same nice streets as middle-class and working-class homeowners of all races. It is tempting to imagine this, but it is only honest to report that no one I have met here holds such expectations.

Whatever good things may happen for the children of another generation are, in any case, of little solace to those who are children now and will not have their childhood to live a second time in the next century. This is particularly the case for those, especially the very young, who are about to lose, or have already lost, their mothers or their fathers to the epidemic that now stalks the neighborhood.

The rapid emergence in New York of thousands of black and Hispanic children of low income who have lost their parents to the plague of AIDS is, says the director of an organization called the Orphans Project, a catastrophe that has no real analogy within our nation in this century. "Only the great influenza pandemic of 1918 . . . offers a partial analogy from diseases of the twentieth century. . . . We are only at the beginning of this phenomenon. We do not yet know its duration."

Already in 1993, when I began to visit in the South

Bronx, some 10,000 children in New York had lost their mothers to the epidemic. As many as 2,000 of these children were believed to live in the Mott Haven area and in three or four adjacent sections of the Bronx. The Orphans Project estimated that, between then and the year 2000, HIV-infected mothers in New York would "give birth to between 32,000 and 38,000 HIV-infected babies" and more than twice as many babies who would not have been infected. If these projections prove to be correct, and if the city continues with its present policy of channeling its sickest and most troubled families, often addicted and quite frequently infected, into housing in this area, it is likely that entire blocks will soon be home to mourning orphans, many of whom will follow their own parents to an early grave.

"The viral path" of AIDS, says *Newsday*, "has crept through the family tree" in many South Bronx neighborhoods, "breaking branch after branch." By the spring of 1993, 1,381 women in the area and 3,428 men had been diagnosed. But thousands of people in the South Bronx "have no personal physician. . . . Infected women still go undiagnosed, their lifespans significantly reduced" because they get no early treatment.

A specialist in pediatric AIDS says he's "seeing things medically that I've never seen before and never thought I would ever see." Speaking of people with "rampant TB and three other types of infection at the same time" waiting at hospitals as long as three days for a bed, he says, "It's like the Middle Ages."

"Right now at Bronx-Lebanon," says Mrs. Washington's doctor, "a quarter of all our *general* admissions—not just on obstetric wards—are known to be positive for HIV." The area served by the hospital, according to a study of blood samples tested at the hospital, "apparently has one of the highest AIDS rates in the world."

According to the city's health officials, 91 percent of children in New York who are born with AIDS are black or Hispanic, as are 84 percent of women who have AIDS. So the racial demographics of Mott Haven, as well as the prevalence of intravenous drug use in the area and an apparent increase in the rate of HIV infection among adolescents here, tend to justify the somber language used by doctors in Mott Haven as they look into the future.

At a walk-in center in Mott Haven, run by the Dominican Sisters, which offers medical help and other services to families with AIDS, a social worker who does "anticipatory grieving" with the children of AIDS patients speaks of a 15-year-old girl who is infected "but is afraid to tell her mother, because her mother is already dying." The girl's ten-year-old sister has AIDS also, says the social worker, "presumably because she was infected perinatally," in which case it is remarkable that she has lived this long. But, she says, "with a ten-year-old you can't be sure exactly *how* she was infected."

The incubation period of AIDS in infants is, she tells me, generally shorter than in adults—an average of three years. Most subsequently die in 18 months. According to physicians, only five percent live to be 12 years old.

In another family in the neighborhood, the social worker says, the father died two years ago and the mother is about to die. The four soon-to-be-orphaned children are being cared for by their 75-year-old grandmother. "One of the children, a nine-year-old, is sick with full-blown AIDS. Another child, seven years old, is less sick but he's been getting IV blood infusions. The six-year-old may be okay. But it's the 13-year-old girl, who *isn't* sick, who's causing the most worries. She's staying out all night, defying her grandmother. She started to do this at 11, when her father died. Recently, this girl had an abortion."

"Thirteen years old?"

"Yes," she replies. "Thirteen years old. You can imagine the risks that child must be taking. . . ."

All of the families she's described, she tells me, live in approximately a 12-block radius of St. Ann's Church, and, she adds, "we're barely scratching the surface of the families in the neighborhood who need our help."

How do children living in this medieval landscape face the losses that they must expect? How do they confront the process of bereavement?

When I had asked Mrs. Flowers how she held up in the

face of all the death and violence within her neighborhood, she had given me a simple answer: "This family talks to God." Many of the orphans of the epidemic talk to God as well. Whether because they are in mourning for a mother or a father who has died or because they know that they are sick as well and are afraid of their own death, many of these children also think and speak a great deal about heaven. Some try to picture it in drawings.

One drawing, by a ten-year-old boy, shows a brick wall with a large gate in the middle. Above it are eight puffy clouds. On each cloud there is a small stick-figure. Next to one is the word "ME" with an arrow pointing to his head. Another arrow indicates "MY FRIENDS." A drawing by a 12-year-old shows heaven as "God's house" with a friendly-looking sun smiling above it. In front of the house are three angels with wings, standing on clouds.

"MEET MR. HIV," writes an 11-year-old child, over a diamond-shaped face from which six scaly legs extend. "He invades your body. This is what he looks like when he does," another child writes over a scary-looking monster that resembles a tarantula. An HIV-infected 12-year-old draws a transparent yellow picture of his body filled with hairy, bloblike creatures that resemble paramecia and amoebae. "I hate you because you do bad things to my body," writes another boy. "Go pick on someone your own size."

The written reflections of the children, which are collected in a recent volume about pediatric AIDS, range from jealousy and anger and confusion to compassion, longing, and acceptance. Some are just fearful. "I am an acorn," writes a nine-year-old. "I am scared of squirrels."

A five-year-old named Cassie, with a grown-up's help, composes this message for her mother, who has died some months before: "Mommy, I want you to know everything. . . . I am going home from the hospital today. . . . I am starting kindergarten next week. I am going to wear my dress which has flowers on it and is black. . . . I wish I could fly up there to the sky to be with you."

A four-year-old says, "My mommy lives in heaven. Her eyelashes go down instead of up because she is . . . in heaven, but I miss her." She feels consoled that her mother "is with God," who, she says, "has pink whiskers, red hair, and two feet. . . . I did not want her to die until I died. I think I am going to die too in a little while."

The knowledge that a stigma is attached to AIDS, however, keeps some children from confiding thoughts like these to other children of their age. A 16-year-old whose mother has AIDS, which some children in New York refer to as "the skinny disease," tells an interviewer she "has never told a single friend" about her mother's illness. "It's like I always carry this big secret. . . ." An eight-year-old says that when he feels afraid or sad while he's at school, he goes into the bathroom, to a toilet stall, and flushes the water so that nobody can hear him cry.

Other children seem to be miraculously free from morbid thoughts and focus with exaggerated energy on the good things life may still afford them. Several children I have met in the South Bronx who have seen their mothers die of AIDS are living with their fathers. Some of their fathers have tested positive for HIV. Others have been afraid of being tested. Despite the fears with which they live, and many other problems that they face, some have used the meager funds they have to make their homes into safe-feeling, happy places.

One of these families of survivors—a father and his daughter—live on a street with many boarded-up, abandoned buildings, close to Yankee Stadium, where they share their small apartment with a puppy by the name of Pork Chop, another dog whose name I do not know, two cats, a turtle, and six goldfish, which, on the day I visit, inhabit a half-foot of water in the bathtub. The father, a former heroin user in recovery on methadone, was forced to move here with his daughter from a nicer neighborhood in Harlem close to Central Park, because the city agency that gave the family rent support as long as the child's mother was alive has cut their rent assistance since her death. "In the eyes of the government the case is closed," explains a social worker from a charitable organization who arranged my meeting with the family.

The family was getting a $900 rental subsidy each month in Harlem. Now, the father says, "I pay $286. It's all we have."

The child, who is nine years old and named for a spring flower, has idyllic memories of Harlem. When I ask her why she liked it there, she says, "Because I could ride my bike in Central Park."

"You don't ride it here?"

"No," she answers. "It's too dangerous to go outside."

"What is the danger?"

"The drug dealers," she replies.

"What do you fear?"

"They snatch children away."

"Where are the drug dealers?"

"Right downstairs there—by the store."

"What are they doing there?"

"Eating powder," she replies.

"Is there any safe place here to play?"

"There's no such thing as safe around here," says her father. "This here is a burial ground. People walk the streets like they're already dead."

"They are tired of living," says the child, "and they have no hope."

The child and her father are avid Yankees fans. She tells me she has dreams of playing for the Yankees when she is grown up. Their house is seven blocks from Yankee Stadium, but the child has never seen a game.

"The tickets are expensive," says her father. He shows me a jar in which they are collecting coins. "We're saving up. Someday we're going to go."

The child shows me her baseball mitt and her stuffed animals and dolls. In her closet there are several pretty dresses.

"Who picks out your clothes?" I ask.

"My daddy does. He buys my clothes. He takes me to the store. He cleans. He cooks. He teaches me. He plays with me. He irons my dress. He combs my hair and cuts my hair."

"Who cuts your daddy's hair?"

"I do," she says, "and sometimes I make coffee for him

in the morning and I make French toast for him and bring it to him in his bed and we have breakfast."

Noting that the father is bilingual, I ask the child if she speaks Spanish also.

"Only an inch," she answers.

There are so many pets in the three rooms! The apartment feels as if it has been pumped with life. I ask her, "Where do all these animals sleep?"

"Pork Chop sleeps with me," she says. "Cecil sleeps with the goldfish in the bathtub. This cat here and that dog there sleep with my daddy. This little kitty has to sleep under the bookcase because she's been bad. She's being punished."

I ask her what she feeds them.

"Cecil," she says, "eats turtle food. The cats eat cat food." Pork Chop and the other dog, she says, "eat beans and rice."

"Why don't you feed them dog food?"

"Beans and rice are cheaper," says her father. "Alpo costs $1.09 a can."

"Do you say your prayers?" I ask the child.

"Yes," she says. "At night. Before I go to sleep."

"What do you pray?"

"I pray for my daddy and my mommy."

"Do you ever try to picture where your mommy is?"

"My mommy is in heaven."

Her father goes into the kitchen to make supper. The smell of rice and beans and spices starts to fill the house. As I leave, he's putting a big pile of shrimp into a frying pan. Ensconced on the sofa with her puppy curled up at her side, the child looks snug and secure.

"I wish I was rich enough to give her everything she wants," her father told a journalist some time before.

Downstairs on the street, as I look up at their apartment building, it occurs to me that he's already giving her a lot—maybe even more than many wealthy fathers give their children. I don't know too many men who iron dresses for their children or who cut their hair. He has told me, however, that he has a heart condition. His two brothers have died of AIDS. He did not tell me if he also is infected, and it may be that he does not know, but I had the feeling that he does not wish to look too far into the future.

Later, I describe this family to a counselor who works with HIV-infected men and women at an agency close to Mott Haven. "I know a great many families who remind me of this man and his young daughter," he remarks. "Really, it is very beautiful to see what happens to these men, to some of them at least. Once they look into the face of death, some of them begin to live for the first time. Even those who know they are infected, and may not have long to live, sometimes go through an inner change that brings to mind a kind of 'resurrection.' I have heard men *use* that word. 'AIDS is my resurrection!' Men who lived in a narcotic cloud for 15 years open their eyes and notice everything. They see the trees and animals and birds! They finally see their children! They learn how to shop and how to cook. Ordinary little things they never knew and never noticed become precious. So, in this way, on the edge of death, they start to live."

His optimism suddenly expires. "For the mothers, of course, these blessings come too late."

He gets up from his chair, walks to the window, and looks out for a long while on an avenue of boarded stores beneath an elevated subway track. I have seen many adults like him, social workers, nurses, teachers, doctors, having to fight off tears this year while we were talking. Some become hardened by the things they see; some become bureaucratized by protocol and jargon; many do not. Their hearts remain open to the suffering that has been packed into their neighborhoods. Even if they live at a good distance from the Bronx, these memories stay with them and some tell me that they find it hard to sleep.

Whenever I feel discouraged by the sheer accumulation of sad stories I've been told, I look for an excuse to go back to the elementary school on Cypress Avenue, because, although the things the children talk about are often sad, their unexpected ways of saying them seem to refresh the world. If possible, I spend time with them also in the playground during recess, since the energy released out in the schoolyard tends to make their comments more spontaneous and natural and less inhibited.

When I look through my notes after a day like this, I'm often fascinated by the names of many of the young black children I have met, especially the little girls. Some are African names, as well as poetically beautiful invented names that have an African sound. Increasingly, however, in the past few years, biblical names have come to be more popular again—or names that, while not literally biblical, evoke a biblical feeling and convey a powerful sense of gratitude to God. Some also symbolize a wish to mark a new departure from the bitterness or sorrows of the past.

"When I left the house of bondage," said Sojourner Truth, whose given name from her slave childhood was Isabella, "I left everything behind. I went to the Lord and asked Him to give me a new name." She did not want, she says, "to keep nothin' of Egypt on me"—"and the Lord gave me Sojourner. . . . Afterwards I told the Lord I wanted another name, 'cause everybody else had two names; and the Lord gave me Truth. . . . 'Thank you, God,' I said. 'Thou art my last master and Thy name is Truth.' "

I have never met a child named Sojourner in New York, but more than one who was named Charity, one in Roxbury named Prudence, one in New Orleans named Felicity (possibly for a street of that name close to where she lived), and a baby girl in the South Bronx named Easter. "She was born in the spring and I was hopeful, prayin' for a better life, for something better," said her mother, who had also, like Sojourner, done domestic work for many years.

One day, in a kindergarten class at P.S. 65, I met a truly angelic-looking child with a round face who was so affectionate and trusting that a mother who was helping in the classroom bent way down impulsively and gave her a big kiss when the child came right up with open arms and hugged her.

During a song-and-story period, the child sat on the floor with the other children, sucking on one thumb and holding her other hand around one of her ears. A boy sitting beside her, a thumb in his mouth too, was sound asleep. His head was resting on her shoulder. When the teacher sang a song to the children but forgot one line, all the children giggled, but this little girl laughed on and on, as if it were the funniest thing that ever could be.

When I asked the mother what this little girl was named, she brought her hands together as if to recite a prayer. "Her name is Destiny! God bless her!"

Destiny's name, I found, was neatly written on a card taped by the teacher to her desk. I later asked if she would copy it for me on a piece of drawing paper. She gripped a pencil in her hand and wrote it once, then reached for a purple crayon and wrote it several times again. She did it slowly and seemed to take tremendous satisfaction in the shaping of each letter.

Destiny's name, although unusual, is no more so than the names of many other children at the school. In another kindergarten class, I met a child, with her hair in beaded cornrows, named Delilah. Later, in a fifth grade class, I met a tall and beautiful child named Mahogany, who turned out to be the older sister of Bernardo Rodriguez. Her eyes were filled with a smoldering anger that intensified her beauty but also made it somewhat frightening.

Some months before, in one of the poorest homes I've ever visited, I met a baby girl named Precious. The chubby infant sat on a sofa by my side, staring at me with the greatest concentration while she held one of my fingers. I asked her mother how she chose this name.

"When I was pregnant," she replied, "I said to God, 'I want a healthy child. I want a pretty little girl who has long hair and I don't want no dummy.' He gave me *exactly* what I ordered!

"For what you want," she said, "you got to be specific. One time I asked Him for a handsome man and that's exactly what I got: a handsome man and nothin' else. No brains, no money, no religion. I cannot deal with an ignorant man who don't believe in nothin'. So I said, 'Next time I got to be specific. . . .'"

I asked her if she belonged to a church.

"I do," she said, "but I don't need to go to church to

pray. If I want, I go in the kitchen and I pray right there. I get on my knees and send it up!"

I asked her what she prays for.

"I pray to God to give my baby a better life, something more interesting. . . . I'm lookin' at a doctor or a lawyer."

"Do you believe God hears your prayers?"

"God hears. He sit up high and look low, even here," she said with confidence.

When I asked about her own job prospects, she said she was in a program at a community college, where she was receiving training in "domestic services." I have since met other mothers in the South Bronx and in Harlem who have told me that they studied "domestic sciences" in high school and also, in one instance, in the Job Corps.

A 30-year-old woman whom I met once on the train, who was returning with her daughter from a trip to Sing Sing, where she had been visiting her husband, a life prisoner, told me she'd attended Taft and felt it had prepared her well for her employment. I asked her what she did, and she replied she was a cook and household maid in Riverdale. Her daughter, a five-year-old, was named Leticia, but, she said, "Her grandma calls her Blessing." She and Leticia sang together in the choir at her church, she told me.

I asked the child, who wore patent-leather shoes and a frilly pink dress of the kind a little girl might put on for a party, if she would sing a song for me.

"You don't need to slay the lamb no more . . . ," the child sang, a gospel song I'd never heard before.

Her mother pinched her cheeks after she sang the song. "She's smart—but pouty! *Aren't* you?" she said, looking at the child. She told me that Leticia would start school the next September.

"I have the highest hopes for her," she said.

On a mild night in early May, rain falls intermittently on Boston Road as I walk up the hill to Mrs. Washington's apartment building from East Tremont.

David isn't home. "He's at Charlayne's," says Mrs. Washington as I come in.

She looks well and says that she's been feeling so much better that she's thought of looking for a job. "I asked my doctor if he knows someone who needs a secretary. He says he's not sure I can do it, but I'd like to try."

Although I tell her I'm not hungry, she insists on cooking a delicious dinner of linguini, lima beans, and chicken. Later, we have ice cream for dessert.

While we eat, I ask her if she got a letter that I sent her with a picture of my parents, which she had asked to see, but she says she never got it. "You go a month or so and get your mail. Then nothing. Then you find somebody else has got your letters and your bills. Or else you find that no one got them. You don't know.

"A couple weeks ago, the mailman said that he was followed in our building by two guys. The word was out. 'They're goin' to get the mailman.' So he kept the mail and held it a few days. He was right. He had no choice. If they steal the bag, they take the checks and cash and throw the rest away."

"Have you lost important mail?"

She laughs. "How can I tell? If it's important and it's lost, I'll never know! The trouble is you lose the letters that you wish you got and get the ones that you don't want.

"Two weeks ago," she says, "I got a letter from my welfare office. Said my check was bein' cut in half. It was a form letter. In the place where they fill in the reason, somebody had put, 'Your son David got married.'

"The letter's got my name misspelled and has my welfare number wrong. It's also got my budget wrong. It says I get $330 and I don't. I get $206, which I get twice a month, plus food stamps—$550 total in a month. That's what I live on. So they got it wrong from one end to the other.

"I wish I had this letter so that you could see it. It looks like a child wrote it. I gave it to David because it was hard to read. He said it looks like it was written by a person in the second grade.

"I called my doctor's social worker and she said to wait three days and see what happens when I go to get my check. I went yesterday to the check-cashing. The man put in my card. Out came a piece of paper. He looked at it, then told me, 'Let me have your card again.' I gave him back my card. He did it four more times and then he said, 'These bastards only gave you $50.' He knows me there. He knows I'm sometimes out of breath. He looked at me and said, 'Are you all right?' I said, 'No. I am not.'

"I was goin' to go and pay my phone bill but I knew I couldn't pay it now, but still I got mixed up when I came out and got on the first bus. After I got my seat I didn't know why I was on the bus, because I live two blocks from the check-cashing. So I got off the bus and came back to the house and stood outside and felt confused and I came in and then I cried. I said to myself, 'I'm tired now. I'm tired.' So I cried for a while. When I stopped crying I got mad.

"If it wasn't the time it was, I would have got back on the bus and gone down to the welfare office, but it was too late. Maybe it's good I didn't go because I think I would have got myself in trouble."

"What do you mean—in trouble?"

"If you go to welfare and you don't have an appointment," she replies, "the guard asks you to leave. I wouldn't have left, because I was so angry. But if you refuse to leave, they sometimes call the cops."

"Have they ever done that to you?"

"Once. Two years ago. The same thing happened. I was cut off for no reason. I went in and asked them what they thought that they were doing and they said they couldn't say because they lost my folder. Lost my name and lost my records. So I said that I would wait and they could look for it. Supervisor said, 'You have a lot of nerve.' She called security. The guard was not too rude to me but he was drunk. Three o'clock in the afternoon. He smelled of wine.

"He asked me, 'Are you goin' to leave?' So I said, 'No.' I lost my temper and I told him, 'Get out of my face. I see that you've been drinking.' So they called the cops. Cops are sometimes nicer to you than the social workers. Cop just told her, 'Find this lady's records.' It only took ten minutes. I said to her, 'You could have done it all along and saved me all this trouble.' She wouldn't look at me. She stepped away. I think that she got scared."

"Got scared of what?"

"Got scared that I would hit her."

"Have you ever hit a social worker?"

"No. I've never done it but there's always a first time. Don't ever say what you would or would not do, because you never know. I hope I'm never forced to that. I think I'm too old to go to jail."

Attached to her key chain on the kitchen table is a can of blinding spray about the size of a fat pencil and a knife the blade of which, she says, is seven inches long. "It's not against the law. The limit is eight inches."

"Have you ever had to use it?"

She doesn't directly answer. "I know how to if I have to."

The thought of her wielding a seven-inch knife, or beating up a social worker, is almost impossible to reconcile with her appearance, which is as middle class as that of my mother and most of my mother's friends. She dresses, in fact, very much the way my mother does: in dark gray skirts and fashionable long sweaters and smart-looking shoes that might have come from Lord & Taylor but which she buys at a discount store on the Grand Concourse. The effort she puts into dressing stylishly, keeping her apartment neat and clean, putting pretty decorations on the walls and happy faces on the door of the refrigerator, like the care she takes to send attractive cards to anyone who's kind to her and to every neighbor who has lost a parent or a child, keeps reminding me of her terrific, gutsy, absolute refusal to allow herself to feel abased by the indignities that have been heaped upon her. Even in telling me some of those stories that involve a great deal of humiliation at the hands of hospital or welfare personnel, she usually manages to find something that's funny in the madness of it all and keeps on saying things that make both of us laugh.

"In February at the hospital," she says, "they had to keep me four days down there in the waiting room. While I was waiting one night by the entrance where the ambulance comes up, a doctor talked with me. He said, 'I think you may be clinically depressed.' Bad as I felt, I had to laugh. There I was, with an IV in my arm, in all this noise, with bloody bodies coming in, police, and everybody crying, looking frantic and upset. He says I seem 'depressed'!

"I asked him, 'How would you like to be here on a stretcher for four nights in all this mess?'

" 'I see your point,' he said.

"I didn't want to hurt his feelings, but the way he said that made me laugh!"

Once she got into a room, she says, "I had a different doctor every day. One day, I had a doctor who was from Nigeria. The next day, I had somebody from Pakistan. That night, I had a doctor from the Philippines or China. I said, 'Excuse me? How many different doctors am I s'posed to have?' One doctor said that I had had heart damage. Another doctor said my heart was fine but that I might have meningitis. Each one told me something different. I told the Pakistani doctor, 'Why don't all of you go out for dinner someplace and decide what's wrong with me, so I will know how I am going to be treated?'

"Some of the doctors are from countries that I've never even heard of. They don't speak English. They speak 'combination languages.' My doctor at the clinic is the only one I know who is American.

"I asked my nurse, 'Where are all the doctors from America?' She made a comment that was not polite.

"Another time, I was up there on the fourteenth floor. It was the middle of the night and I heard someone open up my door. Then it happened a second time, and then a third time. I got up. I didn't want some stranger coming in. You hear of patients bein' raped there in their beds. I turned on the light and there was a grown man staring at me in a wheelchair. He was sittin' right there by my door.

"Ten minutes later, the nurse comes in because she'd heard me scream. This was a nurse I'd never seen before. She says, 'Mrs. Washington, do you have a complaint?' I told her, 'Yes. There was a man I don't know in my room. He was sittin' right there in a wheelchair.' She says, 'Now, Mrs. Washington! Please calm yourself. We don't want you to get a heart attack.' She helped me get back in my bed and took my pulse. She said it was high because I'd been so scared.

"I told my doctor, 'If I ever check out of the hospital real fast, you'll know the reason why.'"

Sometimes humor becomes interwoven with real tenderness. "Another time when I was there," she says, "there was a man in the bed right next to mine. I felt like I was a college student in a coed dorm."

"I didn't know that they put men and women in the same rooms," I reply.

"It's like two rooms—but with the same alcove," she explains. "I was here and he was over there. This man was terminally ill and knew he wasn't goin' to leave. Very thin. He had big tumors on his neck. Kept talkin' about 'Agent Orange' all the time. He said he was a veteran and should have been in the VA. Nobody ever came to see him.

"When my kids came in to visit, I said, 'Go and visit with him too.' He used to say, 'I'm tired. I've been through enough.' He kept on saying he was tired. You know, Jonathan, everyone gets tired.

"In this ward," she says, "you see a lot of older people walkin' back and forth in their pajamas. Some of them are almost naked but they're friendly to each other and they smile. I seen one woman sittin' on another patient's lap. Her arms was around his neck and they were kissing. I think this woman has Alzheimer's. . . .

"The nurses at the hospital," she says, "try hard to be nice to you. They stop and talk whenever they can. But they're worn out. They got too much to do. One of the nurses that I know says that it's goin' to get worse because the city's plannin' to cut back again."

I ask how she reacts each time she hears these statements about cutbacks caused by "fiscal shortages," which, it seems, are now reported in the papers almost every day when budget questions are discussed. "I know that you don't buy these arguments," I add, not wanting to pretend that I do not know something of her feelings on the matter.

"Of course I don't. I've told you that before. This is a rich city. All you need to do is read the ads. I saw an ad for a brassiere that costs $800! Women who pay money like that for a brassiere must think their chest is made of gold. Are you goin' to tell me that these people are too poor to pay their share?"

I mention the term "compassion fatigue," which has also been in the newspapers many times in recent months. "The idea," I say, attempting to explain the way the term seems to be used, "is that it isn't so much lack of money but more like a feeling of exhaustion people get from reading about so many problems and not seeing anything get better."

"I don't understand what they have done to get so tired," she replies with an enjoyable sarcasm. "When I was in the Holland"—the hotel for homeless people near Times Square in which she lived for a short time—"I got tired and my kids got tired carryin' water buckets up the stairs when we were on the seventh floor. Maybe the wealthy people and reporters down there got exhausted just from watching us.

"Somebody once said this is the biggest city with the smallest spirit in the world."

"Do you agree?"

"I don't have no way to know," she says. "I've never lived in any other city. This is the only one I got."

After dinner, we talk about the years when she was growing up in New York City, which were the early 1960s. She speaks of the death of President Kennedy and of the time a few years later when his brother Robert ran for the U.S. Senate from New York. These memories, for both of us, awaken other memories from the same period: Dr. King in Washington and Birmingham, Malcolm X in Harlem, the freedom struggles in the South, the political hopes that soared so high, so briefly, in Chicago and New York.

"Do you think it will happen again?" I ask.

"Nope," she says. "I don't. Not in New York. Not while you and I are still alive." She shakes her head and smiles, maybe with nostalgia, maybe with amusement at my own nostalgia.

"If anything happens, I think it will be more violent than that."

"That sounds a little like Armageddon," I say.

"That isn't what I mean. I told you that I don't believe in things like that. I'm thinkin' of what happened in Los Angeles. Real fires, not imaginary ones."

I do not ask her, as I might have done a few months earlier, if she really believes that this could happen in New York. But she sees the question in my eyes.

"Yes. It could happen. It would only take one little spark to set it off."

"Do you think that wealthy people understand that this can happen?"

"Nope," she says again. "I don't. I think they see poor people broken down so bad they don't think *nothin's* goin' to happen. But people who don't have no hope are dangerous. City's worried about the squeegee men? That ain't nothin'! What if all these mothers and grandmothers that have lost their babies ever got real mad?"

"When they're mad," I say, "it seems like they get mad at their own neighbors. Do you think they really look at anyone downtown?"

She doesn't answer and, instead, brings the discussion to an end, as she has often done when we have talked of things like this before, by bringing our speculations back to solid earth.

"Want some coffee?"

She goes to the stove and pours the coffee into two big mugs and sets them on the table and sits down.

Despite some of the worried statements she has made, there has been a sense of deep serenity, a sweet, relaxed, and happy feeling, in her voice most of the evening. Her daughter, she tells me, is about to graduate from college. David, she adds in an almost hesitant voice as if she fears that talking about something good may make it go away, has just been accepted to City University.

"Did he get financial aid?"

"He got it all. The whole deal. He starts in September."

She stirs her coffee and is silent for a while.

"I lived for this, you know. This is what I dreamed of. Now it's going to be true. He wants to be a prison officer."

"I know," I say.

"I'm proud of him. He had a hard time when we lost our home. He went through things that children shouldn't have to face. He never had nothin' handed to him. But he came out a nice person."

I look at her with curiosity. "Why did you save this up to tell me now? You could have told me this when I came in."

"I don't know why. I was afraid. . . . Sometimes you want to save something awhile and just think of it yourself and not tell anybody else. . . . I wanted to surprise you."

"You succeeded! I'm surprised!" Then, more honestly, I add, "I guess I knew that he'd get in."

"I knew it too. But now it's true. It's there. It's his. And I feel happy."

Then she really cries. "I'm happy," she says, smiling through her tears, and she keeps saying it, "I'm happy. Something good has happened. Something *good!* No one can take that from him now." It is the first time that I've seen her cry this way, without embarrassment, without constraint, without trying to conceal it.

The rain, which has been intermittent all night long, seems almost to have matched the rhythms of our conversation, steady for a while, then really coming down, and now subsiding altogether. By the time I leave, the sky is clear. There are bright stars overhead. The neighborhood seems almost cheerful and the air smells clean.

The next afternoon, Anthony meets me in the garden of St. Ann's and takes me for a walk to see the building where he lives, a few blocks to the west and north, close to Third Avenue, and the building where his grandmother lives, which is a little to the south and which he says he likes to visit because "my grandma feeds me."

His grandmother, he tells me, is "the happiest person that I know."

"Why do you think it is," I ask, "that she's so happy?"

"I don't know why. I think that feeding people makes her happy." Children from the neighborhood, he says, come to her house and she makes icies for them and bakes cookies. "I think that she likes children more than grown-ups."

His uncle, however, who lives with his grandmother, is, he says, "not happy. He has many troubles."

His eyes look worried when he says this.

"Anthony, what troubles does your uncle have?"

"Mr. Jonathan, my uncle is a sick man. He has AIDS."

When I ask how he knows about his uncle's sickness, he replies, "My grandma told me but I thought of it before she told me. Did you ever notice how some people who have AIDS are always eating sweets?"

"I didn't know that."

"Yes. It's true," he says. "Every day is he buying licorice sticks. He eats them all day long. But when he sits at the table at dinnertime, he does not eat at all. He comes to the table stumbled up. His eyes look bad. He falls asleep into his soup."

"What does he do during the day?" I ask. "Does he go out and visit friends?"

"Yes, he goes out. How can I say this? He goes out but he stays in. He stays inside himself. He does not look at people. He looks down. The man looks at the ground. I don't know why. I think that he's afraid to look up at the world."

"Anthony, is your uncle a drug user?"

"That," he answers, "is something that I do not want to know."

"Do you cry for your uncle?"

"Yes, I cry. It's not a sin to cry."

"Do you know other children who cry?"

"Many cry."

"Do you know children who are happy?"

"Truly happy? No."

"Happy at all?"

"Not many. . . . Well, to tell the truth, not any who are happy for more than one day." Then he corrects himself: "No! Not for one day. For 15 minutes." He thinks this over, as if to check that he is being accurate, then repeats, "Not any. That's no lie."

I wonder at times if a sense of the dramatic might lead

Anthony to overstate his answers to my questions, so I challenge him by telling him that I've met children in the schoolyard who seem cheerful.

"Cheerful? Yes. Happy is not the same as cheerful," he replies.

"I think there are certain children who are happy anywhere," I tell him. But he holds his ground.

"Whenever you see a child who enjoys life in this neighborhood, come and see me right away. I'll have to go and see a doctor."

He stops at that moment and waves his hand around him at the neighborhood. "Would you be happy if you had to live here?"

"No, Anthony. I wouldn't."

We walk as far as Alexander Avenue, then circle back. As we walk, we pass a painted memorial to a victim of gunfire that has been partly whited over in one of the periodic cleanups by the city. A name and date can still be read, however. Sometimes, Reverend Overall has told me, the city needs to use sand-blasters to remove these tributes to the dead.

On 140th Street, as we pass the memorial to Moondog, I see the mother of the slain man on the steps of a Lutheran church next door, of which, as it turns out, she is the deacon. Jovial as before, she is surrounded by a group of children. When I introduce her to Anthony, he asks her, "Do you have confession in this church?"

"No," she says.

"Do you have communion?"

"Yes."

"Can I have a glass of water?"

"Of course."

She asks one of the children to take Anthony inside the church. When he comes out, he thanks her and we cross the street and head back to St. Ann's. Passing a mother with her baby in a carriage, Anthony bends very low and peeks under the hood. "God bless her," he whispers. Then, seeing a man with short gray hair staring at a vacant lot ahead of us, he says, "Excuse me, sir. I want to introduce you to my uncle."

Anthony's uncle looks up when he hears his nephew call his name, but seems confused. He stands there on the sidewalk with a razor blade in one hand, carefully held between his forefinger and thumb, and a cigarette in the other. In order to shake hands he drops the razor blade. His reaction to seeing his nephew, and to meeting me, is more like a nonreaction. He does seem, as Anthony said, "inside himself." After an awkward moment, he just nods and then goes on.

"Do you know what the shortest verse in the Bible is?" asks Anthony.

"No," I say. "I don't."

"Jesus wept," he answers.

His uncle moves on toward a corner where a man is selling stalks of sugar cane. The green stalks, which look nearly six feet tall, are tied in bundles of about a dozen each. For those who wish, the man who runs the stand scrapes down a length of cane and puts it through a juicer.

"What does it taste like?" I ask Anthony.

"It's too sweet," he answers. "I don't like it."

Back in the garden of St. Ann's, sitting on a bench, he shows me a little spiral notebook that he carries with him at almost all times. On one page he's written "THEOLOGY" and, next to this, "The science which studies things that God has made."

I ask him if he's ever thought of studying to be a preacher.

He answers, a bit annoyingly, with a question. "Do you know who Samuel was?"

"In the Bible?"

"Yes," he says.

When I tell him that I don't remember very much of Samuel, he replies, "Don't worry. I'll tell you the story." Then, like a Sunday school teacher, he begins, "Samuel had been born by miracle. God had closed his mother's womb. That means she couldn't have a baby. . . .

"So his mother prayed to God. She said, 'Lord, if you let me have a baby, I will give him back to you.' This meant she would put him in God's service.

"Now, wait! One day, while Samuel was doing his job,

whatever it was, he heard a voice calling to him from the sky. 'Samuel! Samuel! Where are you?' said the voice. So he got scared and went to the rabbi, and the rabbi said, 'Next time you hear it, answer, "Here I am! What do you want with me, Lord?" So, the next time he heard the voice, he did what the rabbi said. He said, 'What do you want?' And God said, 'I have chosen you to be my prophet.' So he said, 'Okay.' "

He stops there. So I ask, "What happened next?"

"So he became a prophet! And he prophesied that a boy named David would be king. David was just a shepherd but that didn't matter. God had decided. He told Samuel, 'This is the one. He will be king.' So Samuel said, 'This child will be king.' So David became king. And Samuel became a prophet. And that's the story."

"Anthony, why did you tell me this story? Do you want to be a prophet too?"

"I would be happy if God called on me," he answers. "Happy? No! Let me revise that. I would be excited! I would say, 'Here I am! I'm here, Lord! Over here! I'm down here in the garden.' " But then, thinking it through again, he says, "To tell the truth, if God chose me to be a prophet, I would be grateful but I'd also be a little sad because then I would know I couldn't be a novelist."

"Why not? You couldn't be both?"

"No. I think you have to be one or the other."

With curious eyes he asks me suddenly, "How long does a story have to be for it to be a novel?"

I tell him that I don't know any rule about this.

"Is 22 pages long enough?"

"That may be a little short."

"Oh," he says, and seems quite disappointed.

He mentions that since we met the last time, he's been reading novels of Mark Twain but that he still values Edgar Allan Poe over all other writers and has even bought a picture of the writer's mother, who, he says, "was beautiful."

I try to switch the subject back to some of the more ordinary details of his life by asking him about his mother's home. "Do you still sleep in the living room?"

"Yes," he says.

"Do you mind that you don't have a bedroom?"

"No," he answers. "I don't *want* a bedroom. I am not ambitious for a bedroom."

"What are you ambitious for?"

"I'm ambitious for more books," he says, and rapidly switches the subject back to literary matters. "Mr. Jonathan, I have not told anybody this, but I would like to be buried in the place where Edgar Allan Poe is buried."

"Where is he buried?"

"He's buried in Virginia."

Punctilious, however, about details, he corrects himself again. "No, wait! He was buried in Virginia. That was first. Then they dug his body up and sent it somewhere else."

"Where did they send it?"

"To another city. I don't know which one."

After a moment, he asks me, "Did you know he was adopted?"

"No. I didn't know that."

"Yes, it's true. He was, because his parents were too poor to keep him. Anyway, they were about to die. The only thing they could afford to do was keep his brothers, but not him. But, come to think of it, they couldn't afford his brothers either. So they gave them all away. All he had was a picture of his mother. Even I have a picture of his mother." And he says again, "His mother was beautiful."

Many children in Mott Haven who, like Anthony, do not have a bedroom have a hard time finding quiet places to do homework. I ask him, "Where do you do your writing?"

"In the closet of my brother's bedroom. With a flashlight," he replies.

"When you visit Mr. Castro, do you show him what you're writing?"

"It's like this. I ring the bell. He says, 'Who is it?' I say, 'Me.' Then I go in. We sit in his living room and talk about a lot of things. He reads what I've written and gives me a grade and sometimes he gives me a soda or a glass of juice and tells me what he's written."

"What is he writing now?"

"He's writing a poem about the Incas."

"Do you think that he's a happy person?"

"I think he is pleased with life."

"Do you think of Mr. Castro as a wise man?"

"Very wise, because he's read so many books. How can I put it? Talking to Mr. Castro is like talking to the *Encyclopaedia Britannica*."

"Do you have your own encyclopedia?"

"Yes," he says.

"Which one do you have?"

"*World Book*," he replies.

"How did you get it?"

"From the *defuntos*."

"What does that mean?"

"From the deceased."

I ask him to explain.

"I got it from my aunt—my mother's sister. When she died, she left it to me in her will."

Then, revising himself again, as he's done several times this afternoon, he says, "I think that the real reason Mr. Castro is so wise is probably because he's lived so long. The man is very, very old."

"How old would you like to live to be?"

"That's easy. One hundred and thirteen."

"That number's quite exact," I say. "How did you decide on that?"

"I'm 13. I'd like to live another 100 years."

"Why *exactly* 100 years?"

"I would like to live to see the human race grow up," he says.

He gets up abruptly from the bench and starts to pace around an old tree near us in the garden. "Mr. Jonathan," he says, "I have committed sins."

He stands half-hidden from me by the tree.

"Big sins?"

"Big enough. . . ."

"How big?"

"Well, not murder. . . . But I did some things I'm not supposed to do."

"Anthony, what sins did you commit?"

"I have taken food I wasn't supposed to have," he says. "Are you hungry sometimes?"

"Yes."

"What do you eat for dinner?"

"Oatmeal."

"Hot oatmeal?"

"No. Cold."

"With milk?"

"No. Plain."

"Do you like it?"

"It's not bad."

"What do you do if you're still hungry?"

"I go to my Grandma Ana's or I come here to the church and Mother Martha gives me food."

"Have you ever stolen food?"

"Yes," he says, still standing partly hidden by the tree.

"Did anyone see you?"

"You think that no one sees. But someone sees."

"Do you feel guilty when you do this?"

"Yes."

"What do you do?"

"I pray God to forgive me."

"Do you think that God is angry when you do this?"

He comes out from behind the tree and answers me like this: "When someone commits a sin, God turns His back on you because He's disappointed. He feels sad. But if you ask Him for forgiveness, it's as if you're knocking on His door. 'Hello? Wake up! It's me! Are you still mad?' Then He may turn to you again and give you His forgiveness."

"Do you forgive people who have hurt you?"

"I try, but I am not as strong as God. If I had the power I would give someone a second chance. The only one I wouldn't give a second chance is Pablo Escobar. He is the great drug dealer of the world."

"How have you heard of him?"

"I saw him on TV."

"Do you want him to be sent to hell?"

"Let's not say hell. Let's just say the place where there's no heaven."

I ask him if he ever sees the man whom he called "Mr. Mongo," an addicted man who, he had told me in December, often has tear-filled eyes.

"I have different feelings now. Mr. Mongo's not a happy man, but he sells drugs. I don't feel sorry for him anymore. He tried to get my brother."

"What did he do?"

"There's an old trick they have," he says. "It goes like this." He holds out both his hands wrapped into fists. "Choose one." I pick one hand. He opens it up and looks in his palm and smiles. "It's your lucky day, my friend!"

"What's in his hand?"

"White powder. Whichever hand you pick, there's powder in it."

"You've seen him do it?"

"I was there. He did it twice. I saw it."

"What did you say?"

"I said, 'Please, God, don't let him do it to my brother.' "

"What did your brother do?"

"He turned his back."

"Where is Mr. Mongo now?"

"He's in the jail."

I ask him finally something I'd asked in a different way at Christmas when he spoke about the plague. "Anthony, what would it take to make New York a place where children do not have to cry?"

"To answer that," he says, sitting beside me now with one leg underneath him and his hands around his shoe, "you can't ask somebody like me. I can't explain it, because I don't own it." Still holding his hands around his shoe, he says, "You'd have to go to somebody who owns New York."

"Who owns New York?"

"You'd have to ask that to somebody else. All I know is that it isn't me and isn't Mr. Castro and it isn't Mother Martha."

He gets up then and waves to Reverend Overall, who is coming down the steps that lead into the garden from the church. In her black robe, she walks across the churchyard to the place where we've been talking. When she draws near, he grows a little foolish and, talking too fast, he asks her the same question that he asked me just an hour before. "What is the shortest verse in the Bible?" He says it in a silly voice, as if it were a riddle.

The pastor smiles, as if to say, "You can't fool me! That's one I've heard before!" She pulls him close to her and, hugging him, she looks down at his scruffy hair, cut in a circle like that of a child in a children's book from olden days. Without sentimentality, but holding him very close, she answers, "Jesus wept."

The children in the afterschool program at St. Ann's line up at the kitchen counter in the basement of the church to receive their dinner of chicken nuggets, potatoes, vegetables, and apple juice from several mothers and grandmothers of the church. There are 36 children, two thirds of them girls. Approximately half are black; most of the rest are Puerto Rican. A young Hispanic man with watchful eyes and a solicitous black woman seat the children at three tables. Some of the girls are whispering and giggling. An imposing-looking woman, one of the grandmothers, comes out of the kitchen and just folds her arms. The children quiet down and clasp their hands. Reverend Overall, who is standing by the door, closes her eyes. The children say their prayer in lively unison, as if it were a football cheer:

> *God is good!*
> *God is great!*
> *Thank you for*
> *The food we eat!*
> *Amen!*
> *Be good!*

They dig into their dinner. Those who want get seconds, until all the food is gone. For dessert they get big pieces of chocolate cake with frosting.

Upstairs in her office, Reverend Overall says that An-

220

thony's uncle recently came close to death in Lincoln Hospital. When he recovered, he came to the church and she and Anthony baptized him. Another of Anthony's uncles, she tells me, is in prison.

His father, she says, is a kindly man who is separated from his wife but lives nearby and goes for walks with Anthony on Saturdays and, if he has any money, buys him lunch. He lives on checks from general relief, in exchange for which he works without pay at a park and recreation center for teenagers.

"Anthony's mother," she continues, "is a Pentecostal, so she doesn't come here very much and I don't know her well. I only know that she is a good woman and is desperately poor. She budgets carefully but has a hard time getting by. Just keeping food in the house is a real struggle.

"Do you know," she asks, "what Anthony eats for dinner?"

"He told me—oatmeal."

"Cold oatmeal. Out of the box."

"I can see why he comes here so often," I observe, incautiously.

"I hope that's not the only reason," she replies.

I tell her what Anthony said of his grandmother.

"Anthony's grandma," says the pastor, "is an extraordinary person. She comes to Bible study at the church. She cries, because she's seen what's happened to her son and is afraid for her grandchildren. But she's a pillar of the church. She comes here every Sunday to help out in the soup kitchen."

The dog adopted by the church lies flat on his stomach on her desk and studies her closely as she speaks. Stroking his head, the pastor says, "He has decided that my desk-top is his bed. He sits and stares at me while I am working on my sermons. Sometimes I have to make him move a little so I have some space to write."

While we are talking, the telephone rings. The pastor answers a number of questions about a bus trip that is scheduled to begin here at the church in a few days. When she hangs up, she tells me that the bus is being sent on

Mother's Day to take some of the mothers of the neighborhood to prison so that they can see their sons and daughters.

As day turns into darkness in the window, covered with a metal grate, that looks into the garden, she speaks again of Mrs. Blue, a woman who died two years before of cancer and had lived in Mrs. Flowers's building. Her younger son, who was 12 when she was dying and is now 14, lives with Reverend Overall and goes to junior high school in Manhattan. An asthmatic child during the years when he was growing up on Beekman Avenue, he is free of asthma now, she says, and doing well in school.

"When his mother was dying, there were many days when they did not have food. She went out one night and sold her medication, her prescription drugs, in order to buy groceries. When she was caught, her punishment was to have her 'catchment area' restricted."

She explains that "catchment area," an unpleasant expression I have heard before, is a term used by the health care system to refer to the medical service zone to which a welfare family is assigned. "They actually use this term," she says, "as if our people were like runoff from a sewer." The punishment, she says, restricted her to Lincoln Hospital.

"They think of Lincoln Hospital as a punishment?"

"It seems they do," she says.

In my pocket I have a card I picked up in the subway that announces what the president of the transit system has described as the new "gospel" that New York will henceforth "preach" in regard to subway beggars. "When you're on a train," the card instructs the passengers, "don't give money for *any* purpose. . . . The best way to help end panhandling is not to give. . . . Don't give."

I hand it to her and she looks at it awhile and seems reluctant to react. At last she says, "I'm surprised that he would dare to use a word like 'gospel.'"

The message on the card is cleverly constructed. It does not prohibit charity but recommends an arm's length version. If we feel upset, it says, "Look in the Yellow Pages under . . . Human Services."

I ask her, "Do you think that anyone will do that?"

"Not really," she replies. "I don't think that that's the purpose of it anyway. I don't think the point is charity but self-protection. I mean, emotional protection. Looking into the eyes of a poor person is upsetting because normal people have a conscience. Touching the beggar's hand, meeting his gaze, makes a connection. It locks you in. It makes it hard to sleep, or hard to pray. If that happened, you might be profoundly changed, the way that Paul was changed. Writing a check to the Red Cross or some other charity can't do that. What this card is really telling us is, 'Do not open up your heart. Don't take a chance! Send a check to us and we will do the touching for you.' That's why I think that this is sacrilegious.

"The message of the gospel is unalterably clear. 'Give to him that asketh thee, and from him that would borrow of thee turn not away.' Those are the words of Jesus." No exception, she notes, is made for the stranger who talks too loud in crowded trains, or who may be partially deceiving us about his actual condition, or who offends us by his importunity or by his dirtiness, or color.

"Do you think of this," I ask, "as a Judeo-Christian city?"

"I wish I could say yes, but I don't know. If it were, I doubt that we could lead the kinds of lives we do. I think that we'd be asking questions all the time. 'Where does my money come from? Who pays a price for all the fun I have? Who is left out? Do I need this bottle of expensive perfume more than a child needs a doctor or a decent school? What does it mean, in theological terms, when grown-ups can eat caviar while Anthony eats oatmeal? What does this say about a city's soul?' "

"Do you ever say things like that to rich people?"

"Sometimes. Yes. I once called a very well-known businessman." She names the man, whose photograph is often seen in the social pages of the Sunday papers, where he is described as a philanthropist. "He's one of the investors in the buildings you've been visiting," the complex in which Anabelle and Mrs. Flowers live. "I said, 'I want you to come to the neighborhood and see the way your tenants live.' He was cordial to me, but he said, 'My chauffeur's on vacation.' I'm not sure if he was joking. If he was, it wasn't a good joke."

"What did you think would happen if he came here?"

"I don't know. I guess I simply wanted him to see this for himself. I thought that it might get to him somehow. It's difficult, I think, for people who surround themselves with so much luxury to understand how *very* poor poor people are. I frequently forget it and I find myself surprised. . . .

"Do you know—I am the only member of this congregation with a car?"

"Virtually the only one?"

"The *only* one," she answers.

A child I met here in this church some weeks before had shared with me the Bible parable of the camel and the needle. When I had asked the child to explain it, she had told me, "He's too big. He can't get through the hole, because of his hump. The hump is big. The hole in the needle is too small. That's why the rich man can't get into heaven."

"Why?" I had asked. "Does he have a hump too?"

"I'm not sure about that part," she had replied. "But there's some reason."

When I repeat this conversation to the pastor, she smiles at the child's words but then reminds me that, from the vantage point of children in this neighborhood, anyone who can depart the South Bronx every night to sleep in a safe neighborhood, and certainly any writer who can pay for airline tickets back and forth between New York and Boston, is in a position that might not seem very different from that of the richest millionaire.

"Flying on a plane, sleeping overnight in a hotel, going sometimes into a nice restaurant—all that's like another world for children here," she says.

The dog, his head about eight inches from her face, pricks up his ears at the slight rise in her voice and peers into her eyes, then plops his nose down on the desk again and soon begins to snore.

We talk late. The children have gone home. The church is very still. Sirens can be heard from time to time, some backfires from exhaust pipes, but no gunshots.

224

The pastor rises at five A.M. She seldom seems to finish work much before ten at night. When people are sick, she takes them to the hospital. When their sons are arrested, she goes with them to court. When they are born, she baptizes them. When they die, she buries them. This afternoon I saw her with a wet mop and a pail, washing the church floor. Anthony teased her, so she lifted the mop and shook it in his face. He pretended to be scared and ran and hid behind a chair. She gave him a look, as if to say, "Don't mess with me." If she had remained a lawyer, she could be at home now getting ready to go out for dinner.

I can see why Anthony feels safe when he is here.

"Let the word of my mouth and the meditation of my heart be acceptable in Thy sight, O Lord," says Reverend Gregory Groover, the minister of Bright Temple in Hunts Point, as he stands before the altar at eleven o'clock on Sunday, the most segregated hour in America.

"I had rather be a doorkeeper in the house of my God than to dwell in the tents of wickedness," replies the congregation.

Beautifully dressed for Mother's Day, over 100 black and Hispanic women, many with large straw hats, and dozens of children and quite a few men, mostly Hispanic, fill the small white chapel on one wall of which I read, "I saw Him high and lifted up" and, on the opposite wall, "We are more than conquerors."

A choir of young adults stands in white-and-purple robes next to an organist who wears a bright-red hat and a boy who plays the drums, just to the right side of the altar. On the left side are a dozen children in white shirts or blouses and black pants or skirts. Two vases of pink flowers stand before the altar; in front of each, a child wearing a white surplice holds a Bible and a crucifix.

"O God!" says one of several older women who take turns before the altar. "Help us to be a lighthouse on the corner!"

The pastor introduces a white-haired woman, whom he asks to rise. Standing before her pew, she turns and nods. Then, searching the faces of the many younger women in the room, some of whom, it seems, have not been here before, she says, "I want you to know, if you don't have a mother living, you can find one here this morning in this church."

The children to the left side of the altar sing a fast, hand-clapping song, "All Things Come of Thee," and then surprise the congregation by walking down into the aisles, where they hug and kiss their mothers and grandmothers, after which they sing a slower and more tender song: "I Love You with the Love of the Lord."

After asking one of the poorest congregations in America "to make offerings for those less fortunate than we," and leaving time for the offering plate to pass across the room, Reverend Groover returns to the altar and asks another woman, "Sister Eunice Turtle," to stand up, and then a number of the other senior mothers of the church. Each is given a flower and fruit basket. One of the women, wearing a white dress and white hat with a black ribbon, weeps as she receives her gift.

"We thank you, O Lord, for the gift of motherhood," the pastor says. "We pray you to have mercy for all mothers, even those who may be out there walking in the streets." His voice is tender and not patronizing. "And show mercy, Lord, to the principalities and powers of our city, that they too may know Thy grace and be transformed."

"Somebody say 'Amen!' " he asks.

A woman in the seat beside me, who is cradling a baby in her arms, adds her voice to the voices of others who do as the pastor asks.

Another woman rises briefly to speak of "many who have died this week." Stocky and powerful-looking, with bristling short black hair, she lifts her arms above her. "He has stayed his hand and we are here! Help us to love each other!"

Barbara Ann Groover, a seminarian who is the pastor's wife, rises to give the sermon.

"Genesis 16," she says. "And Sarah, Abraham's wife, had a maidservant whose name was Hagar. And Abraham went in unto Hagar and God told Hagar that she would conceive.

"And Hagar fled into the wilderness. And the angel of the Lord found her by a fountain in the wilderness. And he said, Hagar, Sarah's maid, whence camest thou and whither wilt thou go? And she said, I flee from the face of my mistress. And the angel of the Lord said unto her, Behold, thou art with child and shalt bear a son, and shalt call his name Ishmael, because the Lord has heard thy affliction.

"And Hagar bare Abraham a son; and Abraham called his son's name Ishmael. . . .

"We're not going to worry about the sociologists today," the preacher says as she completes the reading of the lesson. "We're not going to talk about statistics. Hagar was a single mother. We know what the sociologists can tell us about *that*. I look to all the single mothers here today and those who will be mothers. You may not have an Abraham to stand beside you. But I want you to know God blesses every mother on this earth. I want you to know there is a song for *you*. I want you to know that Hagar went down on her knees beside the water in the wilderness and, like a tree standing by the water, she was not afraid, because God spoke to her and *told* her that He had engraved her child's name upon the palm of His own hand. 'Lift up the lad!' He said. And God opened her eyes and she saw the well of water and she went and filled the bottle with the water and she gave the lad to drink. . . .

"God cautioned her that Ishmael would not have an easy life, that he would feel hostility against his brothers. 'And he will be a wild man; his hand will be against every man, and every man's against him.' But God told her also she would raise up a great nation."

With tremendous feeling, more than any other preacher I have heard in many years, she trembles and prays, "In spite of living in Hunts Point, I can still rise and praise my mother and the offspring of my loins. In spite of oppression, in spite of bigotry, in spite of violence, O Lord, I can still thank You for my children!" Looking out beyond the front rows to the younger women in the back, she says to them, "When we are in pain, we ask, 'How can I see? Oh, how can I keep on?' "

In a thrilling and commanding voice, she answers in these words: "Go back and tell your children that, even in the wilderness of the South Bronx, God *sees* a mother and a child! Your children may be drowning in despair today but I want you to know that they will rise in glory! I want you to tell your children there is a song for *them* as well!

"Do not tell me that God does not see this mother! Maybe this 14-year-old girl has nobody to tell her Hagar's story. I want the mothers of this church to take that 14-year-old mother by the hand and comfort her and tell her God will see her too! I want you to tell these boys in prison, 'I am a woman! One day the God I see, you shall see also!' "

In a quieter voice, she says, "Sometimes it's not easy. Even with a father in the house it isn't easy. Still, I ask you to love the Lord that Hagar loved and not to be afraid. I know the Lord sees every mother in this church because your name has been inscribed upon His hand."

With organ music accentuating every shift in mood, she continues in rising and falling cadences for ten or 15 minutes more, then brings the sermon to a stirring end. In the silence following a chorus of "Amens," two young women rise from pews near the back of the church and walk shyly to the front. They are immediately surrounded by a number of older women, who embrace and welcome them. As the young mothers start to pray and weep and the older women stroke their heads and pray with them, the organist begins the most familiar of all gospel songs. At first nobody sings. Instead, the pastor speaks the words in a soft voice as some of the women move their lips. Around me, many women also move their bodies in their seats and start to sway.

Amazing grace! How sweet the sound
That saved a wretch like me.
I once was lost and now am found
Was blind but now I see.

Then the organ becomes louder and the congregation rises and the verse that Reverend Groover spoke is turned to music and the whole room sings. They end with the hopeful words of the fourth verse that I have read now several times at home. But reading it in Massachusetts and hearing it sung by people in Hunts Point are not the same.

When the service ends, people turn to those around them and shake hands and say, "God bless you." The woman beside me says, "God bless you" to her baby and then turns and says the same to me, but I am afraid to say it in return.

Reverend Groover invites me to have lunch upstairs with members of the church. After lunch, a couple who grew up here but now live out in the suburbs offer me a ride back to Mott Haven. I sit for the rest of the afternoon in the garden of St. Ann's and think for a long time of the sermon I have heard.

The preacher told the mothers of the church to tell their sons in prison, "I am a woman! One day the God I see, you shall see also!" She told the mothers, "I want you to know there is a song for *you*. . . . Your children may be drowning in despair today but they will rise in glory!"

I write this question on the back of the church program: "Then where is He? What is He waiting for? Come on, Jehovah! Let's get moving. Where's your sword?"

As soon as I write this down, I feel embarrassed by these thoughts. The words of the gospel songs I heard in church, like a stern reprimand, keep going through my mind.

There are children in the garden. Their playfulness is like a reprimand as well. The sweetness of the hour and the voices of the children soon dispel the feeling of irreverence I had fallen into. Their voices are like summer songs, not songs of pain. Several boys are walking single-file on the top rung of a wooden structure, daring one another to go all the way to a small platform at the end. Precariously balanced, they shout challenges to one another. How long will they be content to stay within this garden?

When it gets dark, I fish in my pocket for two quarters and go out on St. Ann's Avenue and buy an icie and walk up to Beekman Avenue, hoping to see Anabelle, but see no children there and head off finally to Brook Avenue, then to the train and the hotel, then to the Delta terminal, and then the plane. As the plane takes off, I try to get a look at Rikers Island, but I'm on the wrong side of the plane and it climbs fast into the clouds.

I look at my notes as the plane crosses Connecticut. I'm looking forward to getting home and sitting at my desk and trying to make sense of everything I've learned. But I don't really think I will make sense of anything and I don't expect that I'll be able to construct a little list of "answers" and "solutions," as my editor would like. I have done this many times before; so have dozens of other writers; so have hundreds of committees and foundations and commissions. The time for lists like that now seems long past.

Will the people Reverend Groover called "the principalities and powers" look into their hearts one day in church or synagogue and feel the grace of God and, as he put it, "be transformed"? Will they become ashamed of what they've done, or what they have accepted? Will they decide they do not need to quarantine the outcasts of their ingenuity and will they then use all their wisdom and their skills to build a new society and new economy in which no human being will be superfluous? I wish I could believe that, but I don't think it is likely. I think it is more likely that they'll write more stories about "Hope Within the Ashes" and then pile on more ashes and then change the subject to the opening of the ballet or a review of a new restaurant. And the children of disappointment will keep dying.

I think that Mrs. Washington is right to view the years before us with foreboding. I have never lived through a time as cold as this in the United States. Many men and women in the Bronx believe that it is going to get worse. I don't know what can change this.

Epilogue

On a hot weekend in July, I go back for a reunion with some of the friends that I have made in the South Bronx.

The children in the St. Ann's summer program have been taken to the country on the day that I return and Reverend Overall is with them. Because I have some hours free, I take a long walk in St. Mary's Park, the southern tip of which begins at Beekman Avenue.

A retired teacher who works as a reading volunteer at P.S. 65 told me a few months before that she grew up here in the neighborhood, attended P.S. 65, and used to spend her weekends in the park.

"They used to have little ponies and the children went for pony rides on Sundays. There was a balloon man. I remember that he used to put something like salt in the balloons to make a rattling sound. It was a wonderful place to spend an afternoon. There used to be beautiful flower beds and men who walked around with pointed sticks to pick up trash. There were trash baskets everywhere. The park was kept immaculate."

I asked her when this was.

"The 1940s," she replied.

The park is still a magnet for some families on a weekend afternoon, but instead of carefully tended flower beds and children riding ponies, one finds a tired-looking place with an apparently unseeded lawn, green in some spots, brown in others, and a baseball field surrounded by the concrete skeleton of bleachers from which half the wooden benches have, for some reason, been removed along one side.

Close to the Beekman Avenue side, on the day I visit, there is an antiviolence rally going on, sponsored by the Parks Department and the officers from Precinct 40.

Speeches are given by some politicians and officials lined up on a stage. A woman with a handheld microphone tells a crowd of about 400 children, "You can't control what you were born as, but if you can control *yourself*, our life will be more peaceful." A white official from the Parks Department tells the children, "Don't believe the things you hear. The Bronx is coming back."

A disc jockey from a radio station tells the crowd, "If you want a Hot 97 T-shirt, you got to come up and do a rap against crime." A man wearing a costume of McGruff the Crime Dog tells the children, "Just say no! Just say no!" The children are then asked by a policewoman named Officer Dandridge to chant in unison, "No!" to drugs and violence and "Yes!" to something else, which I can't hear because of static on the microphone.

Afterward, there is to be a double dutch competition; but the people from the city who are supposed to run the competition never do show up. A group of girls with jump ropes, wearing jerseys that say "Summer Fun," wait a long time and seem disappointed.

Finally, I walk back on a path littered with trash to Beekman Avenue, where a man with a metal hook for a right arm sits on a battered car-seat on the sidewalk. In his left hand he holds a bottle in a paper bag, which he lifts to his mouth from time to time. At 141st Street, the building opposite Anabelle's apartment house is blasted out: windows broken, some covered with plywood, some wide open. On the ground floor of the building, there are two windows covered with iron bars. A pair of mean-looking dogs sit in the openings of the windows with their slobbery, droopy faces sticking through the bars.

Near the end of the next block, I find myself walking directly toward a gray-haired man who, I realize when we're close, is Anthony's uncle. He's walking quickly with a nearly empty bottle in one hand and doesn't seem to see me. After I pass him, I stop and turn around to see where he is heading. At the moment I turn, he turns too. He looks a little puzzled, hesitates, then walks back several steps to shake my hand. "I met you at the church . . . ," he says, trying to place me, then goes on.

It is probably unrealistic to anticipate a time when ponies will return with the balloon man to St. Mary's Park. With overflowing waste bins, "rats as big as squirrels" foraging for food, "long-abandoned sandboxes . . . knee-deep with weeds," the *Daily News* observes, many of the hills and walkways of the park have come to be "hunting grounds" for murderers and drug dealers. The park's sole toilet, says a man who's come here since he was a child, is open only "a few days a month" and it is years since many of the drinking fountains worked. A bleak photograph in the paper bears the caption, "Children play amid garbage at St. Mary's Park."

In one of those minor details sometimes dug up by a diligent reporter, the paper notes that "239 of 277 swings" for children in Bronx parks aren't "in place" or "need repair." Trivial as it is, this disappointing detail seems to say it all.

Sometimes in St. Mary's Park, which I have revisited several times when I've been in New York, I have tried to picture what it would be like with flower beds in bloom, friendly men with pointed sticks walking around and stabbing bits of paper, grown-ups and their children having picnics, music playing, the lady who sells *coquitos* at her stand nearby. I've tried to picture Anthony and Anabelle and Reverend Overall and Mrs. Flowers and their friends and neighbors sitting together on the grass. I try to imagine a wave of excitement going through the crowd, the children jumping up and rushing down the hill toward St. Ann's Avenue, then coming back, their voices thrilled, ecstatic, telling everyone, "The ponies have come back!" Then the ponies enter the park. They come in a procession like something I've seen in Mexico, all on their own, with nobody to guide them, shaking their heads and jingling their bells, and then the balloon man comes and gives balloons to all the children. No politicians are giving speeches about guns. Nobody is chanting "No" to anything. Anabelle is jumping out of her mind. "There they are! There they are! The ponies have come back to be with us!" she cries.

* * *

At five o'clock, the children have returned to St. Ann's Church. Anthony is in the pastor's office, sitting on the floor beside the dog who has become the full-time tenant of the building.

"Guess what?" he asks as I come in.

"What?" I say.

"I'm going to Jerusalem!" he answers.

I don't even try to fathom what he means by this, but I must have a dubious expression on my face because he repeats it when the pastor comes into the room, as if he still is waiting to hear my response.

"It's the truth," she says. "The bishop decided to include him in a group that goes there every fall. I hope nothing goes wrong. It would be awful if they changed their minds."

A few weeks earlier, the TV news reported that a comet was expected to collide with Jupiter. "When Anthony heard this," Reverend Overall had told me on the phone, "he became alarmed and asked me to confess him. His grandmother told him the explosion might have some effect upon the earth and he was petrified." When the explosion turned out not to do the damage that he feared, she says, "he was tremendously relieved."

Talking with him in the garden, where we take the dog to have a walk, I ask him why the comet had alarmed him.

"My Grandma Ana said that the explosion from it could burn up the earth," he says—"and bye bye, world! No more this one [pointing to me], no more that one [pointing to the dog]. No more Anthony. No more Grandma Ana.

"It didn't happen. We're still here."

Like many kids his age, he's taken to wearing a Walkman, though he says he only has one tape. He's also had a haircut that has left him nearly bald along the sides but with a circle of dark hair still left on top. The humorous impression his appearance gives is of a Spanish friar from another century who wandered by mistake into the age of tape cassettes.

Once, some months before, when Anthony and I had talked, I had shared with him some of the things that other children in the neighborhood had said in trying to imagine heaven, which he refers to sometimes as "God's kingdom." When I told him what Anabelle had said, he pulled rank of 13 years of teenage wisdom over Anabelle, who was just 11, and he said, although politely, that he thought her comments immature. "I think that she's too young to understand."

With the unforgotten habits of a teacher, I had immediately proposed he write a paper for me to correct her misimpressions.

"A report?"

He suddenly looked put-upon.

"You could think of it more like a letter," I suggested, to placate him.

"Oh no!" he said.

"What's wrong?"

"Spelling!" he replied, making a bad face.

"Don't worry about spelling. I'm not giving you a grade. Just let me know your thoughts. You could do it during your vacation."

Smacking his head in a clownish way, he said, "Only I in all the world will have to do a homework paper in the summer!"

To my surprise, however, when I see him at the church, he says, "I did it." And he takes three pages from his spiral notebook, which, I notice, have many words crossed out and copied over. "Mother Martha," he confesses, "helped with spelling."

It turns out that my visit isn't timed too well because he has to go off somewhere with his mother for the evening. After he's gone, I stay in the garden and sit down and read what he calls his "report."

"God's Kingdom," it begins, much like a homework paper. "God will be there. He'll be happy that we have arrived.

"People shall come hand-in-hand. It will be bright, not dim and glooming like on earth. All friendly animals will be there, but no mean ones.

"As for television, forget it! If you want vision, you can use your eyes to see the people that you love. No one will

Anthony's heaven

look at you from the outside. People will see you from the inside. All the people from the street will be there. My uncle will be there and he will be healed. You won't see him buying drugs, because there won't be money. Mr. Mongo will be there too. You might see him happy for a change.

"The prophets will be there, and Adam and Eve, and all of the disciples except Judas. And, as for Edgar Allan Poe, yes, he will be there too, but not like somebody important. He will be a writer teaching students.

"No violence will there be in heaven. There will be no guns or drugs or IRS. You won't have to pay taxes. You'll recognize all the children who have died when they were little. Jesus will be good to them and play with them. At night he'll come and visit at your house.

"God will be fond of you.

"How will you know that you are there? Something will tell you, 'This is it! Eureka!' If you still feel lonely in your heart, or bitterness, you'll know that you're not there."

At the bottom of the last page he has written, "Check in back." I turn it over. On the back there is a picture of a bird with flapping wings. From the mouth of the bird, which is elongated and wide-open like the mouth of an alligator, he has drawn a line to a bubble, as in a cartoon. Inside the bubble he has written in big letters: "NEVER MORE!"

Anthony's Uncle Carlos dies in late October when cold weather comes. Anthony is prepared for it. His Grandma Ana says that Carlos was at peace before he died, but Reverend Overall says that he looked very tired at the end, "the way that people do when they are simply 'sick of being sick,' hoping perhaps they'll wake up in the morning and discover that it all had been a dream."

At his uncle's funeral, Anthony reads a passage he has chosen out of Revelation. "And I saw a new heaven and new earth, for the first heaven and the first earth were passed away. . . . And I heard a great voice out of heaven saying, Behold . . . , I make all things new. . . . And there shall be no more death, neither sorrow nor crying, neither shall there be any more pain: for the former things are passed away. . . .

"And God shall wipe away their tears."

He recently sent me a Polaroid picture of himself wearing a pair of funny glasses with a plastic nose attached, which makes him look like Groucho Marx. He's holding up a pencil, and tapping it, as if it were a cigar. His head is tilted and he has a goofy grin. Like the picture of the raven he had drawn after he finished his report on heaven, the Groucho glasses remind me of the playful nature of his personality and, of course, remind me too that he is just 13 years old, in many ways mysterious and even mystical and still a fairly normal kid and not a "child prophet," neither Samuel nor Isaiah, but a thoughtful person nonetheless who has been forced by life to think more often about death than are most children of his age.

At night, in Mr. Castro's home on St. Ann's Avenue, the poet speaks with pride of Anthony.

"The solitary figure of this child touches me tremendously," he says. "His mentality, as you have noticed, is not organized and that is part of his attraction. When he rings my bell, it pleases me. He reminds me by his earnestness of Don Quixote.

"He brings me his stories and he asks me for a grade. I always give him a good mark because I don't want to discourage him.

"He told me once, 'If I could not write, I would go crazy.' Well! He likes to overstate things, but there's something in it. Children long for this—a voice, a way of being heard—but many sense that there is no one in the world to hear their words, so they are drawn to ways of malice. If they cannot sing, they scream. They are vessels of the spirit but the spirit sometimes is entombed; it can't get out, and so they smash it! (violence)

"But life," he says, "is a complicated school. Not all of the powerful are happy. Not all the children of this neighborhood are sad. There are many who surprise you. They have faces sometimes that are like *iluminadas*. Light surrounds them. No one yet has clipped their wings.

"I saw a movie once about the children in a concentration camp in Germany. Most of them looked down because they knew they were about to die. Their eyes were hollow. But one little girl—you can't forget the power of her eyes! She did not seem pathetic. There was something different in her gaze. She looked at the camera with these penetrating eyes. We see her only for ten seconds but we can't forget her. There is a light reflecting from her. It is like the illumination of the angels. She tells us, 'There is something in me you cannot destroy.'"

I ask him why the children in the Nazi camps came to his mind when we were speaking of this neighborhood. He answers with a caution I have heard from others, Mrs. Washington included, when a reference to the Holocaust was made. "It is not the same," he says. "But there are some similarities. There is the feeling of eclipse. There is the likelihood of death for many. There is the sense of people watching from outside but seeming paralyzed and doing nothing. And there are the miracles."

Hesitant to interrupt, but needing to check the accuracy of something that I wrote down in December, I ask if he knew the children who were murdered in this building two years earlier.

"Oh yes. . . . That was up on the fourth floor."

"How old were they?"

"Fourteen, 15, 16. . . . They were schoolboys. I'd known them as children. But these children had no dialogue with grown-ups. They would never look at me or answer when I spoke. God forgive me! Sometimes you feel glad when you are told that it is over. You start to hate them and the chaos they create because you see that they disturb the order of the universe.

"This apartment where they lived was like a brothel. No matter what the hour of the night or day. You couldn't ever tell who really lived there but I think it was the daughter of a friend of mine. She was the one who found them. She came in and saw them on the floor and thought it was a joke. She thought they were pretending. 'Come on, guys! Stop kidding me!' She kicked her foot at one of them and saw his head roll over and she saw the blood and screamed. She screamed like holy hell! I heard it from downstairs.

"The killers, it seems, had made them lie flat on the floor and gave each one a bullet in the brain.

"God forgive me," he says again. "My wife and I were shocked but I was also so *relieved!* Goings and comings. Comings and goings! Every hour of the night. We couldn't sleep for weeks because of all the noise."

He mentions that the man believed to be the paid assassin of the boys was recently convicted of the murder of another person, at a corner store on Cypress Avenue, the bodega where some of the kids from P.S. 65 go after school to buy potato chips and sodas.

"He walked in with a pistol, shot him in the nose and killed him, and walked out. . . .

"I'm told that in the beginning of the Christian era there was a terrible place like this in Rome. The poet Martial wrote of this. I could help you find the passage if you want."

Going into the kitchen to take out a bottle of red wine, then setting two glasses on the table in the living room, he sits down again. "I want to pass something on to you that you may find of interest. I was told this by a man named Herman Klein, a Jewish man from Hungary who escaped the Nazis."

"Was he your teacher?"

"No. He was my boss. He owned a chain of stores to do dry cleaning. He hired me to work for him. When he saw I was a poet, he encouraged me. He used to say, 'Don't hide your talent in a drawer. If you write in English, show it to people who read English. If you write in Spanish, show it to people who read Spanish. If you can make music, play your music in the park where everyone can hear.' So this is the first time that I thought, 'Yes! I can make something worthwhile.' "

"Do you still play music in the park?"

"Yes," he says. "I play with a small band. We play sometimes on Sunday in Crotona Park." He shrugs. "It's not a very nice environment, but possibly it gives the people there some pleasure."

"Is Mr. Klein still living in New York?"

"That," he says, "I do not know. For a long time I

don't see him. But I don't forget him. He was the first person in New York who *asked* if he could read my poems.

"There is one thing I learned from Mr. Herman Klein that you may find of value. He told me never to rush when I am writing. If you don't take time, it gets too turbulent. There will be too much foam. This is why I tell Anthony to write more slowly. I tell him, 'Your mind is like a crowded room. Let your stories come out quietly and calmly. There will be time for every little thought to make its own escape.'"

"You told me once that you left school after eighth grade."

"That's so," he says.

"How did you learn to write?"

"I had no one to teach me," he replies. "I had to educate myself out of experience. I had to build my own shield, but I tried not to allow this shield to be too hard. I don't like overcertainty. The dirt of doubt and ambiguity is where the ore is hidden."

Like many in the neighborhood, he says that he has grown uncomfortable with New York City's mayor, Rudolph Giuliani, but his criticism has to do with style more than politics. "The man turns flowers into stones," he says. "He is too dry and brittle, like the cold judiciary out of which he came. He has the mechanism of the law, but not its spirit. He tells the beggar, 'Don't sleep on the grass.' He should explain, 'This grass is sacred. Don't defile it. It is the banquet of our Creator.' It may be he does not understand the human factor. He is too absolute. There is something missing in his personality."

"What is it?" I ask.

"Love of the divine in man," he answers.

Speaking of the social commentators on the radio talk shows in New York, whom he dislikes and calls "uncultured and too coarse," he says, "There are people who are so incomplete that they will not be content until the whole world is as incomplete as they. They offer bitterness, and bitter people call them for that reason: to have a conversation with *la bestia*. So they enrage poor people with each other and they leave us vibrant with their gall."

I ask, "What is *la bestia*?"

"The beast of the Apocalypse," he answers but does not explain it further.

He speaks sardonically about the major churches of New York, which, he believes, have been neglectful in their obligation to confront and counteract the selfishness and meanness of the city, and he appears to have a deep distrust of organized religions; but when I press him on his own beliefs, he grows less combative.

"We would be very lonely without God," he says, "but I think that God would also be quite lonely without man. Writers need readers. Musicians need listeners. God needs human beings to be admirers of His creation.

"The universe too, I think," he says after a pause, "would be a lonely place without spectators."

Since this conversation in the summer, we have corresponded with each other frequently. His letters are pungent with humorous and often scathing comments about life in New York City. Not long ago, he sent me a dialogue he'd written in which Plato, Socrates, and Aristophanes debate at length on what to do about drug dealers—"people who sell the poppy flower of Morpheus" and "corrupt the youth of Cypress Lane." In a recent letter, he mentions that his health has not been good. But he says he still goes out to play his accordion in the park on Sundays. Anthony still visits him sometimes on weekday afternoons and reads him stories he has written.

"The truth is," says the poet, "I enjoy the child's conversation and his company. I find that I look forward to his visits."

"Do you think America likes children?" Mrs. Washington asks me the next evening in her kitchen after we have dinner. It is the last time I will see her for a long while.

"What do you think?" I say, turning back her question, as I probably do too often.

"I don't think so," she replies, and hands me a clipping she has saved. The story, which is from *Newsday*, is about an abandoned steel plant that is going to be used this fall as a school building. The factory, which is next to a cemetery and beside a pipeline that carries "combustible fuel," is in an area, according to a Board of Education engineer, that "appears to be a dumping ground" for "tires, rugs, and parts of bodies." Because of unexpected overcrowding, some 500 children will be forced to go to school there.

In the margin, next to a sentence that says the site of the building is "a haven" for rats, Mrs. Washington has written, "This is the rock-bottom. So what else is new?"

Another clipping she has saved describes a school in which another group of children will be having classes in a bathroom next to urinals. "That ain't new either," she remarks, as I fold up the clippings to put in my pocket.

For dessert she cuts in half a honeydew melon, putting each half in a bowl with red clown pictures on the sides. "I love honeydew!" she says. "I could eat a honeydew a day if I had money." She instructs me, "When you buy a honeydew you have to press it to make sure it's ripe. It tastes best when it looks as if it's rotten."

After taking away the plates from dinner and putting mugs of coffee on the table, she talks about her mother, who, she says, taught her to cook Italian food. "I don't know why. She loved Italian dishes. She made her own pasta. Wouldn't buy it in a box. Wouldn't buy frozen foods. Hated things that came in cans.

"She liked German dishes too. Sauerbraten. You make it with sauerkraut and boiled ribs and new potatoes. Used to make a Spanish dish. Red rice with little bits of bacon. . . .

"She'll be gone now 22 years next month. Died on a Monday at nine-thirty in the morning. I was there alone. My father at the time was in the VA. Even now when I go up there by Jacobi Hospital, I get a funny feeling and I start to cry because that's where she died.

"Do you know I talk to her sometimes? I hope that you don't think that's crazy."

"I don't think it's crazy."

"I don't either but my daughter teases me. She tells me, 'Ma, you're one can less than a full pack.' I don't mind.

I get comfort out of talking with my mother."

"What do you say to her?"

"I tell her the news. 'Ma,' I'll say, 'do you see what's goin' on? Do you see what's happened over here today?' "

"Is this when you read the paper?"

"No. Before I go to sleep. I like to talk to my mother while I braid my hair. It helps me concentrate my thoughts."

"Do you think of her in heaven?"

"I don't know why—I do. I didn't believe in that when I was young but I believe it now. It helps to know that I'll be seeing her someday."

The children I've been meeting speak an awful lot about the Bible miracles. Although I try to be respectful, sometimes I feel guilty since I'm much too skeptical to think these stories are believable. When I mention this to Mrs. Washington, she says, "I don't believe them either. No. To me, that's superstition. There's only one miracle I know. To me, a baby is a miracle. You know where it comes from. But nobody knows what makes it beautiful and pure. That part is the miracle. When I see a baby, that's the only time I'm sure that I believe in God."

Whenever we get together now, the mood is so much more relaxed than when we started having these long talks a year before that I don't often like to press her for specific information; but, because she has brought up the subject more than once, I ask her to explain one detail that has always puzzled me about the time when she was in a shelter near Times Square.

"You said you had to go out to a bar across the street in order to get water. How did you do this? Was there some arrangement with the bar? Or did people just walk in and ask?"

"No. They wouldn't have let us in. It was arranged by the hotel. They gave you a bucket. Then somebody from the bar sat outside on the sidewalk with a hose and everyone lined up there with their buckets."

"This was on 42nd Street?"

"Right there. A block or two from Times Square."

"Plastic buckets?"

"No. Metal. You know the kind you use to mop the floor?"

"Were they clean?"

"I didn't drink the water to find out! We used it for the toilet—and to wash."

"You carried it yourself?"

"No. All of us together. I couldn't do it on my own. Water's heavy! With no elevator workin'. Water spillin' in the stairs. . . . David, me, and Charlayne would take turns."

"I never saw that in the paper."

"I didn't either," she replies with a good helping of sarcasm, "but you know, Jonathan, that you don't need to read things in the paper to find out if they are real. Take it from me. Believe me. I was there. I have a good memory and I don't get things wrong."

One of the things that's often worried me about the interviews I've had with children and adults in the course of writing books over the years is that they do not tend to reflect the shifting moods and changing points of view of people I have talked with. They end up, inevitably, as "one-time snapshots." Most journalistic interviews are like that. I have often thought there was a certain arrogance about the act of "freezing" people in this manner. "I came on a Tuesday. This is what she said, so this must be what she believes." I often find on Friday she does not believe exactly what I thought I heard on Tuesday; people also simply change their minds, as I find that Mrs. Washington does frequently.

"I want to correct something I told you once," she says. "You asked me once if I thought white people wish that Puerto Rican and black people would just die or go away. I thought it over and I changed my mind. I don't think they wish that we would die. I think they wish that we were never born. Now that we're here, I think they don't know what they ought to do. I think that that's the biggest problem in their minds about poor people." She adds politely, "I'm not talkin' about *all* of the white people. Some of them feel this way. Some of them don't. Some of them don't feel nothin'. Some are nice people but they can't get nothin' done and so they put it out of mind."

I tell her of Mrs. Roiphe's belief that a degree of cruelty in writing off poor people may be "part of the energy, part of the delight" of living well in New York City, that it may even be "the fuel that powers the palace."

"Go through that again?"

I do; and, when I'm done, she says, "Who is this woman?"

"She's a well-known writer," I reply.

"Come on!" she says, then adds, "At least she's honest. I'll say that. But, you know, bein' honest doesn't make a person nice." After a few more moments, she remarks, "People should be very careful using talk like that. They might give poor people the idea that cruelty's not bad."

The hardening of feelings toward poor people in New York, which is apparent in the words of Mrs. Roiphe, is present also in the words of government officials who increasingly appear to see themselves as having been assigned the role of the "defenders of civility" against the insubordination or the pathos of the poorest of the poor. "We have to cut off the head of the enemy and the enemy is the homeless," said the commanding officer of the police in Central Park a couple of weeks before, a statement Mrs. Washington immediately repeated to me on the phone.

"He's got a goddamn nerve!" she said.

When I ask her now how she explains the climate that permits these kinds of statements to be made with relative impunity, she speaks with less resentment of the officer. "I guess he's doin' what the politicians and newspapers want." She adds, "You have to wonder sometimes what these people teach their children. What will their kids be like when they grow up?"

"Some of their children may rebel against this," I remark.

"Let's pray for that. Let's hope that that's what happens."

She stirs her coffee thoughtfully. "Do you know—did they have the Fresh Air Fund this summer?"

"I think they have it every year."

"How many children do you think they send to camp?"

"Maybe 5,000 or 10,000."

"How many poor children is there in New York?" she asks, then answers her own question. "I bet close to a million." Then she says, "It's nice they do it. For the ones that get it, it must be like heaven to get out and see some grass."

In this rather quiet mood, she speaks about her doctor, whom I've never met, although we've talked once on the phone. "You don't see many people like him nowadays. He's like the doctors that they used to have when we were young. He could go anywhere he wants but he stays here.

"Last time I was in the clinic building at the hospital, I saw him crying."

"Where did you see that?"

"In the waiting room. I don't think he realized I was there. A patient died in his examining room. Her stepfather and her mother both had AIDS. She was only 17. He came out into the waiting room and cried.

"I could tell he was embarrassed that I saw him. He said, 'I have to leave.' He went out of the room awhile and then came back. He's a very sentimental man. He grows attached. I think he works too hard. He doesn't take a break for lunch. Sometimes at night he can't go home. He sleeps right there.

"People say the reason that he's like that is because he's married to a Puerto Rican woman, so he feels more for poor people; but I don't think that's why. I just think he cares about his patients. He gave me his home number. I don't know too many doctors who would do that.

"He told me once that he became a doctor to save lives. It seemed like a funny thing to say. Why else would somebody become a doctor? I guess that's obvious. But I liked it when he said that. He said he didn't know then about AIDS. Nobody did.

"I don't know what I would do if he was not my doctor."

David is at his sister's house again. It seems he's spending more time there now than at his home. Although this puzzles me, and worries me a bit, I don't comment on it. Mrs. Washington makes more coffee and we spend the rest of the evening talking about ordinary things that are entirely unrelated to the worries and the problems of the people in the neighborhood. We never had nights like this when we first met. A feeling of emergency was always in the air. Now, with the respite in her illness, she seems more at peace. Perhaps something has changed in me as well.

At two A.M., she walks with me to the East Tremont station. Then, however, because it's so late, she says she doesn't want me to go back by train and so she helps me to flag down a cab.

I have always told myself that I was here as a "researcher" of some sort, maybe a "social anthropologist" or an "oral historian," something of professional significance, that this was my job and I would do my best to get her words down right and be as faithful as I could to everything she told me. But there has been more to this than research and, of course, I feel it now that I am really leaving.

"God bless," she says. As usual, I feel afraid to say it in return. She gives me a hug, and although I often am embarrassed by my feelings, I hug her too, as closely as I can, and suddenly feel panicky and don't want to let go. The taxi-driver makes a grumbling sound and seems impatient. I have never been good at knowing how to say goodbye.

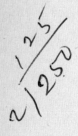

In Memoriam

BERNARDO RODRIGUEZ, JR., eight years old, died in the elevator shaft of his apartment building, 140th Street near Cypress Avenue, 1994.

LOREL POUNCIE, eight years old, died with his five-year-old brother, Christian, in a fire in his apartment building, 140th Street near Brook Avenue, 1994.

EBAN RAMOS, ten years old, died with his mother in a fire in his apartment building, 138th Street near Brook Avenue, 1994.

ROBERT CALLAHAN, five years old, died in a fire in his apartment building, Morris Avenue near 150th Street, 1994.

EBONY WILLIAMS, 13 years old—"her teachers said that she was always dirty," says Mrs. Washington, "but she had a pretty smile"—incinerated in a Pampers box under the Bruckner Expressway at 165th Street, 1993.

"TONY," 18 years old—"I can't remember his last name," says Mrs. Flowers—shot and killed in the lobby of Mrs. Flowers's house, Beekman Avenue, 1990.

DAVID GRAVES—"I think that he made 22," says Mrs. Flowers—shot and killed in the lobby of his apartment building, Beekman Avenue, 1991.

SEAN TAYLOR—"he made 16," says Mrs. Flowers—shot and killed in the schoolyard of P.S. 65, Cypress Avenue, 1993.

ANTHONY GREEN, 17 years old, shot and killed, Beekman Avenue, 1991.

JIMMY KNOTT—"another young one, I cannot recall his age," says Mrs. Flowers—shot and killed, corner of Beekman Avenue and 141st Street, 1992.

ANGEL ROSA—"we called him Choco"—19 years old, shot and killed in front of the bodega, corner of Cypress Avenue and 141st Street, 1993.

DAMON LEE, 16 years old, shot and killed in the lobby of Mrs. Flowers's house on Beekman Avenue as she was coming up the stairs to her apartment, New Year's Eve of 1994.

"A BEAUTIFUL TEENAGE GIRL—I can't recall her name, but I knew her and her sister. Fell four flights and died in the elevator shaft of her apartment house. Yes, another faulty elevator door," says Mrs. Flowers—138th Street close to Cypress Avenue, 1992.

JUDSON DUKES and STEVEN DUKES: "They were brothers, both young men. One fell off the roof of his apartment building. The other died of illness in the hospital, both in the same year. I knew their mother. This was something awful hard for her. They lived on Beekman Avenue, next door to me. This was in 1992," says Mrs. Flowers.

DANNY SANTIAGO, 15 years old, executed in Mr. Castro's house, St. Ann's Avenue near 141st Street, 1992.

OTIS LAMONT BLAIR, 16 years old, killed in the same execution, St. Ann's Avenue, 1992.

DAMIAN SALGADO, 15 years old, killed in the same execution as his friends Otis and Danny—"yes, I knew these boys," says Mr. Castro. "Remember them with kindness. It was not their choice to live and die in the South Bronx."

CHRISTOPHER HERNANDEZ, 15 years old, shot and killed on the floor of his apartment building with two of his friends and three adults—"another execution," Mrs. Washington says—Prospect Avenue near 150th Street, Valentine's Day, 1993.

ANNETTE MEDINA, 17 years old, killed in the same execution, Prospect Avenue, 1993.

EDWIN SANTIAGO, 17 years old, killed in the same execution as Annette and Christopher, 1993.

ROBERTO ROBLES, 16 years old, lived on 138th Street, a student at Morris High School, shot by mistake while walking through a playground near the school, 1994.

ALICIA APONTE—"another beautiful girl who died," says Mrs. Washington—19 years old, also a student at Morris High School, fatally shot in the head in the same crossfire, also by mistake, 1994.

ISABEL LOPEZ, 17 years old, died in a fire at a nightclub known as Happy Land—"right up from my house," says Mrs. Washington. "It happened in the spring of 1990. In all, I think that 87 people died that night. Their mothers still put flowers out in front."

THESE WERE NEW YORK CITY'S CHILDREN TOO

KALLIE BLUE, 50 years old, beloved friend of Mrs. Flowers and Reverend Overall, lived in Mrs. Flowers's house on Beekman Avenue, died of breast cancer, 1992.

JUAN CARLOS ÁVILES, Anthony's uncle, 41 years old, mourned by his nephew and his sisters and his mother, died of AIDS in Bronx-Lebanon Hospital, 1994.

GEORGE CALDERON, heroin-addicted at the age of ten, druglord, employer, and philanthropist, shot and killed when he was 35 years old, 161st Street near Yankee Stadium, 1992.

LOURDES CINTRON, called "Sugar," George Calderon's sister, who tried to carry on the family business, shot and killed when she was 27, 146th Street near Brook Avenue, 1992.

MOONDOG: "His name was José Luis Ortiz," says his mother, Ruth Ortiz. "He was born on January 15, 1969. He died on October 1, 1989. He loved dogs." Shot and killed protecting a pregnant woman in the doorway of his house, 140th Street, between Brook Avenue and Willis Avenue.

IN OUR HEARTS WE'LL REMEMBER

Notes

3 RICHEST, POOREST CONGRESSIONAL DISTRICTS: U.S. Bureau of the
Census, cited in *Congressional Districts in the 1990s: A Portrait of
America* (Washington, D.C.: Congressional Quarterly, Inc., 1993).
POPULATION AND RACIAL MAKEUP OF SOUTH BRONX: Until some
years ago, the term "South Bronx" was used to speak of four pre-
dominantly black and Hispanic community districts south of the
Cross-Bronx Expressway. Newspapers in recent years, however,
have tended to apply the term to a somewhat larger area, including all or part of three additional districts that lie to the north of
the expressway. In this book, the term is used to refer to all seven
of these districts. In five of them, white people make up fewer
than 2.5 percent of the population. In the other two, they made
up, respectively, 14 and 24 percent of the population in 1990,
according to the U.S. Bureau of the Census, but these percentages have declined significantly since. (See note for page 192.)
The total population of these seven community districts is about
610,000 people. The primary source of this data is *Demographic
Profiles: A Portrait of New York City's Community Districts* (New York
City: Department of City Planning, 1992). See also *New York
Times*, August 4 and December 25, 1994; *The New Yorker*,
December 21, 1992; *The Village Voice* (cover story by Camilo José
Vergara), March 27, 1990.

POPULATION AND RACIAL MAKEUP OF HARLEM AND WASHINGTON
HEIGHTS: *Demographic Profiles,* cited above; offices of Manhattan
borough president Ruth Messinger and United States represen-
tative Charles Rangel.

MOTT HAVEN DEMOGRAPHICS: Mott Haven is part of a community
district that contains two additional neighborhoods (Melrose and
Port Morris). Press reports sometimes inaccurately cite the district's total population (77,000) for Mott Haven. According to Lee
Stuart of South Bronx Churches, Mott Haven's population is
48,000 people, who live in roughly 18,000 households. Of this

number, 1.7 percent were white in 1990. (*Demographic Profiles,* cited above; *New York Times,* November 5, 1991; *Newsday,* May 25, 1993; "Mott Haven Profile-at-a-Glance," Mayor's Office for Children and Families, New York, 1990.)

MEDIAN HOUSEHOLD INCOME OF MOTT HAVEN $7,600: *New York Times,* November 5, 1991. The figure corresponds closely to the monthly welfare payment granted to a family of three people—a fairly typical family size in the Mott Haven area—which, including cash benefits and food stamps, is $577 in New York, or about $6,900 a year. The *Times* (December 25, 1994) also notes, however, that the poorest 20 percent of families in the Bronx, a disproportionate number of whom live in Mott Haven, had incomes of only $3,700 at the beginning of the 1990s. The federal government defined a family of three people as "poor" in 1991 if their income fell below $10,860, according to the U.S. Bureau of the Census ("Weighted Average Poverty Thresholds for Families of Specific Size, 1959–1993").

BLOCKS ADJACENT TO ST. ANN'S CHURCH POOREST IN NEW YORK CITY: *Newsday,* May 31, 1993.

PERCENT OF PEOPLE IN NEIGHBORHOOD WHO ARE POOR: Interviews with Reverend Martha Overall (St. Ann's Church), Manuel Rodriguez (principal of P.S. 65), James Roundtree (St. Benedict the Moor). The U.S. Bureau of the Census places the figure for the St. Ann's census tract at 60 percent; but, because so many people in the neighborhood are distrustful of governmental inquiries and refuse to fill out census forms, and because census-takers do not dare to enter numerous buildings and are unable to gain entrance to others, and often cannot reach people by telephone because so many families have no phones, the census figures for Mott Haven, as for many similar neighborhoods in the United States, are in general discredited by knowledgeable people in the area.

4 HEROIN USE IN SOUTH BRONX: New York City Department of Health, cited in unpublished memorandum of August 27, 1993, Hunter College Center on AIDS, Drugs, and Community Health; New York State Division of Substance Abuse Services, cited in "Reaching Low-Income Women at Risk of AIDS," by Nicholas Freudenberg and other staff members of the Hunter College center, in *Health Education Research,* Vol. 9, No. 1, 1994; author's interviews with staff members of the center. The estimate of nearly 4,000 intravenous heroin users in Mott Haven is the lowest of several estimates I have seen, some of which exceed 7,000.

ONE QUARTER OF WOMEN TESTED IN OBSTETRIC WARDS HIV POSITIVE: *The New Yorker,* December 21, 1992; author's interviews with doctors at Bronx-Lebanon Hospital. Also see *Newsday,* May 26, 1993. PEDIATRIC AIDS: See notes for pages 194, 195.

NEARLY TWO THIRDS OF HOUSING IN MOTT HAVEN CITY-OWNED: *New York Times,* November 5, 1991.

CONDITIONS FOUND IN MOTT HAVEN HOUSING: *Newsday,* May 24, 1993; *New York Times,* November 6, 1991, December 25, 1994.

4, 5 FAMILY SLEEPS IN SLEEPING BAGS: *Newsday,* December 9, 1992.

5 "DEADLIEST NEIGHBORHOOD IN NEW YORK CITY": *New York Times,* October 13, 1992; *Washington Post,* November 8, 1992. A vivid description of the effects of violence in the neighborhood of Beekman Avenue and 141st Street is given in the *New York Daily News,* November 11, 1993.

MURDERS IN SOUTH BRONX, MOTT HAVEN, ST. ANN'S NEIGHBORHOOD: Hunter College Center on AIDS, Drugs, and Community Health, unpublished memorandum of August 27, 1993; *New York Times,* November 5, 1991; *Newsday,* October 13, 1992, May 25, July 15 and 25, August 16 and 31, September 12 and 17, 1993; *New York Daily News,* July 25 and August 1, 1993. Also see the weekly police blotter published in the *Bronx Times Reporter,* which typically shows approximately twice as many homicides and other crimes of violence in Precinct 40, in which St. Ann's Church is located, as in other precincts of the Bronx.

7 MEDICAL WASTE INCINERATOR ON LOCUST AVENUE: *Newsday,* October 16, 1991, March 21, 1992, November 7, 1993; *New York Daily News,* July 22 and September 2, 1992; *New York Times,* November 2, 1991, September 8, 1992; *Bronx Press Review,* May 27, 1993; *Riverdale Press,* February 4, May 13 and 20 and September 16, 1993.

11 RESETTLEMENT OF HOMELESS PEOPLE INTO SOUTH BRONX NEIGHBORHOODS: The city's resettlement policy, which began to be implemented as early as 1986, accelerated as shelters in Manhattan were shut down during the next three years. Between 1989 and 1992, more than 3,000 additional homeless families, including over 10,000 children and adults, were moved into Mott Haven and three other South Bronx neighborhoods. (*New York Times,* November 6 and 8, 1991; *Newsday,* March 24, 1993; *City Limits,* April 1993; author's interviews with employees of the city's welfare department, shelter providers, and homeless families.)

15 HOSPITALS IN BRONX AND HARLEM: For background data and discussion of conditions in these and other public hospitals in New York City, see the *New York Times,* October 28, 1988, April 7,

1991, May 6 and September 23, 1994, March 5, 6, 7, 1995; *Healthweek,* November 4, 1991.

16 "DO NOT TAKE ME TO HARLEM HOSPITAL": *New York Times,* April 7, 1991.

18 FIRE IN NIGHTCLUB: The fire, which was at the Happy Land nightclub, took place, according to Mrs. Washington, in 1990. An informally organized group of relatives and friends of survivors continues to place flowers at the site.

21 LAWRENCE MEAD CITED: *New York Times,* May 19, 1992.

Chapter Two

27ff. CHILDREN'S TEXT ON HISTORY OF SOUTH BRONX: Lisa Garrison, *The South Bronx and the Founding of America: An Activity Book for Teachers and Students* (New York: The Bronx County Historical Society, 1987).

29 MORRIS HIGH SCHOOL: See note for pp. 151, 152.

PORT MORRIS INDUSTRIAL PARK: The *New York Times* (November 7, 1991) says that 80 percent of the 20,000 people employed at the industrial park live in the Bronx, a figure repeated frequently. What is difficult to ascertain is the percentage of these people who are South Bronx or Mott Haven residents. In an off-the-record conversation, an official of the New York State Department of Labor informs my colleague Cathy Foley that many of the companies in the industrial park have "a hard time" finding "even two percent" of their employees in the area. Neighborhood parents and clergy in Mott Haven tell me that they have to struggle hard to think of anyone they know who works there.

32 PUBLIC SCHOOLS ATTENDED BY CHILDREN IN FEATHERBED LANE NEIGHBORHOOD: P.S. 204 is the elementary school housed in a former synagogue. P.S. 4, which was temporarily housed in the same former synagogue in 1991 and is now in another location, "scored dead last" in reading in 1991, according to *Newsday,* April 12, 1991.

36, 37 MALCOLM X AND TRAGEDY: "My Brother Malcolm," by Veronica Chambers, *New Youth Connections Alumni Edition* (a student-written New York City periodical), February 1993.

41, 42 RADIO TALK-SHOW HOST: Jay Diamond, a broadcaster on WABC, New York, is cited from transcript of his broadcast of November 17, 1993, provided by Fairness and Accuracy in Media, an organization in New York that monitors the press.

47 CHURCH CONSUMED BY FIRE: *New York Daily News,* November 7, 1993; *New York Times,* November 8, 1993.

48 CHILD RAPED, INCINERATED: The 13-year-old was named Ebony Williams. *Newsday,* October 17, 1993.

52   "A SCENE OUT OF DICKENS": Mario Cuomo, *An Experiment in Democracy* (New York: Crown, 1994).

Chapter Three

59   "A GOOD VEIN FOR INJECTING": "What Works," undated pamphlet, distributed by St. Ann's Corner Harm Reduction Center, 312–314 Cypress Avenue, Bronx, New York 10454. Joyce Rivera-Beckman is the founder and director of the center.

60   GEORGE CALDERON: *Newsday,* May 25, 1993; *New York Daily News,* November 8 and December 17, 1993; *New York Times,* July 23, 1994, April 10, 1995.

61   DIEGO-BEEKMAN HOUSING, CONTINENTAL WINGATE: *New York Daily News,* November 11, 1993, February 4, 1994; *New York Times,* March 25, 1973, May 7, 1978; *New York Daily News,* February 4, 1994.

61ff.   SECURITY DIRECTOR OF DIEGO-BEEKMAN HOUSING CITED: The security director at the time was Leonard Hicks.

71   ST. VINCENT DE PAUL: The citation is translated from Jean Anouilh's faithful portrayal of St. Vincent in the screenplay that he wrote for *Monsieur Vincent,* a 1947 film by Claude Renoir and Maurice Cloche.

73   "THE KILLER IS NOT A SONG": unnamed rap musician cited, *MacNeil-Lehrer NewsHour,* Public Broadcasting System, January 3, 1994.

90   FIRST HOMICIDE OF 1994: *New York Times,* January 2, 1994.

      FORMER ACOLYTE AT ST. ANN'S CHURCH ARRESTED FOR MURDER: *New York Times,* January 8 and 17, 1994.

Chapter Four

99   BERNARDO RODRIGUEZ, JR., DIES IN ELEVATOR SHAFT AND DESCRIPTION OF THE BUILDING THAT HE LIVED IN: *New York Daily News,* January 16 and February 4, 1994.

100   SHORTAGE OF DRUG TREATMENT SERVICES: According to *City Limits* (May 1994), "there are currently 50,000 treatment slots available" for "an estimated 600,000 hard-core addicts" in New York. Also see *New York Daily News,* June 23, 1994; *New York Times* (op/ed article by Michael Massing), October 22, 1993.

      CUTS IN VARIOUS PUBLIC SERVICES ANNOUNCED OR ANTICIPATED: *New York Times,* January 27, February 3, 16, 28, March 2 and 14, April 19, May 1 and 11, 1994; *New York Daily News,* March 15, April 1 and 20, May 4 and 11, June 23, 1994; *City Limits,* March 1994; *Newsday,* May 6, 11, 20, 1994. For the effects of certain of these cutbacks on poor children, see columns by

Joyce Purnick in the *New York Times*, September 19 and October 31, 1994.

EFFECTS OF CUTS ON PUBLIC HOSPITALS: The chairman of the board of directors of the city's Health and Hospitals Corporation is cited in the *New York Times*, February 16, 1994.

CUTS IN AIDS SERVICES: The most extensive discussion is in *City Limits*, March 1995. Also see *New York Daily News*, April 20, 1994; *New York Times*, July 3, 1994.

CUTS WOULD HURT POOREST, HELP RICHEST: *New York Times*, March 2, April 19, May 11, 1994.

THREATENED CUTS IN AIDS SERVICES "INTOLERABLE": *New York Times* (editorial), April 5, 1994, and (commentary), April 4, 1994.

DEPUTY MAYOR CITED: *New York Times*, January 27, 1994.

REACTION ON WALL STREET: *New York Times*, May 11, 1994.

100, 101   IMPACT OF CUTS ON BLACK AND HISPANIC WOMEN: *New York Amsterdam News*, March 19, 1994; *Newsday*, May 23, 1994.

101   CASELOADS OF SOCIAL WORKERS ALREADY HIGH: *New York Times*, February 23, 1989. Also see *New York Times*, March 18, 1995.

MANHATTAN BOROUGH PRESIDENT RUTH MESSINGER CITED: *New York Amsterdam News*, March 5, 1995.

MAYOR EXHORTS STUDENTS TO HELP THEMSELVES: *New York Times*, February 16, 1994.

CITY CUTS JOBS FOR YOUTHS AND AFTERSCHOOL PROGRAMS: *New York Daily News*, April 19, 1994; *New York Times*, May 1, 1994.

MAYOR WANTS TO FINGERPRINT WELFARE RECIPIENTS: *City Limits*, March 1994.

"GREEN UNIFORMS" FOR 1.2 MILLION WELFARE RECIPIENTS: Deputy Mayor John Dyson is cited from the *New York Daily News*, February 9 and March 15, 1994; the *New York Observer*, February 21, 1994; and his confidential memorandum of December 19, 1993.

103   JESUS' WALK TO CALVARY COMMEMORATED: This description is based upon "Easter's Coats of Many Colors," a survey of Easter preparations, by Charisse Jones in the *New York Times*, April 1, 1994.

107   NUMBER OF SCHOOL DOCTORS 20 YEARS AGO AND NOW: *New York Daily News*, June 22, 1993.

NUMBER OF RAT EXTERMINATORS AND HOUSING INSPECTORS DIMINISHED: *New York Times*, May 10 and 11, 1994, May 22, 1995; *City Limits*, March 1994; WWOR-TV (news report), May 23, 1995.

108   PREDICTED CONSEQUENCES OF THESE CUTS: *City Limits*, March 1994.

109   "ALL THE PEOPLE OF THE CITY": Mayor Giuliani cited in *New York Times*, January 27, 1994.

EFFECTS OF SANITATION CUTS LIKELY TO BE HARSHEST IN POOR NEIGHBORHOODS: For examples of the effects of previous cuts on poorest neighborhoods, see *New York Times*, April 18, 1993.

PRESIDENT OF TIMES SQUARE IMPROVEMENT DISTRICT CITED: *New York Times,* March 25, 1994.

HOMELESS PEOPLE REMOVED FROM IMPROVEMENT DISTRICTS, SOMETIMES FORCIBLY: *New York Times,* July 6, 1995.

AN EXAMPLE OF "REINVENTED GOVERNMENT": Deputy Mayor John Dyson is cited by the *New York Times,* March 25, 1994.

111 WALL STREET MONEY MANAGER: George Soros earned $850 million in 1992 and more than $1 billion in 1993. Several other investors in 1993 had individual earnings in excess of those of all the people in Mott Haven put together. The combined income of the 18,000 households of Mott Haven, each year between 1991 and 1994, was less than $200 million. (*The Nation,* January 23, 1993; *Forbes,* May 24, 1993; *Financial World,* July 5, 1994; *New York Times,* November 5, 1991, December 25, 1994.) Also see *New York Times* (column by Russell Baker), September 17, 1994.

113 OFFICIALS OF MUNICIPAL ASSISTANCE CORPORATION CITED: *New York Times,* May 15, 1994; *New York Observer,* August 1, 1994.

113, 114 ANNE ROIPHE CITED: *New York Observer,* January 24, 1994.

114 RATS ATTACK CHILD IN CRIB: The incident Mrs. Washington describes here was reported in the *New York Daily News,* March 4, 1994.

116 MAYOR GIULIANI'S ANNOUNCEMENT OF INTENTION TO ELIMINATE AIDS AGENCY: *New York Times,* April 4 and 5, 1994; *New York Daily News,* April 11, 1994. Some of the consequences of the mayor's ultimate decision to diminish (not eliminate) the agency are described in the *New York Times,* July 3, 1994, January 24 and February 15, 1995.

122 ARREST OF CALDERON'S MOTHER: *New York Daily News,* May 27 and June 5, 1994.

124 POVERTY OF CHILDREN AT P.S. 65: See notes for page 3.

READING SCORES OF CHILDREN AT P.S. 65: *New York Daily News,* January 7, 1994.

128 RADIO TALK-SHOW HOST: Bob Grant, a broadcaster on WABC, New York, is cited in *New York Amsterdam News,* March 26, 1994; *New York* magazine, October 24, 1994; *EXTRA* (newsletter of Fairness and Accuracy in Media), January/February 1994; transcript of his broadcast of March 2, 1992, provided by Fairness and Accuracy in Media. Also see *New York Times,* November 18, 1994.

"I DIDN'T BREED THEM": *The Nation,* April 18, 1994, citing the *New York Times.*

132 "FIERY TOMB FOR TWO BRONX KIDS" AND OTHER HEADLINES: *New York Daily News,* April 6, May 4, 5, 6, 1994.

132, 133 TEN-YEAR-OLD DIES WITH HIS MOTHER IN 138TH STREET FIRE: *New York Daily News,* April 6, 1994; *New York Times,* April 6, 1994. The child was named Eban Ramos. The *Times* quotes the mother's cry as "Mommy!" But a woman who knew the family tells me that the word was the Hispanic "Mami!"

133 EIGHT-YEAR-OLD BOY DIES IN 140TH STREET FIRE: *New York Daily News,* May 8, 1994. The child was named Lorel Pouncie.

136 NUMBERS OF SHELTERS, SOUP KITCHENS, FOOD PANTRIES: A compilation based on interviews with service providers, as well as "Where to Go for Help," a listing of services in the South Bronx, distributed by churches in the area. The numbers provided here are only for agencies in walking distance of the areas in which this book takes place.

136, 137 ANA OLIVEIRA CITED: Ms. Oliveira, at the time, was Director of Program Services at The Osborne Association, described in note for page 146.

137 TRANSFORMATION OF CHILDREN'S PARK: The primary initiative in development of the new park, now known as Padre's Park, was taken by Stefan Zucker, a veteran member of the faculty at P.S. 30, a nearby elementary school. The park has evolved into a safe, attractive place for children and is also used by people living at St. Benedict the Moor, which is next door to the park on St. Ann's Avenue.

Chapter Five

141 CYPRIAN AND MCNEILL CITED: William H. McNeill, *Plagues and People* (New York: Doubleday, 1976).

142 "A 415-ACRE ALCATRAZ": *New York Times,* June 5, 1994.

$58,000 EACH ADULT INMATE: *Newsday,* December 23, 1993; *Crane's,* November 29, 1993.

$70,000 EACH JUVENILE: *New York Times,* June 25, 1994.

SPENDING ON CHILDREN IN NEW YORK CITY PUBLIC SCHOOLS: The *New York Times* (March 12, 1995) places the figure at $7,150.

143 NUMBER OF GUARDS AND OTHER EMPLOYEES AT RIKERS ISLAND: Author's interviews with Sandi Franklin of Fresh Start (an agency that runs educational programs on the island), representatives of The Osborne Association (see note for pages 145, 146), and with employees on the island. See also *New York Times,* May 15, 1995, and *Rikers Review* (a periodical written by Rikers Island inmates), Summer 1994.

INCREASE IN NUMBER OF PEOPLE INCARCERATED, TOTAL NUMBER INCARCERATED IN ANY ONE YEAR: "Cause for Alarm," Federation of Protestant Welfare Agencies, New York, September 1991; "AIDS in Prison and Jail Fact Sheet," the Correctional Association of New York, May 1993; "Prisoner Profile," the Correctional Association of New York, February 1994.

STATE PRISON POPULATION: *New York Observer,* November 22, 1993; *New York Times,* April 4, 1994; interviews with representatives of The Osborne Association (see note for pages 145, 146).

NEARLY THREE QUARTERS OF STATE INMATES ARE FROM SEVEN NEW YORK CITY NEIGHBORHOODS: "Cause for Alarm," cited above.

NUMBER OF BLACK MEN IN NEW YORK CITY UNDER THE CONTROL OF CRIMINAL JUSTICE SYSTEM COMPARED TO NUMBER OF THOSE IN COLLEGE: *Education for the People,* Winter 1993.

RELATIVE NUMBERS OF NEW YORK CITY INMATES IN INCARCERATION OR JUVENILE DETENTION WHO ARE BLACK, HISPANIC, OR WHITE: "Cause for Alarm," cited above.

143, 144 NATIONAL STATISTICS FOR BLACK MALES INCARCERATED OR EARNING COLLEGE DEGREES: *New York Times,* April 21, 1992, June 12, 1994. Also see Andrew Hacker, *Two Nations* (New York: Charles Scribner's Sons, 1992).

145, 146 DOCUMENTARY FOOTAGE FILMED ON RIKERS ISLAND: "Lock Up: The Prisoners of Rikers Island," produced and directed by Nina Rosenblum and John Alpert, a production of Home Box Office, 1994.

BACKGROUND INFORMATION AND DATA ON RIKERS ISLAND: The most consistently reliable and thorough sources of information on matters pertaining to inmates and their families are Elizabeth Gaynes and other staff members at The Osborne Association, 135 East 15th Street, New York, NY 10003. An overview of issues related to the incarceration of black men in New York City and elsewhere in the nation is found in Gaynes's essay "The Urban Criminal Justice System," *Fordham Urban Law Journal,* Vol. XX, No. 3, 1993. Other consistently accurate sources of information on inmate life and prisons in New York and elsewhere are the Correctional Association of New York and *The Angolite,* a brilliantly edited periodical written by inmates at the Louisiana State Penitentiary in Angola, but with a national perspective.

146 BURIALS AT POTTERS FIELD: Interviews at Rikers Island and later with employees of Osborne Association, cited above. The cost of children's coffins was reported by the *New York Times,* July 24, 1994. See also *New York Times,* July 6 and 31, 1994.

PEOPLE WITH AIDS IN PRISON IN NEW YORK AND ELSEWHERE IN THE NATION: "AIDS in Prison and Jail Fact Sheet," cited above; *New York Times,* March 7, 1994; *The Progressive,* November/December 1993.

146, 147 "IS THAT WHAT WE DO?": The nun is cited in an article on inmate mothers by Jill Kirschenbaum in *City Limits,* November 1993.

148 SCHOOL SEGREGATION IN NEW YORK VERSUS OTHER STATES: The Harvard study is cited in the *New York Times,* December 14, 1993.

"TWO THIRDS OF AMERICA'S BLACK CHILDREN": *New York Times,* December 15, 1994. For further discussion of school segregation in New York and other cities, see Jimmy Breslin, *Newsday,* May 17, 1994; Nat Hentoff, *Village Voice,* May 31, 1994; and Douglass Massey and Nancy Denton, *American Apartheid: Segregation and the Making of the Underclass* (Cambridge: Harvard University Press, 1993).

"THE SHIP IS FLOATING BACKWARD": Gary Orfield cited, *New York Times,* December 14 and 15, 1993.

VICTOR HUGO: cited in Valerie Polakow, *Lives on the Edge* (Chicago: University of Chicago Press, 1993).

150, 151   "I COUNT THE GRADUATING CLASS": City University professor Michelle Fine is cited from *Equity and Choice,* Fall 1991.

151   "PAY TO APPEAR": *New York Times,* September 19, 1994.

151, 152   MORRIS HIGH SCHOOL GRADUATION RATE: *New York Times,* March 24, 1994. A teacher working at the school tells me, in early 1996, that long-delayed repairs are at last nearing completion. Morale, she says, is a great deal better, although drop-out numbers remain high.

152   TAFT HIGH SCHOOL: *Newsday,* November 23, 1993; *New York Times,* January 4, February 20, 1994; *New Youth Connections,* May/June 1994.

CONDITIONS IN OTHER NEW YORK CITY SCHOOLS: *New York Times,* November 7, 12, 13, 1993, May 9 and June 8, 1994; *Newsday,* January 24, 1993.

BLACK, HISPANIC CHILDREN 75 PERCENT OF NEW YORK HIGH SCHOOL ENROLLMENT: *New York Times,* August 13, 1993, March 18, 1995.

BLACK, HISPANIC ENROLLMENT AT STUYVESANT HIGH SCHOOL: "Stuyvesant High School Annual School Report, 1993–1994." Also see *New York Times,* March 18, 1995.

DISTRICT 7 ADMISSIONS TO STUYVESANT AND OTHER SELECTIVE HIGH SCHOOLS: *New York Times,* March 18, 1995.

CRITERIA FOR ADMISSION TO STUYVESANT: Telephone interview with Stuyvesant admissions department, March 1995.

152, 153   DESCRIPTIONS OF STUYVESANT HIGH SCHOOL, PRINCIPAL AND STUDENT CITED: *New York Times,* September 10, 1992, November 7, 1993; *Technos,* Vol. 2, No. 3, Fall 1993; *New Youth Connections,* November 1993; Mario Cuomo, cited above.

PRISON BARGE IN SOUTH BRONX: *New York Times,* July 12, 1994; author's interview with correctional officer at barge.

153, 154   MARIO CUOMO CITED AND PH.D.'S OBTAINED BY STUYVESANT STUDENTS: See note on Governor Cuomo for page 52.

154   CHARLES MURRAY CITED: *Losing Ground* (New York: Basic Books, 1984).

155   PROVISIONAL TEACHERS, TV CABLES, OVERCROWDING OF SCHOOLS: *Newsday*, January 24, 1993; *New York Times*, June 8, 1994, March 1, 1995.

155, 156   LEAD POISON IN CITY-OWNED APARTMENT BUILDINGS AND IN INNER-CITY NEIGHBORHOODS: *Newsday*, March 25, 1991, June 5, 1995; *New York Times*, August 25, 1994, March 21, 1995.

    LEAD POISON IN SCHOOLS; JOHN ROSEN CITED: *Village Voice*, December 22, 1992; *New York Times*, September 15, 1993; *New York Daily News*, July 27, 1994; WWOR-TV (news report), September 16, 1994.

160   CORNEL WEST: *Prophetic Reflections* (Monroe, Maine: Common Courage Press, 1993).

    HENRY LOUIS GATES CITED: *Narrative of Sojourner Truth* (New York: Vintage, 1993). Professor Gates is cited in the introduction by Margaret Washington.

163, 164   KENNETH CLARK CITED: *Dark Ghetto* (New York: Harper & Row, 1965).

168, 169   MURDER, DRUGS ON BEEKMAN AVENUE: *New York Times*, November 5, 1991, September 16, 1993; *Newsday*, October 11 and 13, 1993.

171   ASTHMA AND PNEUMONIA RATES: Charts prepared by United Hospital Fund of New York and Health System Agency of New York City, included in "Analysis of Hospital Utilization Patterns, Bronx, New York," an unpublished study by John Billings, March 1990. Also see "Poverty, Race, and Hospitalization for Childhood Asthma" in *American Journal of Public Health*, Vol. 78, No. 7, July 1988; "Inner-City Asthma," *CHEST*, June 1992; *Newsday*, October 10, 1993; *New York Times*, October 10, 1993.

    ASTHMA MORTALITY, BRONX AND STATEN ISLAND: "Variations in Asthma Hospitalizations and Deaths in New York City," *American Journal of Public Health*, Vol. 82, No. 1, January 1992.

172   MEDICAID MILLS IN MOTT HAVEN: *Washington Post Weekly Edition*, July 15–21, 1991.

    DR. ROBERT MASSAD CITED: Dr. Massad is chairman of the Department of Family Medicine at Montefiore Medical Center in the Bronx.

172, 173   NUMBERS AND QUALIFICATIONS OF DOCTORS: *Newsday*, October 1, 1990, May 26, 1993; *New York Times*, October 18 and November 14, 1993, May 8, 1994; *The Nation*, February 28, 1994; *Emerge*, September 1991.

173   HOMES WITHOUT TELEPHONES IN BRONX: "Among the nation's 100 most populous counties, Bronx County, New York, contains the highest population of families without phone service . . . according to the 1990 U.S. Census." (*Atlantic Monthly*, June 1994.)

173, 174   JESUS GILBERTO SIERRA CITED: Mr. Sierra, at the time, was executive director of the Segundo Ruiz Belvis Neighborhood Family Care Center in Mott Haven.

176ff.   SEGREGATION OF PATIENTS AT MOUNT SINAI HOSPITAL: *New York Daily News,* October 18, 19, 20, 1993, March 10 and April 30, 1994. Also see *New York Times,* October 19, 1993.

182   "WE HAVEN'T BEEN FAIR": David Elwood, a professor at John F. Kennedy School of Government at Harvard University, is quoted from a telephone conversation with my colleague Cathy Foley, 1995.

Chapter Six

186   ST. VINCENT CITED: See note for page 71.

186, 187   INCOME LEVELS, INFANT MORTALITY, PHYSICAL AND SOCIAL DIFFERENCES NORTH AND SOUTH OF 96TH STREET: *New York Times,* September 30, 1990, November 5 and December 25, 1994; *Newsday,* October 6, 1993, and November 6, 1994; *New York Daily News,* May 20, 1994.

LUXURY GROCERS ADVERTISE DELIVERY SOUTH OF 96TH STREET: See, for example, the advertisement for Jefferson's Market in the *New York Observer,* April 10, 1995, and routinely on other weeks in the same paper.

187   "CROSSING 96TH STREET": Newsletter of the Booker T. Washington Learning Center, Church of the Resurrection, East Harlem, Summer 1994.

MANHATTAN BOROUGH PRESIDENT RUTH MESSINGER CITED: Conversation with author, 1994.

190   "A SOUTH BRONX RENAISSANCE": *New York* magazine, November 21, 1994; *New York Times,* November 13, 1994. Also see *Newsday,* February 28, 1993; *New York Daily News,* June 5 and July 12, 1994; *New York Times,* June 8, July 11, 29, 31, 1994, May 2, 1995.

191   SIMILAR STORIES, OPTIMISM, DISAPPOINTMENT, IN PAST DECADES: *New York Times,* June 4, 1972, March 25, 1973, December 1 and May 7, 1978, September 3 and November 10, 1987, July 18, 1988; *Village Voice,* October 4, 1988 (recapitulating earlier stories).

HERMAN BADILLO CITED: *New York Times,* June 4, 1972.

PUBLIC SCHOOLS OF THE SOUTH BRONX, "A FEW REMARKABLE EXCEPTIONS": One of the notable exceptions is P.S. 30 on 141st Street. The school's principal, Aida Rosa, has been able to assemble an impressive staff, which has developed close ties to the parents in the neighborhood. There are a number of excellent teachers at P.S. 65 as well. By and large, however, elementary schools in the South Bronx remain close to the bottom by all indices and standards of success or failure.

LINCOLN HOSPITAL: The long-embattled hospital, at which I've talked with several dedicated and experienced physicians, now faces the loss of 25 percent of its entire budget, according to Dr. Harold Osborn, chief of Lincoln's emergency services department, with whose staff I met in May of 1996.

192 DEMOGRAPHIC PROJECTION: *New York Times,* March 29, 1995. The combined black and Hispanic population of the Bronx, Washington Heights, and Harlem at the start of the next century will be approximately 1.6 million. The population of Houston is 1.69 million, according to the *Statistical Abstract* of the United States (U.S. Bureau of the Census, 1994).

193 DIRECTOR OF THE ORPHANS PROJECT CITED: Carol Levine, *A Death in the Family: Orphans of the HIV Epidemic* (New York: United Hospital Fund, 1993).

194, 195 NUMBER OF NEW YORK CITY CHILDREN ORPHANED BY AIDS: *New York Daily News,* February 27 and March 30, 1994. The most authoritative source for this and related information is The Orphans Project, cited above.

"THE VIRAL PATH" OF AIDS AND PEDIATRICIAN CITED: *Newsday,* May 26, 1993.

"APPARENTLY . . . ONE OF THE HIGHEST AIDS RATES IN THE WORLD": David McBride, *From TB to AIDS* (Albany: State University of New York Press, 1991).

PERCENTAGES OF CHILDREN AND WOMEN WITH AIDS IN NEW YORK CITY WHO ARE BLACK OR HISPANIC: *New York Times,* September 24, 1990; *Newsday,* May 26, 1993; "New York City AIDS Surveillance Report, October–December 1994," New York City Department of Health, January 1995.

PEDIATRIC AIDS IN NEW YORK CITY AND SOUTH BRONX: The pediatric AIDS rate, measured in terms of AIDS cases per 100,000 children, is 144 in New York City but 176 in the Bronx, believed to be the highest rate for any highly populated area in the United States. Up to the start of 1994, 30 percent of pediatric AIDS cases in New York were in the Bronx, a percentage that rose to 35 percent during the next 12 months. ("New York City AIDS Surveillance Report, October–December 1994"; *Newsday,* June 22, 1993; author's discussions with staff members of the Hunter College Center on AIDS, Drugs, and Community Health, and with other health agency workers in Mott Haven.) Also see "The AIDS Outcasts," by Nat Hentoff, *Village Voice,* March 6, 1990; *New York Daily News,* November 30, 1993, February 7, 1994.

PROGNOSIS FOR HIV-POSITIVE INFANTS: *Newsday,* May 26, 1993; *New York Daily News,* February 27, 1994; *Village Voice,* March 6, 1990 and June 7, 1994; author's interviews with service providers at

Bronx-Lebanon Hospital, with staff of Hunter College Center on AIDS, Drugs, and Community Health, and with staff of Dominican Sisters Family Health Service in Mott Haven.

196, 197 CHILDREN'S WORDS AND DRAWINGS: "Children Speaking with Children and Families about HIV Infection," by Lori Wiener, et al., included in Philip Pizzo and Catherine Wilfert, *Pediatric AIDS* (Baltimore: Williams and Wilkins, 1994). A somewhat different presentation of most of these writings and drawings is found in a book compiled by Lori Wiener and two associates, *Be a Friend: Children Who Live with HIV Speak* (Morton Grove, Ill.: Albert Whitman and Company, 1994).

CHILDREN AFRAID TO SHARE FEARS WITH FRIENDS: See *Pediatric AIDS,* cited above; and *New York Daily News,* February 27, 1994.

199 "I WISH I WAS RICH ENOUGH TO GIVE HER EVERYTHING SHE WANTS": The father was cited in a story about the family in the *New York Times,* December 5, 1993. My visit with the family was made possible by the Children's Aid Society.

200 "AIDS IS MY RESURRECTION": The counselor cited is Dicxon Valderruten, Director of HIV Services at El Rio, an agency in the South Bronx affiliated with The Osborne Association (see note for pages 145, 146).

201 SOJOURNER TRUTH CITED: Carleton Mabee, *Sojourner Truth: Slave, Prophet, Legend* (New York: New York University Press, 1993).

222 THE NEW "GOSPEL" REGARDING BEGGARS: *New York Times,* January 11, 1994.

CARD DISTRIBUTED IN SUBWAY: "Panhandling in the Subway," Metropolitan Transportation Authority, New York, 1994.

Epilogue

235 ST. MARY'S PARK: *New York Daily News,* July 18 and 19, 1994.

240 MURDER OF THREE BOYS IN MR. CASTRO'S BUILDING: According to information I received after the publication of this book, the boys may not have been the actual targets of this execution. I'm also told that they did not live in the apartment where they died but had been visiting the woman who resided there.

244 SCHOOL IN FORMER STEEL PLANT: *Newsday,* May 23, 1994.

247 "THE ENEMY IS THE HOMELESS": The statement, apparently made by the officer in mid-July, is cited in the *New York Times,* July 20 and 24, 1994.

248 POOR CHILDREN IN NEW YORK CITY: In 1992, the Community Service Society of New York placed the number at 800,000, nearly 40 percent of all children in the city. (*New York Daily News,* June 10, 1992.)

Acknowledgments

From its initial conception through its multiple revisions, this book has been beneath the guiding hand of Cassie Schwerner, my closest co-worker for many years, whose personal investment of herself within this work was limitless. She has been, as always, my most loyal friend and patient critic. I am deeply grateful.

I am also indebted to the many people who have examined this writing as it has evolved, including some people in the South Bronx whom I am unable to thank by name. Among those readers whom I am able to name, and who have helped me greatly, are Rabbi David Saperstein, Marian Wright Edelman, Mary Frances Berry, Charles Schultz, Sylvia Ann Hewlett, Dennis Kalob, Safir Ahmed, Steve and Nancy Schwerner, Ruth and Victor Sidel, Frances Fox Piven, Ruth Conniff, Lynn Nesbit, Laurie Stark, and my editor James Wade.

Robert Bonazzi and Elizabeth Griffin, who are the literary trustees of my friend John Howard Griffin, devoted many months to an examination of this text, as did my trusted colleagues Marilyn Weller, Tisha Graham, and Cathy Foley.

There are also people I do not know but whose work has had an impact on my thinking or has helped to lead me to some of the neighborhoods I visited. The writings of Felicia Lee, Celia Dugger, David Gonzalez, Isabel Wilkerson, Lynda Richardson, Charisse Jones, Kimberly McLarin, Joyce Purnick, Don Terry, Bob Herbert, and Jason deParle, all of the *New York Times,* photographer and essayist Camilo José Vergara, the investigative team of *Newsday* journalists who reported on life in several South Bronx neighborhoods in 1993, investigative writers for the *Village Voice, City Limits, Daily News,* and *Amsterdam News,* as well as recent books by Valerie Polakow, Luis Rodriguez, Laurie Abraham, Kai Erikson, Nicholas Lemann, Samuel Freedman, Andrew Hacker, Brent Staples, Patricia Williams, John Hope Franklin, and Alex Kotlowitz have shaped the state of mind in which I wrote this book.

My deepest debt is to the people who have welcomed me into their churches, shelters, clinics, schools, and homes in the South Bronx: particularly Blanca Picart, the wise young aunt of Bernardo Rodriguez; Shirley Flowers Alston and her family and their friends on Beekman Avenue; Gizelle Luke and those who carry on her work at Featherbed Lane; Gregory Groover and the congregation of Bright Temple A.M.E.; Dicxon Valderruten of El Rio; James Roundtree of St. Benedict the Moor; and Juan Bautista Castro, the poet of Mott Haven.

I was also assisted by Mary Brodsky of the Children's Aid Society, Sandi Franklin of Fresh Start, Jacqueline Pitts and David Jones of the Community Service Society of New York, Peggy Shepard of West Harlem Environmental Action, Bronx borough president Fernando Ferrer, Manhattan borough president Ruth Messinger, Earl KooperKamp of the Church of the Intercession, and Elizabeth Gaynes of The Osborne Association.

Most of all, of course, I am grateful to the woman I call Alice Washington and her son, whom I call David, to the children, mothers, and grandmothers who are the soul of St. Ann's Church, to their pastor, Martha Overall, and to the children of P.S. 65 on Cypress Avenue. I do not know how to thank Anabelle for her smile, or the children in the schoolyard for their jump-rope rhymes, or Destiny for the way she held a purple crayon. I do not know how to thank Anthony for his honesty and decency and inner grace. This book is my best effort to give thanks to all these children. I pray that many will lead long and happy lives and that their deepest dreams may be fulfilled.

Index

277

JONATHAN KOZOL has spent much of his life talking with and listening to children. His first book, *Death at an Early Age,* won the National Book Award. His book about homeless families, *Rachel and Her Children,* won the Robert F. Kennedy Book Award. His most recent book, *Savage Inequalities,* was a finalist for the National Book Critics Circle Award and became a national bestseller. Mr. Kozol lives near Boston, Massachusetts.